RECONSTRUCTION IN A GLOBALIZING WORLD

RECONSTRUCTING AMERICA
Andrew L. Slap, series editor

Reconstruction in a Globalizing World

David Prior, Editor

Fordham University Press

New York   2018

Fordham University Press has no responsibility for the persistence or accuracy of URLs for external or third-party Internet websites referred to in this publication and does not guarantee that any content on such websites is, or will remain, accurate or appropriate.

Fordham University Press also publishes its books in a variety of electronic formats. Some content that appears in print may not be available in electronic books.

Visit us online at www.fordhampress.com.

Library of Congress Cataloging-in-Publication Data available online at https://catalog.loc.gov.

Printed in the United States of America

20 19 18   5 4 3 2 1

First edition

for Tiffany and Isaac

Contents

Foreword

Ian Tyrrell

The Reconstruction period is usually considered one of the most inward-looking periods in American history. When considered in international comparison, the years from 1865 to 1877 have a reputation as unique in mounting a thorough attempt to replace the institutions of slavery and institute liberal forms of equality. Momentous though the period was in the expropriation of slave-owners' property and in granting freedom and civil rights to African-American people, that observation should not exclude historians from setting the Reconstruction period in the context of world history. The transition from unfree labor of various shapes and forms to free labor occurred across the Americas from the 1830s to 1880s, and also in Russia with the emancipation of the serfs between 1861 and 1866. Moreover, in the realm of national consolidation and state-building, the United States can be situated within the broader phenomenon of nationalism, both in Europe and beyond. Still another comparison can be found in the patterns of racial domination and new forms of coerced labor and racially stratified citizenship that replaced slave labor in the Americas.

Not all these matters are included in these essays, but a good many are. These contributions show that the actors in the great drama of Reconstruction often had an eye on what was going on abroad—both in the adjustment of relations between slave and free, and between "democracy" and forms of privilege that republican ideology described as "aristocracy." The global re-shaping of the economic and political order as the world moved toward patterns of greater representation and inclusiveness of oppressed people as citizens is both a backdrop to American events and a way of better understanding those events. By highlighting these transnational connections, historians can re-enter the actual world that people inhabited. This was not a world of hermetically sealed units in which people thought only of nations, but a world of nations in the making, in which individual journeys across national boundaries, both material and intellectual, were common. Of course, the variations in these experiences of the 1860s and 1870s in different countries were numerous, but these chapters show how events in Europe impacted American Reconstruction, and how foreigners were influenced by what they saw, heard, and read of the United States. Whether in the form of immigrant identification with German or Irish homelands, or common experiences of racial hierarchy in Africa and the United States, or models for modernization of education and gender relations drawn for use abroad from the exposure of foreign reformers to American conditions, ideas and cultural experiences flowed across the political boundaries within the Atlantic world. Even the very term "Reconstruction" was circulating in Europe, and the ways it was used were duly noted by Americans intent on their own reforms of the polity.

This set of essays builds upon the tendency in scholarship of the past two decades to see American history in terms of the wider world. This scholarship is partly comparative history, setting up national and regional comparisons between units considered as separate for the purposes of study. But it also increasingly singles out the exchanges between and across national units of analysis, and treats national borders as porous. The two approaches are not mutually exclusive, though these essays give prominence to the flows of people, goods, ideas and institutions across national boundaries, a methodological strategy central to transnational analysis. For the period in question, the relevant "wider world" is mostly taken to be Europe, though some contributors extend their gaze to a hemispheric inclusion regarding Latin America and Canada. Transnational history does not, even when focused on the United States, exclude unique American stories and traditions. It is clear that the transatlantic flows of information induced international comparisons used to hone understandings of difference. Indeed, in many instances these comparisons served to bolster American exceptionalism through a Republican Party narrative of the triumph of freedom over slavery.

Another feature of transnational history is the shifting of chronological categories. Time and space are intricately linked, and the different spatial conception that transnational analysis opens up draws our attention to somewhat different points at which Reconstruction might be said to end, or indeed begin. In these papers, there are hints that the Civil War and Reconstruction should be considered together. A broader sense of Reconstruction might also include what is formally Reconstruction's aftermath because the period's eddies abroad continued after 1877. These influences centered on the global circulation of ideas and techniques of racial oppression such as literacy tests that made the American South, British Natal, and Queensland, Australia in some measure fit together as instances of the racial readjustments in citizenship, in territorial boundary-making, and in the uses and forms of coerced labor.

I hope that these careful studies will inspire others to look beyond the prism of nation-centered analysis. The wider perspective of the new transnational scholarship will likely come in the future to encompass the modernization of mid-nineteenth-century polities as a global phenomenon. That might include, for example, the Japanese Meiji Revolution, struggles against the subaltern status of the subjects of the British Empire in Ireland and India, as well as the national unification in such diverse cases as the Dominion of Canada and Imperial Germany. Historians such as the late Carl Degler urged broad perspectives of these kinds, and in the essays presented in this volume we see the signs of empirical work to give substance to such historiographical generalizations.

Introduction

David Prior

Reconstruction in a Globalizing World strives to deepen the engagement between transnational history and scholarship on America's Reconstruction. Its approach is to illustrate how archival, historiographical, and conceptual work can firmly connect these two fields. The chapters here offer nuanced studies of topics that scholars rarely group together or view in relation to Reconstruction. Collectively, they call attention to the diverse and multilayered transnational connections that existed throughout the 1860s and 1870s and tease out the relationships of these to themes integral to Reconstruction scholarship. By immersing themselves in their own subjects, these chapters underscore just how much grist there is for our mills.

This focus begs the question of how to define and delimit these two fields. Is *trans*national history the same things as *inter*national, *global*, and *world* history? What was it that was being reconstructed in the United States and did this process define a period of American history? Is transnational history a subject, method, or, as Sven Beckert has termed it, a "way of seeing"?[1] What were Reconstruction's chronological and geographical boundaries? For all the competing answers to these questions, we should not lose sight of underlying points of agreement about the subject matter at the heart of these two fields. Transnational history is possible because of the connections—cultural, economic, political, intellectual, and otherwise—that have stretched across the borders of nation-states throughout modern history. If there had been no cross-border connections in the modern era—if all of modern history had been contained in discrete, hermetically sealed national territories—it would be impossible to do any kind of transnational history.[2] For all the various definitions of Reconstruction, no one has aimed to decouple the concept from the intertwined collapses of the Confederacy and southern slavery. These two events and the developments that followed on their heels occupy a prominent place in even the most expansive and original formulations of Reconstruction.[3] Starting with what is not in dispute, this volume addresses how connections that stretched across the United States' borders intersected with and took shape from the pattern of events wrapped up with and following from slavery's demise and the Confederacy's defeat.

This approach does not resolve all the interpretive challenges facing specialists in these fields. Starting with these general points of agreement does, however, lay bare the halting, uneven, but also promising nature of the conversation between these two fields over the last twenty or so years. Over this period, the study of Reconstruction has been on the leading edge of several scholarly trends, such as gender and cultural history.[4] Simultaneously, interest in transnational connections has spread across the historical profession. Yet by at least four measures, these two fields have become only lightly integrated with each other, if they are now more so than in 2006 when Mark M. Smith surveyed scholarship on Reconstruction and foreign affairs in his essay, "The Past as a Foreign Country."[5] First, the number of monographs and think pieces that place themselves at the nexus of these two fields, if recently buoyed by Andrew Zimmerman's essay on labor and capitalism, "Reconstruction: Transnational History," is modest when compared to outward-looking scholarship on the Civil War and Gilded Age.[6] Second, narratives of Reconstruction and America's place in world history touch only lightly upon each other. In essence, the two fields are telling separate stories.[7] Third, the two fields have yet to produce a series of mutually engaging historiographical debates concerned with events and processes of common interest. Scholars in these two fields have not, cheerfully or otherwise, brought their distinctive expertise together to answer questions of mutual interest. Fourth, neither field has posed a major challenge to how the other conceptualizes itself. Altogether, transnational history and Reconstruction scholarship have yet to develop a self-sustaining conversation.

It is, of course, possible to overstate how wide the gulf is between these two fields and to underestimate how much momentum there may now be behind mutual engagement. Reconstruction scholarship has long addressed, if usually briefly, topics like Republican diplomacy and Confederate emigration.[8] With the current wave of transnational history, a handful of studies, such as those by Philip M. Katz, Moon-Ho Jung, Jay Sexton, Alison Efford, and Greg P. Downs, have connected the two fields.[9] Works covering longer time periods have also discussed topics relevant to both fields, including especially the racial politics surrounding the proposed annexation of the Dominican Republic.[10] Smith's essay, although it has been largely neglected, proposed a unifying focus for this literature in the social construction of foreignness and domesticity.[11]

Moreover, current research trends provide grounds to hope that the engagement between these fields is expanding. A resurgent interest in political economy may flesh out our understanding of the complex relationships between international markets and the postbellum South.[12] Indeed, recent works, echoing scholarship from the 1930s and 1940s, have underscored that the birth of a free labor South unfolded alongside the rise of industrial capitalism. The current literature in this mode tends to call attention to the Civil War's disruption of global cotton markets and then the exporting of political and economic models from what has conventionally been understood to be the post-Reconstruction South. That said, this literature nonetheless points the way to a new view of Reconstruction as part of an emerging global economy.[13] Likewise, decades after W. E. B. Du Bois suggested that the collapse of Reconstruction contributed to the global rise of racial imperialism, the ongoing revitalization and transformation of diplomatic history may spark more debate on Reconstruction's geopolitical implications.[14] This topic connects to another emerging issue: whether the conquest of Native American polities in the western United States forms a part of Reconstruction proper, its broader national story, or its international context.[15] Recent works have also revived interest in the symbolic meaning of international events to people in the United States, a topic better developed for the Antebellum Period and the Civil War.[16] The converse—how outsiders, including ex-pats, imbued developments in the United States with meaning, whether from afar or based on firsthand observations—has also sparked interest, especially if one considers the Union's turn to emancipationist policies during the Civil War as a part of Reconstruction.[17]

But these points should not obscure the persistent challenges facing dialogue between these two fields. The greatest potential value of this volume lies with bringing these two fields closer together without trivializing the reasons they have remained distant. So, what then accounts for the gulf? Why have these two fields not overlapped more in terms of monographs, narratives, historiographical debates, or conceptual innovations? One could make a case for a variety of factors that are incidental, rather than intrinsic, to the two fields. Many transnationally minded scholars of American history, for instance, have perhaps gravitated toward fields with an eye-catching hook. The postbellum years, for example, though rife with transnational connections, lack an overseas conflict that features dramatic, large-scale U.S. involvement. Likewise, there was no prospect of a European diplomatic intervention in the United States during Reconstruction, as there had been, arguably, during the Civil War. Historiographically speaking, Reconstruction scholarship lacks a brilliant, auspicious transatlantic study akin to Bernard Bailyn's *Ideological Origins of the American Revolution* (1967), which rolled off the presses just as university faculties were mushrooming and the pace of academic publication accelerating.[18] Such a work on Reconstruction might have helped spark a tradition of Atlantic history akin to that which developed on colonial North America. It may also be that, right before the current wave of transnational history took off in the 1990s, the waning prestige of economic, agricultural, and diplomatic history combined with some shifts of emphasis within these fields to tamp down interest in some of Reconstruction's most obvious connections.[19] Such factors would suggest that there is no reason that transnational history and Reconstruction scholarship will not gradually come into greater dialogue with each other.

Yet deeper issues are also at play. One, which is addressed further in Chapter 7, is that Reconstruction narratives have long been divided between two loosely formed "southern" and "national" approaches that, together, tend to marginalize interest in transnational connections. Another issue is the distinctive concerns that have animated these two fields. Reconstruction scholars and transnational historians of course share commonplace academic values, and both groups include individuals with diverse motivations. But the two fields have also tended to prioritize different goals, and if neither adheres to an authoritative agenda, they are oriented in different directions. Inspired by the Civil Rights Movement and history from the bottom up, much Reconstruction scholarship has, for the last several decades, been devoted to recovering the experiences and agency of freedpeople (those former slaves who became free during and immediately after the Civil War).[20] U.S. historians engaged with transnational history, although by no means uninterested in experience and agency, have been more drawn to macro-level processes and abstractions such as globalization, modernity, and capitalism.[21] What is more, Reconstruction scholars' emphasis on civil rights has led them to foreground the tragic exclusion of African Americans from equal citizenship in the United States. That has reinforced the centrality of the nation to how Reconstruction scholars frame their research, envision their audience, and strive for eloquence. In contrast, transnational historians have had an ambivalence about the nation, with some viewing the concept as an ideological construct that narrows perspective rather than as a reliable unit of analysis.[22]

Interestingly, this last issue actually suggests why Reconstruction scholarship represents an important historiographical reference point for transnational historians. There is much to consider in transnational historians' warnings about the biases and exclusions of national history. Such arguments, however, tend to gloss over the dominance of social and cultural history in the profession from the 1960s into the early 2000s, or roughly the period prior to and then coinciding with the current wave of transnational history. To be sure, throughout these decades, social and cultural historians worked within fields of study that were typically delimited in national terms. This, however, likely reflected institutional inertia more than a broadly shared commitment to the nation as the primary subject of historical inquiry. Indeed, a good case can be made that over the last six decades few social and cultural historians deemed nations to be the quintessential subjects of modern history, preferring instead to focus on much smaller scales of analysis. Several trends, moreover, including the cultural turn's deconstructionist leanings, the complex and contested place of American exceptionalism in historical scholarship, and the New Left's conflicted stance toward patriotism should make scholars suspicious of any easy characterization of the relationships between social and cultural history on the one hand and national history on the other.[23] On this front, Reconstruction scholarship demands attention from transnational scholars because its social and cultural historians have often been explicitly concerned with America as a nation, in part because it was the nation that freedpeople demanded equal membership in. More so than most fields of study, Reconstruction scholarship might provide transnational historians opportunities to expand upon and substantiate the novelty of their approach to studying the past.

That noted, it bears emphasizing that freedpeople had little and often no discretionary access to the wider world. They rarely if ever got to choose the grounds on which they engaged with transnational developments. That makes it genuinely difficult to write a transnational history that focuses on their agency. For former slaves, freedom of movement was one of the most palpable and immediate consequences of abolition.[24] Yet, in the decades immediately following the Civil War, freedpeople had few means to travel internationally and only a small proportion of southern African Americans joined the Gilded Age's massive long-distance labor migrations, moving most often to the West or North when they did.[25] Likewise, a fascination with international affairs was integral to Civil War–era political culture, but impoverished freedpeople most often lacked formal education and had limited resources with which to consume and produce printed commentary on foreign events.[26] Finally, the second half of the nineteenth century would become a period of remarkable transatlantic intellectual and artistic exchange, but freedpeople largely lacked the means to travel to locations like Paris, Rome, or Berlin to participate in the ferment, especially during the 1860s and 1870s.[27] If one opts for a "long" definition of Reconstruction that stretches it into the late nineteenth and even early twentieth century, then these interpretive difficulties diminish somewhat as opportunities increased on all these fronts in interesting and complex ways. But that would not alter the fact that most freedpeople never had chances to seek better opportunities abroad, publish commentaries on the period's global events, or exchange ideas with kindred spirits around the globe. It is no wonder that few of the many recent works of African American history that have taken Atlantic and transnational approaches have concentrated on Reconstruction.[28]

Indeed, the freedpeoples' limited discretionary access to the wider world goes a long way to explaining why it has been difficult to parley Reconstruction scholarship's tradition of comparative study into a robust agenda for transnational history.[29] As Ian Tyrrell notes in his *preface* to this volume, in general, transnational and comparative history are compatible with each other and in fact often go hand-in-hand.[30] The contributors here at points combine the two approaches. When it comes to the postbellum decade, however, those societies that were comparable to the southern United States in terms of their histories of race and/or labor were typically better connected to European economic and imperial centers than to the South. This is all the more true if one foregrounds the experiences and agency of oppressed, often racialized, workers in these societies. Even the most proximate slaveholding and post-slavery societies, including Cuba, Haiti, and Mexico, let alone more distant places like the Russian countryside, were beyond the reach of the vast majority of freedpeople. Whereas comparative history has in general played an important role in fueling the rise of transnational history, with Reconstruction scholarship, a smooth transition has proved elusive, especially when it comes to a focus on freedpeople.

At first glance, these issues would seem to put scholars seeking to connect Reconstruction and transnational history in a bind. To those Reconstruction scholars who aim to recover the agency of freedpeople, most transnational history would seem to move too far afield. If transnational historians are concerned with historical processes that reach beyond national borders, then Reconstruction scholarship's highly localized social and political histories of freedpeople in the South would seem off topic. The emphasis of this volume is to push back against this assumption through empirical research. The postbellum United States was so struck through with transnational connections that it seems impossible that they were not relevant to Reconstruction, however one defines it. As the essays here show, several themes long integral to Reconstruction scholarship and obviously relevant to freedpeoples' lives—education, racial ideologies, grassroots political culture, intellectual currents—had fascinating but neglected transnational dimensions. Yet some scholars may nonetheless be unsatisfied with this approach, suggesting that the volume is more about Reconstruction's broad context than it is about Reconstruction's essential, defining topic. The contributors here were not tasked with tackling this potential criticism, which brings with it a number of complicated, even philosophical issues. Still, I would like to suggest that this interpretive dead-end—the seeming impossibility of writing a transnational history of freedpeoples' experiences and, even more so, their agency—is in fact a vista from which to see a way forward.

Not only can scholars write a transnational history of Reconstruction that keeps freedpeople front and center, but doing so would prompt us to think deeply about the relationships between connection and isolation and between agency and the systemic, structural forces that constrain and channel individual action.[31] Both Reconstruction scholars and transnational historians should take interest in how freedpeople were not only isolated from the rest of the world in powerful ways following the Civil War, but also how these forms of isolation entwined with equally important, if not always desirable, forms of connectedness.[32] This was evident, most obviously, in the decisions freedpeople had to make, precisely because most could not leave the South, about how much labor to devote to the production of global cash crops such as cotton. But this interplay of insularity and embeddedness also permeated much of postbellum southern life. Southern politics centered on town, county, and state offices, but European credit markets shaped state spending and thereby elections.[33] Freedpeople fought most of their battles locally, mobilized through person-to-person social networks and face-to-face political meetings. But the ideas they invoked, contested, and refashioned, including claims about race, democracy, equality, nationality, and citizenship, had developed and continued to evolve through transatlantic conversations.[34] Left alone by the world to confront a regional strain of white supremacy, freedpeople contended with racist stereotypes that were often explicitly international in content, referencing purported barbarism among equatorial Africans, Hottentots, Haitians, and others.[35] Since freedpeople resided overwhelmingly in the South, the forces that they struggled to manage and bend to their favor by definition came together in that region. But in a broader sense the causal terrain they inhabited was at once local, state-wide, national, transatlantic and, for those growing agricultural commodities such as rice, cotton, and sugar, global.[36]

Such a perspective helps us understand not only the freedpeoples' predicament but also the general significance of globalization in the second half of the nineteenth century. In retrospect, we can see that the period's rising volume and intensity of cross-border connections added up to a decades-long process of globalization. On the ground, however, this broader process could appear far from an expansive, uniform, and continuous trend. Scholars are right to call attention to those individuals with the richest transnational experiences. Indeed, some of the most interesting recent studies touching on Reconstruction uncover stories of exceptionally mobile working-class people who traveled to or from the South.[37] But we should not lose sight of how these and more prosperous travelers were more indicative of where things were headed than representative of the normal conditions of their times. With hindsight we can make a strong case for the importance of globalizing trends, such as increasing immigration, trade, intellectual exchange, and tourism, and remark at the scale of these relative to those from earlier moments in history. On the ground, however, changes of scale could often be imperceptible and their immediate impact on individuals modest in absolute terms.

As a result, for many people in the United States and elsewhere, as with freedpeople in the U.S. South, isolation and connection often went hand-in-hand. The same act of immigration that made the world a more tightly integrated place could ensconce a person in a new locality while attenuating their ties with an old one. Some states, businesses, and religious organizations exerted far flung influence, but such powers were hard wrought and tended to operate through bureaucracies that left most people rooted in place. A growing number of consumers could revel in goods from around the world and published accounts of "exotic" locales, but only a small share of these consumers traveled internationally or had substantial social contact with people abroad. Political partisans might associate their domestic struggles with others outside the nation, but such views often elided subtle and even not-so-subtle differences and only occasionally eventuated in lasting cross-border friendships. The point is not to trivialize transnational connections or the study of them, but instead to stress that these powerful causal currents often flowed through narrow channels.

In general, personal involvement in the processes of globalization was most often fleeting in nature, mediated by institutions and networks that operated beyond an individual's physical realm of existence, or both. In the second half of the nineteenth century, people encountered sweeping historical changes that connected them to a wider world, but often in an erratic and piecemeal fashion, with the personal significance of those changes left hinging on all sorts of local and regional factors. Indeed, we might go so far as to suggest that, while freedpeople had less control than most of their contemporaries over when and how they engaged with transnational processes, few individuals anywhere could claim much lasting discretion over those processes, or of globalization itself.

I hope that these brief reflections illustrate that a transnational history of Reconstruction is possible and that such a history does not necessarily require that scholars remove freedpeople from the center of the story. The aim here is not to argue that this would be the only way to write a transnational history of Reconstruction, or to imply that scholars of Reconstruction have always focused on only the experiences and agency of freedpeople. As specialists know well, Reconstruction scholarship encompasses diverse topics, ranging from the crafting of federal law to electoral politics to southern white identities following emancipation. But certainly a focus on freedpeople has been integral to modern Reconstruction scholarship and that focus represents a genuine interpretive challenge for scholars seeking to engage the field with transnational history. Foregrounding how insularity and embeddedness cohabitated the same historical moments offers one way forward that draws on transnational history's concern with abstract processes that dwarf the individual and Reconstruction scholarship's focus on deliberate action on the ground. Such an approach does not require scholars to either exaggerate the range of choices confronting most freedpeople or to abandon transnational history's focus on cross-border connections.

The chapters here showcase each scholar's research while addressing topics and themes central to transnational history and Reconstruction scholarship. The result is not a comprehensive survey but a series of explorations that get us closer to understanding Reconstruction's place in a globalizing world. This volume will leave specialists with a sense of how much more work there is to do: There are many archival leads to track down, concepts to debate, and stories to tell. In calling attention to these seven topics, the volume opens up possibilities and encourages debate. The only topic it will put to rest, I hope, is whether greater dialogue between transnational history and Reconstruction scholarship is possible and necessary.

The first two chapters, by Evan C. Rothera and Matthew J. Hetrick, examine the nexus of race and education. Rothera begins by considering the interest of Argentine statesman and reformer Domingo F. Sarmiento in importing practices from America's Reconstruction. In particular, as Rothera shows, Sarmiento's time in Washington, D.C. and New England following the Civil War exposed him to the campaigns to send white northern teachers, many of them women, south to educate freedpeople. Sarmiento had already taken interest in the idea of female teachers, in part because of an earlier visit to Boston where he befriended leading educational reformers Horace and Mary Mann. Again taking a page from developments in the United States, Sarmiento now became intrigued by the prospect of bringing white, blond-haired women from New England to Argentina. As Rothera shows, Sarmiento's efforts to do so speak not only to his place in a hemispheric and transatlantic community of reformers, but also in a similarly expansive community of racial thinkers. Looking at Sarmiento's interest in northern, white female teachers also affords a chance to understand the permutations of racial and liberal thinking across the Americas and the Atlantic as well as a forgotten pan-American moment.

In Chapter 2, Hetrick examines the tumultuous early history of Liberia College in Monrovia, Liberia. The college came to life in 1862, amidst dramatic transformations on both sides of the Atlantic, through financial backing from northern philanthropists. In the United States, the coming of the Civil War and then wartime emancipation dampened African American enthusiasm for emigration to Africa and raised new hope for equality at home. In Liberia, local leaders struggled over the course of their newly independent country (1847), dividing over skin color, class, and policy toward the interior. Liberia College embodied tensions from both of these contexts. Much to the chagrin of Martin Freeman, a key figure in the College's small faculty and an ally of Martin Delany, the College would find itself fighting for support and sympathy from northerners and African Americans. Freeman and his colleagues at the College, Alexander Crummell and Edward Wilmot Blyden, would also find themselves railing against and ultimately outmaneuvered by Liberia's "mulatto clique." Yet the College's history also points to continuities between developments in Liberia and the United States that in turn reflected shared beliefs. In both societies, key groups of elites held that education was necessary to civilize and uplift degraded populations, and, in both societies, these groups faced internal debates about competing ideas about liberal and mechanical education.

The next two chapters, by Mitchell Snay and Alison Efford, turn our attention to reform causes in federal politics. Snay's chapter focuses on the northern radical Republican press and its reactions to the British Reform Act of 1867. The Reform Act, which considerably expanded the suffrage in Britain, namely to middle- and working-class men, appeared to northern Republicans as one of two great democratic acts of 1867. The other was the Republican Party's own set of congressional Reconstruction Acts, which enfranchised southern African American men to vote in elections for state constitutional conventions that would in turn remake state voting laws. As Snay demonstrates, radical newspaper editors followed British politics surrounding the Reform Act closely, celebrating reformers such as John Bright and even, at times, appreciating the role of Conservatives such as Benjamin Disraeli. Yet radical editors in the North, Snay shows, tended to understand the Reform Act through their own contradictory ideology. This included seeing British reformers as united with antislavery forces in the United States in a common campaign against aristocracy. It also, however, led them to contrast the allegedly progressive and enlightened nature of their own country, now free of slavery, with a more hierarchical, hidebound Britain. The same optimism that led radical editors to link their struggles against slavery with the cause of British Reform could also blur into an exceptionalist vision of the United States. Just such a vision, argues Snay, would come to lay the groundwork for American imperial ventures later in the nineteenth century.

Efford turns our attention from the heady days of Reconstruction legislation to the moment where federal politics moved away from radical priorities. Focusing on the Liberal Republican movement and its concern with political corruption, Efford recovers a largely forgotten scandal involving American arms sales to E. Remington & Sons, who were in turn under contract to the French government during the Franco-Prussian War (1870–71). Pioneered by Carl Schurz, the scandal focused on three interconnected issues: whether the federal government had violated neutrality by selling weapons to France; whether members of the Ordnance Bureau were guilty of malfeasance; and the meaning of the arms sales to German-Americans. As Efford shows, the scandal stalled out despite Schurz's efforts, but even as it failed to equal those surrounding Crédit Mobilier, "Boss" Tweed, or the Whiskey Ring, it did help signal another, deeper change. In making his case, Schurz lauded Prussian probity, as did many of his senatorial critics. As Schurz and other Liberal Republicans pursued a broader campaign for civil service reform, international comparisons increasingly held up Prussia, and Britain, as models of progress. Such critical comparisons began a process of transatlantic borrowing that predated and led into the era of social politics addressed by Daniel T. Rodger's *Atlantic Crossings*, and also departed from a longer tradition of bolstering American national pride through comparisons abroad.

Caleb Richardson and Julia Brookins then turn our attention to Reconstruction's political culture and the grassroots activities of immigrant ethnic communities. Both essays are particularly valuable for underscoring how much more there is to say even about well-known topics such as the Fenian movement to free Ireland and Texas's violent, multiethnic politics. As Richardson shows, many scholars have turned their attention to the Irish and Irish-American Fenian Brotherhood, focusing on its secretive organization, divided leadership, and failed paramilitary activities. Yet for all this research, Richardson points out, we have missed what may be the single most important facet of the American-wing of this movement. Far from being just a clandestine organization, American Fenians relied on picnics and similarly public events to call attention to their cause, raise funds, rouse their spirits, and, at least occasionally, enjoy themselves. Such a mixing of politics and entertainment was integral to Reconstruction-era politics and reflected just how American many Irish immigrants had become. Indeed, this transformation was lost on the Fenians's American leadership, who could not understand that effusive public demonstrations did not signal a willingness of the mass of Irish-Americans to risk their well-being invading Canada. Adding some comparative perspective, Richardson points out that the incredibly public nature of Fenian picnics could not have been more different from what was possible in Ireland and the British Empire, where partisans faced violent repression much as freedpeople did in the American South, if for different reasons.

Brookins offers a social and political history of the postbellum career of German-Americans in Texas. As Brookins demonstrates, German-Americans formed an important constituency in the state's Reconstruction politics, playing an outsized role during the brief period in which former Confederates lost much of their political power. A small minority of Texas's population, German-Americans exercised influence in part because they were so eager to see federal authority and the Union Army return to the state. More likely than their Anglo-Texan peers to settle in towns, practice skilled trades, and run businesses, German-Americans had developed close economic and social ties with federal soldiers and officers before the war. During it, German-Americans stood out for their ambivalence toward the Confederate cause, in part because they were typically less committed and even hostile to slavery. Yet even as German-Americans seized these new, postbellum political opportunities, some of them squandered their energies on schemes to partition the state. If the Reconstruction moment got away from German-Americans, it also reforged bonds between them and the federal state and reunified nation. In the coming decades, old and new German immigrants would contribute pivotal technical and scientific skills to the incorporation of the American West.

In the volume's final chapter, I turn to the history of the word *reconstruction*, tracing its meanings in Europe, its adoption in the Civil War–era United States, and its evolution in scholarship. In Europe, by the 1840s the term *reconstruction*, with a small "r," had come to refer to two different types of historical processes. It could refer to the resurrection of polities that had been conquered, partitioned, or otherwise made to disappear; and it could refer to the transformation of the very fabric of society, such as was advocated by socialists. When Americans began to use the term *Reconstruction*, with a big "R," to refer to something specific to the United States, they ultimately incorporated and transformed both of these meanings. In conversation mostly with themselves, Americans came to use *Reconstruction* to refer to the reunification of the country through Union victory and the transformation of southern society through the destruction of slavery. This ambiguity in the meaning of *Reconstruction* has shaped the field's scholarship ever since by allowing for the creations of two loosely formed rival approaches to narrating Reconstruction, one national and the other southern. Tracing the evolution of these two approaches through five historiographical moments, this chapter suggests the irony of this outcome. As scholars have sought to elaborate the national and southern approaches to Reconstruction, they have marginalized transnational connections in their understanding of their subject, and all because of the word's transatlantic history.

Notes

1. See Beckert's comments in C. A. Bayly et al., "*AHR* Conversation: On Transnational History," *American Historical Review* 111, no. 5 (December 2006), 1441–64, especially 1454, 1459.

2. There is considerable diversity in how historians have attempted to define transnational history. Diego Olstein, for example, makes the case for distinguishing between transnational history, which focuses on non-state connections, and international history, which focuses on connections that center around states; see Diego Olstein, *Thinking History Globally* (New York: Palgrave Macmillan, 2015), 15–18. Ramón A. Gutiérrez and Elliott Young, in contrast, argue that transnational history is about transnations, meaning the cultures and societies that exist across borders, adding that transnational history problematizes the history of nation-states in a way that international history does not; Ramón A. Gutiérrez and Elliott Young, "Transnationalizing Borderlands History," *Western Historical Quarterly* 41, no. 1 (Spring 2010): 27–53. Much ink could be spilled moving through many other definitions of transnational history. For a sense of the diversity of perspectives on this topic, see Bayly, "AHR Conversation," especially 1441–50; and David Armitage, et al., "Interchange: Nationalism and Internationalism in the Era of the Civil War," *Journal of American History* 98, no. 2 (September 2011): 455–89, especially 457–60, 462–63, 464. The broader subject that these authors share, however, is the tremendously rich and complex components of modern history that took place across the borders of individual nation-states. The aim here is to engage Reconstruction scholarship with that broad topic, and hence the volume, to start, plays down some finer-grained distinctions. In this sense, this volume's approach is closest to that in Ian Tyrrell, "Reflections on the Transnational Turn in United States History: Theory and Practice," *Journal of Global History* 4, no. 3 (November 2009), 453–74, especially 453–54, 459–61.

3. Chapter 7 of this volume addresses in greater depth how scholars have defined and delimited Reconstruction. See also O. Vernon Burton, David Herr, and Matthew Cheney, "Defining Reconstruction," in Lacy Ford, ed., *A Companion to the Civil War and Reconstruction* (Malden, Mass.: Blackwell, 2005), 299–322. The claim here applies even to scholarship positing that the conquest of the American West was integral to Reconstruction; see especially Heather Cox Richardson, *West from Appomattox: The Reconstruction of America after the Civil War* (New Haven: Yale University Press, 2007); and Elliot West, "Reconstructing Race," *Western Historical Quarterly* 34, no. 1 (February 2003): 6–26.

4. Several essays have surveyed literature on these topics. See, for example, those in Ford, *A Companion to the Civil War and Reconstruction*; Thomas J. Brown, *Reconstructions: New Perspectives on the Postbellum United States* (New York: Oxford University

Press, 2006); and John David Smith, ed., *Interpreting American History: Reconstruction* (Kent: Kent State University Press, 2016).

5. Mark M. Smith, "The Past as a Foreign Country: Reconstruction, Inside and Out," in Brown, *Reconstructions*, 117–40. On the limited engagement between the fields, see also Steven Hahn, "Afterword: What Sort of World Did the Civil War Make?" in Gregory P. Downs and Kate Masur, *The World the Civil War Made* (Chapel Hill: University of North Carolina Press, 2015), 337–56, especially 338–39, 347–48, 350.

6. With monographs, the argument here is necessarily impressionistic. There are multiple think-pieces and discussion forums that speak to the possibility of a transnational history of Reconstruction, but such comments tend to come as part of larger discussions of the Civil War Era. Only Smith, "The Past as a Foreign Country," and Andrew Zimmerman, "Reconstruction: Transnational History," in Smith, ed., *Reconstruction*, 171–96, place Reconstruction front and center. Scholars who opt for a "short" or traditional definition of Reconstruction as ending in 1877 will find much of Zimmerman's essay pertains to subsequent developments. On the broader Civil War Era, see Jay Sexton, "Toward a Synthesis of Foreign Relations in the Civil War Era, 1848–1877," *American Nineteenth Century History* 5, no. 3 (2004): 50–73; David Quigley, "Emancipation, Empires, and Democracies: Locating the United States in the World, 1840–1900," in Peter Stearns, ed., *Globalizing American History: The AHA Guide to Re-Imagining the U.S. Survey Course* (American Historical Association, 2008), 73–92; Armitage, et al., "Interchange"; Douglas R. Egerton, "Rethinking Atlantic History in a Postcolonial Era: The Civil War in Global Perspective," *Journal of the Civil War Era* 1, no. 1 (March 2011): 79–95; David Prior, et al., "Teaching the American Civil War Era in Global Context," *Journal of the Civil War Era* 5, no. 1 (March 2015); Robert E. Bonner, "The Salt Water Civil War: Thalassological Approaches, Ocean-Centered Opportunities," *Journal of the Civil War Era* 6, no. 2 (June 2016): 243–67.

7. Chapter 7 of this volume addresses Reconstruction narratives in greater depth. The leading overviews of America's place in world history treat Reconstruction briefly; see Thomas Bender, ed., *Rethinking American History in a Global Age* (Berkeley: University of California Press, 2002); Bender, *A Nation Among Nations: America's Place in World History* (New York: Hill and Wang, 2006); and Ian Tyrrell, *Transnational Nation: United States History in Global Perspective Since 1789* (Basingstoke: Palgrave Macmillan, 2007).

8. Chapter 7 of this volume addresses this earlier literature in slightly more detail. Two works of note that predate the rise of the current wave of transnational history include Lucy M. Cohen, *Chinese in the Post-Civil War South: A People Without a History* (Baton Rouge: Louisiana State University Press, 1984); Daniel E. Sutherland, "Exiles, Emigrants, and Sojourners: The Post-Civil War Confederate Exodus in Perspective," *Civil War History* 31, no. 3 (September 1985): 237–56.

9. Philip M. Katz, *From Appomattox to Montmartre: Americans and the Paris Commune* (Cambridge, Mass.: Harvard University Press, 1998); Moon-Ho Jung, *Coolies and Cane: Race, Labor, and Sugar in the Age of Emancipation* (Baltimore: Johns Hopkins University Press, 2006); Jay Sexton, "The United States, the Cuban Rebellion, and the Multilateral Initiative of 1875," *Diplomatic History* 30, no. 3 (June 2006): 335–65; Greg P. Downs, "The Mexicanization of American Politics: The United States' Path from Civil

War to Stabilization," *American Historical Review* 117, no. 2 (April 2012): 387–409; Alison Efford, *German Immigrants, Race, and Citizenship in the Civil War Era* (New York: Cambridge University Press, 2013); and Sexton, "William Seward in the World," *Journal of the Civil War Era* 4, no. 3 (September 2014): 398–430.

10. See Eric T. Love, *Race Over Empire: Racism & U.S. Imperialism, 1865–1900* (Chapel Hill: University of North Carolina Press, 2004), Chapter 2; Allison L. Sneider, *Suffragists in an Imperial Age: U.S. Expansion and the Woman Question, 1870–1929* (New York: Oxford University Press, 2008), Chapter 2; Nicholas Guyatt, "America's Conservatory: Race, Reconstruction, and the Santo Domingo Debate," *Journal of American History* 97, no. 4 (March 2011): 974–1000; and Christopher Wilkins "'They had heard of emancipation and the enfranchisement of their race': The African American Colonists of Samaná, Reconstruction, and the State of Santo Domingo," in David T. Gleeson and Simon Lewis, eds., *The Civil War as Global Conflict: Transnational Meanings of the American Civil War* (Columbia: University of South Carolina Press, 2014), 211–34.

11. Smith, "The Past as a Foreign Country."

12. On the relationship of quantitative economic history, which rose to prominence in the 1960s and 1970s, and the more recent interest in the history of capitalism and political economy, see Peter A. Coclanis and Scott Marler, "The Economics of Reconstruction," in Ford, *A Companion to the Civil War and Reconstruction*, 342–65; and Sven Beckert, et al., "Interchange: The History of Capitalism," *Journal of American History* 101, no. 2 (September 2014): 503–36. For a work that points the way forward for Reconstruction, see Scott P. Marler, *The Merchants' Capital: New Orleans and the Political Economy of the Nineteenth-Century South* (New York: Cambridge University Press, 2013).

13. For a recent overview of this approach, see Zimmerman, "Reconstruction: Transnational History." See also Zimmerman, *Alabama in Africa: Booker T. Washington, the German Empire, and the Globalization of the New South* (Princeton: Princeton University Press, 2012); Sven Beckert, *Empire of Cotton: A Global History* (New York: Alfred A. Knopf, 2014); and Steven Hahn, *A Nation without Borders: The United States and the World in the Age of Civil Wars, 1830–1910* (New York: Viking, 2016).

14. On diplomatic history and Reconstruction, in general, see Smith, "The Past as a Foreign Country," 120–27. Chapter 7 offers some additional comments on how Reconstruction narratives have treated diplomatic history. For Du Bois's comments, see W. E. B. Du Bois, *Black Reconstruction in America, 1860–1880* (New York: Free Press, 1992), 9, 15–16, 30, 206, 632, 706; Eric Foner, "*Black Reconstruction*: An Introduction," *South Atlantic Quarterly* 112, no. 3 (Summer 2013): 409–18, especially 411, 414–15, 416; Moon-Ho Jung, "*Black Reconstruction* and Empire," *South Atlantic Quarterly* 112, no. 3 (Summer 2013): 465–71. There are many monographs focusing on individual diplomatic events during the period conventionally associated with Reconstruction (1865–77), although few of these address Reconstruction in detail or have garnered much attention from Reconstruction scholars. For overviews of diplomacy and the Reconstruction presidents, see Richard Zuczek, "Foreign Affairs and Andrew Johnson," and Stephen McCullough, "Avoiding War: The Foreign Policy of Ulysses S. Grant and Hamilton Fish," in Edward O. Frantz, *A Companion to the Reconstruction Presidents, 1865–1881* (Malden, Mass.: Wiley-Blackwell, 2014), 85–120 and 311–27; and the recent dissertations, Stephen

McCullough, "Foreshadowing of Informal Empire: Ulysses S. Grant and Hamilton Fish's Caribbean Policy, 1869–1877," Ph.D. Dissertation, University of Alabama, 2007, and Christopher Wilkins, "American Republic, American Empire: The United States, Post-Civil War Reconstruction, and the Annexation of Santo Domingo, 1869–1871," Ph.D. Dissertation, Stanford University, 2012. The complex relationship between Reconstruction-era politics and imperialism can be seen by reading Gordon H. Chang, "Whose 'Barbarism'? Whose 'Treachery'? Race and Civilization in the Unknown United States— Korean War of 1871," *Journal of American History* 89, no. 4 (March 2003): 1331–65 alongside John Schrecker, "'For the Equality of Men—For the Equality of Nations': Anson Burlingame and China's First Embassy to the United States, 1868," *Journal of American-East Asian Relations* 17, no. 1 (March 2010): 9–34. It is interesting how little discussion Reconstruction has received in the literature on the rise of American imperialism, as Smith, "The Past as a Foreign Country," 123, notes. There is, for example, no article on Reconstruction with a sweeping argument equivalent to that of Walter L. Williams, "The United States Indian Policy and the Debate over Philippine Annexation: Implications for the Origins of American Imperialism," *Journal of American History* 66, no. 4 (March 1980): 810–31. For an overview of the literature on the rise of American imperialism, see Eric Rauchway, "The Global Emergence of the United States, 1867–1900," in William L. Barney, ed., *A Companion to 19th-Century America* (Malden, Mass.: Blackwell, 2001), 104–17. Two recent essays that speak to this topic through detailed case studies are Mark Elliott, "The Lessons of Reconstruction: Debating Race and Imperialism in the 1890s," and Natalie J. Ring, "A New Reconstruction for the South," both in Carole Emberton and Bruce E. Baker, *Remembering Reconstruction: Struggles Over the Meaning of America's Most Turbulent Era* (Baton Rouge: Louisiana State University Press, 2017), 139–202. Several scholars have seen America's war with Spain in 1898 as bringing about sectional reconciliation, with Heather Richardson treating that reconciliation as a part of a longer Reconstruction; see Richardson, *West from Appomattox*, especially Chapter 9. Also of note on Reconstruction and diplomatic history is Samuel L. Schaffer, "'A Bitter Memory Upon Which Terms of Peace Would Rest': Woodrow Wilson, the Reconstruction of the South, and the Reconstruction of Europe," in Emberton and Baker, *Remembering Reconstruction*, 203–24.

15. On this point, consider Brian DeLay, "Indian Polities, Empire, and the History of American Foreign Relations," *Diplomatic History* 39, no. 5 (November 2015): 927–42; Claudio Saunt, "The Paradox of Freedom: Tribal Sovereignty and Emancipation During the Reconstruction of Indian Territory," *Journal of Southern History* 70, no. 1 (February 2004): 63–94; Smith, "The Past as a Foreign Country," 136–39; Steven Hahn, "Slave Emancipation, Indian Peoples, and the Projects of a New American Nation-State," *Journal of the Civil War Era* 3, no. 3 (September 2013): 307–30; and C. Joseph Genetin-Pilawa, "Ely S. Parker and the Paradox of Reconstruction Politics in Indian Country," in *The World the Civil War Made*, ed., Downs and Masur, 183–205, especially 184–85, 193–94, 195, 197, 200.

16. See, of course, Katz, *From Appomattox to Montmartre*; and also David Prior, "'Crete the Opening Wedge': Nationalism and International Affairs in Postbellum America," *Journal of Social History* 42, no. 4 (June 2009): 861–87; David Prior, "Reconstruction Unbound: American Worldviews in a Period of Promise and Conflict, 1865–1874"

(Ph.D. Dissertation, University of South Carolina, 2010); Efford, *German Immigrants, Race, and Citizenship in the Civil War Era*; Downs, "The Mexicanization of American Politics"; Brandon Byrd, "Black Republicans, Black Republic: African-Americans, Haiti, and the Promise of Reconstruction," *Slavery & Abolition*, 36, no. 4 (2015): 545–67; and the much earlier John Gerow Gazley, *American Opinion of German Unification, 1848–1871* (New York: Columbia University Press, 1926). The literature on the Antebellum Period and the Civil War is too extensive to cite here, but see especially Don H. Doyle, "The Global Civil War," in Aaron Sheehan-Dean, *A Companion to the U.S. Civil War*, 2 vols., II: 1103–20.

17. On this general topic, see Eric Foner, "Andrew Johnson and Reconstruction: A British View," *Journal of Southern History* 41, no. 3 (August 1975): 381–90, especially 381; and Wilkins "They had heard of emancipation and the enfranchisement of their race," 211–16. The literature on foreign views of federal emancipation is quite substantial; see most recently; David T. Gleeson, "Failing to 'unite with the abolitionists': The Irish Nationalist Press and U.S. Emancipation," *Slavery & Abolition* 37, no. 3 (September 2016): 622–37. For a work that focuses on later years, see Teresa Cribelli, "A Modern Monarch: Dom Pedro II's Visit to the United States in 1876," *Journal of the Historical Society* 9, no. 2 (June 2009): 223–54.

18. Bernard Bailyn, *The Ideological Origins of the American Revolution* (Cambridge, Mass.: Belknap Press, 1967). The closest relevant comparison to Bailyn's work would be Robert Kelley, *The Transatlantic Persuasion: The Liberal-Democratic Mind in the Age of Gladstone* (New York: Knopf, 1969), which unfortunately says little about Reconstruction. Greater attention to Reconstruction, and in particular northern Republican policy making, would have sustained a more nuanced interpretation of the career of liberal ideas in the United States in which both major parties, Democrats and Republicans, made their own claims to represent the cause of liberalism. Reconstruction scholarship does, of course, have several early and influential comparative histories, but as noted further in the text, this tradition of comparative work has not translated into an equivalent interest in transnational connections.

19. On these points, consider David B. Danbom, "Reflections: Whither Agricultural History," *Agricultural History* 84, no. 2 (Spring 2010): 166–75; Thomas W. Zeiler, "The Diplomatic History Bandwagon: A State of the Field," *Journal of American History* 95, no. 4 (March 2009): 1053–73 and the responses in the same issue; and John Majewski, "U.S. History in a Statistical Age," *The American Historian* (November 2014).

20. For a helpful overview of this literature, see John C. Rodrigue, "Black Agency after Slavery," in Brown, *Reconstructions*, 40–65.

21. Consider Bayly, et al., "AHR *Conversation*," 1450–52, 1453–54, 1455–60. There are, of course, transnational historians interested in history from the bottom up and civil rights; on the latter, see especially Zeiler, "The Diplomatic History Bandwagon," 1069–71. The tendency to abstraction applies to teaching the Civil War era in global context as well; consider Sarah Cornell's, Robert Bonner's, and Andre Fleche's comments in Prior, et al., "Teaching the Civil War Era in Global Context," 141–42, 145.

22. The best critical overview of transnational scholars' ethical critique of national history is Johann Neem, "American History in a Global Age," *History and Theory* 50, no. 1 (February 2011): 41–70. Also helpful are Michael Kazin, "The Vogue of

Transnationalism," *Raritan* 26, no. 3 (Winter 2007): 155–67; Tyrrell, "Reflections on the Transnational Turn in United States History," 458–59, 469–74; Jay Sexton, "The Global View of the United States," *The Historical Journal* 48, no. 1 (March 2005): 261–76, especially 275–76; and Bayly, et al., "AHR *Conversation*," 1445–46, 1449, 1454. For a broader treatment of the origins and evolution of transnational history, consider especially Marcus Gräser, "World History in a Nation-State: The Transnational Disposition of Historical Writing in the United States," *Journal of American History* 95, no. 4 (March 2009): 1038–52, and Olstein, *Thinking History Globally*, Chapter 2.

    23. Consider Michael Kazin and Joseph A. McCartin, introduction to *Americanism: New Perspectives on the History of an Ideal*, edited by Kazin and McCartin (Chapel Hill: University of North Carolina Press, 2006); Michael Kammen, "The Problem of American Exceptionalism: A Reconsideration," *American Quarterly* 45, no. 1 (March 1993): 1-43; and the ironic treatment of nationalism in David Waldstreicher's cultural history, *In the Midst of Perpetual Fetes: The Making of American Nationalism, 1776–1820* (Chapel Hill: University of North Carolina Press, 1997).

    24. The classic treatment on this theme is William I. Cohen, *At Freedom's Edge: Black Mobility and the Southern White Quest for Racial Control, 1861–1915* (Baton Rouge: Louisiana State University Press, 1991).

    25. For some transatlantic perspective on this lack of mobility, see José C. Moya, "Modernization, Modernity, and the Trans/formation of the Atlantic World in the Nineteenth Century," in Jorge Cañizares-Esguerra and Erik R. Seeman, *The Atlantic in Global History: 1500–2000* (New York: Routledge, 2007), 179–97, especially 186–87. For African-American emigration immediately after the war, see Steven Hahn, *A Nation Under Our Feet: Black Political Struggles in the Rural South, from Slavery to the Great Migration* (Cambridge, Mass.: Belknap Press, 2003).

    26. See Ian Tyrrell, *Transnational Nation: United States History in Global Perspective Since 1789* (Palgrave, 2007), 90. On the difficulties facing the Republican press in the South, including African American editors, see Richard Abbott, *For Free Press and Equal Rights: Republican Newspapers in the Reconstruction South* (Athens: University of Georgia Press, 2004).

    27. Again consider Moya, "Modernization, Modernity, and the Trans/formation of the Atlantic World in the Nineteenth Century," 190–91 and 191–93. See also Daniel T. Rodgers, *Atlantic Crossings: Social Politics in a Progressive Age* (Cambridge, Mass.: Belknap Press, 1998).

    28. On this literature, see Keisha N. Blain, "A Bibliography of Black Internationalism," African American Intellectual History Society, http://www.aaihs.org/a-bibliography-of-black-internationalism/.

    29. Smith, "The Past as a Foreign Country," suggests that Reconstruction's comparative studies may have diverted the field's attention from foreign affairs; see 118. Important comparative studies that address Reconstruction include but are not limited to, Eric Foner, *Nothing but Freedom: Emancipation and Its Legacy* (Baton Rouge: Louisiana State University Press, 1983); Steven Hahn, "Class and State in Postemancipation Societies: Southern Planters in Comparative Perspective," *American Historical Review* 95, no. 1 (February 1990): 75–98; and Rebecca J. Scott, *Degrees of Freedom: Louisiana and Cuba*

after Slavery (Cambridge, Mass.: Belknap Press of Harvard University Press, 2005); Peter J. Kolchin, "Comparative Perspectives on Emancipation in the U.S. South: Reconstruction, Radicalism, and Russia," *Journal of the Civil War Era* 2, no. 2 (June 2012): 203–32; and Kolchin, "Reexamining Southern Emancipation in Comparative Perspective," *Journal of Southern History* 81, no. 1 (February 2015): 7–40.

30. See also Tyrrell, "Reflections on the Transnational Turn in United States History," especially 456–58.

31. For an article that addresses some of the limitations of the concept of agency as it has been deployed by scholars of nineteenth-century African American history, see Walter Johnson, "On Agency," *Journal of Social History* 37, no. 1 (October 2003): 113–24.

32. A number of transnational historians have reflected on their fields' engagement with the topic of isolation or disconnection. Patricia Seed has suggested that transnational history addresses transnational connections as well as who gets excluded from access to such connections; see her comment in "AHR *Conversation*," 1458. In contrast, Jürgen Osterhammel has a more skeptical take on the field, claiming that "global historians sometimes see *only* mobility, networking, and cosmopolitanism"; Osterhammel, *The Transformation of the World*, 117. Ian Tyrrell has suggested that using multiple "framing contexts" can help historians attend to the interplay of transnational forces with more localized developments in Tyrrell, "Reflections on the Transnational Turn in United States History," 463–64.

33. Mark Wahlgren Summers, *The Ordeal of the Reunion: A New History of Reconstruction* (Chapel Hill: University of North Carolina Press, 2014), 278–79, 289–90, and Nicolas Barreyre, *Gold and Freedom: The Political Economy of Reconstruction*, trans. Arthur Goldhammer (Charlottesville: University of Virginia Press, 2015), 201–2 offer insightful comments about European financial markets, state bonds, and Reconstruction.

34. There is no book-length work that focuses on placing Reconstruction in the context of transatlantic and global intellectual currents. Several of the chapters in this volume, including those by Evan Rothera, Matthew Hetrick, Mitchell Snay, Alison Efford, and David Prior, address racial and reformist thought and survey relevant literature. In addition to these, works that point toward such a synthesis include Amy Dru Stanley, "Slave Emancipation and the Revolutionizing of Human Rights," and Andrew Zimmerman, "From the Second American Revolution to the First International and Back Again: Marxism, the Popular Front, and the American Civil War," both in Gregory P. Downs and Kate Masur, eds., *The World the Civil War Made* (Chapel Hill: University of North Carolina Press, 2015), 269–303 and 304–35. For classic treatments of African-American political mobilization during Reconstruction, see Eric Foner, *Reconstruction: America's Unfinished Revolution, 1863–1877* (New York: Harper & Row, 1988), and Hahn, *A Nation Under Our Feet*.

35. Reconstruction scholars are well aware of the pervasiveness of such stereotypes, although discussion of them is scattered across the literature; the field lacks studies that focus specifically on the global imagination of postbellum white supremacists. Reconstruction scholars can follow the lead of works such as Robert E. Bonner, "Slavery, Confederate Diplomacy, and the Racialist Mission of Henry Hotze," *Civil War History* 51, no. 3 (September 2005): 288–316.

36. On the last point, see most recently, Richard J. Follett, et al., *Plantation Kingdom: The American South and Its Global Commodities* (Baltimore: Johns Hopkins University Press, 2016).

37. See, for example, Jung, Introduction to *Coolies and Cane*; Kira Thurman, "Singing the Civilizing Mission in the Land of Bach, Beethoven, and Brahms: The Fisk Jubilee Singers in Nineteenth-Century Germany," *Journal of World History* 27, no. 3 (September 2016): 443–71.

1

Our South American Cousin

Domingo F. Sarmiento and Education in Argentina and the United States

Evan C. Rothera

Forty years ago, Eric Foner bemoaned that the "interesting comments on internal American affairs contained in the dispatches of foreign diplomats based in Washington have generally been neglected by historians of the period [Reconstruction]."[1] His critique still stands, particularly for Domingo F. Sarmiento, president of Argentina and one of Latin America's leading liberals. Sarmiento was an admirer and biographer of Lincoln and Horace Mann, a booster of the United States, and an important educational reformer. In addition to visiting the United States in 1847, Sarmiento spent three productive years (1865–68) observing and traveling throughout the country as Argentine Minister Plenipotentiary and Envoy Extraordinary. During this time, Sarmiento paid careful attention to the development of Reconstruction and reflected on what he saw.[2]

Sarmiento's writings and career merit attention from historians of the United States for several reasons. For one, Sarmiento provides a counterpoint to an essay written by Edward L. Ayers, entitled "Exporting Reconstruction." Ayers focused on attempts by the United States to reconstruct other nations and asserted, "If we can see the familiar story of America's Reconstruction as an episode with counterparts, parallels, and resonances elsewhere, we might be able to make better use of this piece of our national history as we navigate our own times and we might understand our own Reconstruction a bit better."[3] Sarmiento illustrates how people in other countries observed, processed, imported, and modified aspects of Reconstruction to suit their own contexts, needs, and desires.[4] Sarmiento was especially struck by northern white protestant female missionaries and teachers who traveled south to teach African Americans. His observations of these teachers caused him to alter his ideas about women and education.[5] While he had earlier advocated for female teachers on the principle that women were cheaper to employ, Sarmiento came to espouse a more racialized and sexualized set of principles. Furthermore, when elected president of Argentina in 1868,

Sarmiento brought white female teachers from the United States to work in Argentine schools, thus using one element of Reconstruction in the United States as a model for Argentina.

Sarmiento's life and work also demonstrate the international nature of the world in which he lived. Many people who lived during the mid–nineteenth century, whether in the United States, Argentina, Mexico, Great Britain, or elsewhere, were well aware of the transnational world around them, one marked by flows of people, goods, and ideas.[6] In this world, it was perfectly natural for an Argentine diplomat to author a biography of Abraham Lincoln, for people in the United States to fashion a "usable Sarmiento," just as Sarmiento created a "usable Lincoln," and for reformers from the United States, England, France, and Argentina to consider themselves part of a broader community. Sarmiento and many northern reformers and Republicans were immersed in the same transatlantic intellectual and political currents. Sarmiento's ability to borrow from and connect with people like Horace and Mary Mann reflected shared values and ideas. Put simply, Sarmiento, northern reformers, and Republicans were in dialogue with one another, were shaped by common intellectual movements and traditions, and clearly considered themselves part of what *Harper's Weekly* called "the great liberal party of the world."[7]

In recent years, historians have become much more attentive to this "great liberal party," although many studies of liberalism still foreground connections between the United States and Northern Europe. Among others, Leslie Butler, Daniel Rodgers, Robert Kelley, and, in this volume, Mitchell Snay persuasively argue that historians must understand the transatlantic dimensions of liberalism in order to form a complete picture of the era.[8] Rodgers contends that the period between the end of the Civil War and World War II was one dominated by sea lanes, in which people and ideas crossed the Atlantic with great rapidity. Despite the important nature of this work, the "great liberal party" was not merely a collection of United States and Northern European politicians and reformers, but a broader group of people stretching throughout the Atlantic World. Thomas Bender argues that the postbellum era was not so much marked by static sea lanes between the United States and Europe, but rather by webs of connections radiating throughout the world.[9] This chapter builds on Bender's analysis, as well as the point by historians Philip Morgan and Jack Greene that "there is also no reason why east-west lines of influence should predominate over those that ran in a north-south direction" to analyze both the "great liberal party of the world" and the great liberal party of the Western Hemisphere.[10] Thus, this chapter will, whenever appropriate, include comparisons between the United States, Argentina, and Mexico to underscore that many of the issues in the United States, such as anti-Catholicism and anti-clericalism, found analogs elsewhere in the new nations of the New World. This hemispheric community of liberals was neither homogenous nor of one mind. Although Sarmiento, northern reformers, and Republicans agreed on many issues, they differed on others, specifically in their opinion of cities versus the country and the impact of state centralization.[11]

While Sarmiento and many of his contemporaries belonged to the "great liberal party of the world," this chapter does not offer a story of people in the New World unquestioningly imitating the Old. Nor is it a story of people in the Americas ignoring each other to focus on Europe. There is no question that people in the Americas often looked to Europe. As Mitchell Snay skillfully demonstrates, Radical Republican analysis of the struggle over the British Reform Act of 1867 mirrored their views of Reconstruction.[12] Similarly, Alison Efford argues that the reform ethos of the Liberal Republicans "heralded a new style of transnational comparison in which Americans became more comfortable drawing political inspiration from European sources."[13] This chapter offers a complement to Snay and Efford's chapters by focusing on people who found more to admire and emulate in New England and Argentina than they did in Europe.

Even as a young man, Sarmiento could have claimed membership in the "great liberal party of the world." He admired Europe, read European writers, and initially considered Europe a lodestar. However, when he visited Europe to study schools, he became disillusioned by what he encountered. When he traveled to the United States, on the other hand, Sarmiento quickly became entranced by the young republic and discovered kindred spirits—Horace and Mary Mann. When Sarmiento became President of Argentina, he called on the friends and acquaintances he had made in the United States and they helped him recruit female teachers for Argentina and promoted his projects. Thus, Sarmiento's ideas about education and female teachers, ideas he modified based on what he saw in the United States, highlight the existence and importance of a hemispheric liberal party, composed of people like Sarmiento, Horace and Mary Mann, Henry Barnard, and Benjamin Apthorp Gould, among others, who focused their attention on the New World rather than the Old. Some of them admired elements of Europe but, on the whole, they were more interested in establishing hemispheric relationships.

Cooperation among the members of this hemispheric liberal party showcases an important episode of pan-Americanism. Historians do not usually think of Reconstruction as a time of pan-Americanism. Two prominent pan-American moments occurred decades before and after Reconstruction. In the 1810s and

1820s, people in the United States celebrated Latin American revolutions and Henry Clay and John Quincy Adams argued for closer relations among the nations of the New World. In the late 1880s and early 1890s, James G. Blaine created the Pan-American Conferences to facilitate access to Latin American markets. Reconstruction, on the other hand, is often analyzed as a time when people in the United States looked inward. Sarmiento and the Manns offer a very different story.[14] This episode of pan-Americanism differs from others because it was not initiated by the United States. United States teachers in Argentine schools could be an example of "soft power" except, as Karen Leroux observes, the United States government did not play a role in recruiting or sending them to Argentina.[15] Despite pervasive anti–Latin American and anti–United States sentiment, people throughout the Americas rejected these ideas and strove to create closer bonds among their respective countries. Sarmiento's life and work not only demonstrate how people in other countries appropriated and modified elements of Reconstruction but also how they were aided in this endeavor by people in the United States who, in turn, appropriated elements from other countries. This was not simply a time when people in the United States looked exclusively inward to solve the problems raised by the Civil War. Rather, this was a time when people looked both inward and outward, a time when liberals throughout the Americas exchanged ideas and, in addition, a forgotten moment of pan-Americanism.

In his 1852–53 report "The State of the South American Republics at Midcentury," Sarmiento grandly asserted that his purpose in life was to "educate the mass of the South American population" and that he had devoted his entire existence to this purpose.[16] By the end of his life, Sarmiento had an international reputation for doing exactly this. In 1881, the Buenos Aires *Standard* extolled Sarmiento as the "Father of Education in South America."[17] Four years later, the distant *Morning Oregonian* praised him as both "the founder of the public school system in the Argentine Republic" and "the leading advocate of the higher education of women in South America."[18] Historians have generally echoed these encomiums. Lewis Hanke, for example, proclaimed that Sarmiento would always be remembered as "'a soldier in the never-ceasing battle for the liberty of men's minds,' who considered the schoolroom the most important battlefield in America."[19]

Sarmiento was born in 1811, in the province of San Juan, to a poor family and from these humble beginnings rose to the zenith of Argentine politics, a Horatio Alger story that he readily employed. As a young man, Sarmiento, like one of his heroes, Benjamin Franklin, read widely and educated himself in an attempt to better his own situation.[20] Sarmiento worked a variety of jobs in his early years including as a teacher, a clerk, and a mine foreman. In addition, Sarmiento participated actively in Argentina politics.

For much of Sarmiento's life, two factions dominated Argentine politics. The Unitarios believed in a strong centralized government and the Federales favored a weaker central government and more powerful provincial governments.[21] Conflict between centralists and federalists played an important role in Mexican politics as well.[22] This conflict was not so cut and dried in the United States. Federalists, and later Whigs and Republicans, often opted for a stronger central government, while Jeffersonian Republicans and later Democrats usually favored a weaker central government and stronger state governments. However, there are many examples of Federalists, Whigs, and Republicans preferring a weaker central government and Jeffersonian Republicans and Democrats embracing a stronger one. Although the same fault line existed in all three countries, the political contexts in the United States, Mexico, and Argentina were quite different. In Argentina, dictators such as Juan Manuel de Rosas, the Governor of Buenos Aires and the caudillo of the Río de la Plata, were proponents of decentralization. In the United States, on the other hand, at least when it came to rhetoric, the widespread fear was that excessive centralization would lead to a dictatorship. In Mexico, Antonio López de Santa Anna and Porfirio Díaz began their lives as *federalistas*, men who favored a weaker central government and stronger states, but, once they gained power, heartily embraced centralization.[23]

The two factions in Argentina were bitter enemies and did not hesitate to use force against each other. The fighting between the two groups lasted for nearly half a century and engendered hatred on both sides. Federales usually banded together under the leadership of regional caudillos (strongmen), men such as Juan Facundo Quiroga and Rosas. Quiroga, a fierce and impetuous man nicknamed the "Tiger of the Plains" (El Tigre de los Llanos), controlled the province of La Rioja for several years until political opponents assassinated him. Rosas, a wealthy landholder, was initially elected Governor of the province of Buenos Aires but quickly assumed dictatorial powers and ruled the province from 1828 to 1832 and from 1832 until his defeat in 1852 at the battle of Caseros.[24] Federales and caudillos resisted the centralizing tendencies of Sarmiento and the Unitarios, causing them tremendous problems.[25]

As a teacher in San Juan, Sarmiento was a proponent of education, viewing it as the key to destroying the power of dictators like Rosas, a man who, in Sarmiento's eyes, was the "the most barbarous representative of barbarism."[26] Many people in the United States, as well as Atlantic reformers, shared Sarmiento's belief that education was a bulwark against tyranny. Sarmiento likely developed this view through his own experiences and from what he read. Like many of his contemporaries, Sarmiento was a voracious reader and devoured a variety of books.[27] In addition to Franklin's autobiography, we know that Sarmiento read books by John Stuart Mill, an advocate of education, and that he kept abreast of European reform literature.[28] Sarmiento and northern reformers read many of the same books and newspapers so, despite living on opposite ends of the world, they shared a common intellectual background and arrived independently at many of the same ideas.[29]

Sarmiento's anti-caudillo and anti-Rosas ideas eventually led him to take up arms with his fellow Unitarios in San Juan. This resort to arms did not end well; after the Federales besieged and captured the city of Mendoza from the Unitarios, Sarmiento's family placed him under house arrest in 1829–30 to save him from a firing squad. Several months later, Sarmiento fled to Chile. Although he returned to Argentina shortly thereafter, Sarmiento again fled to Chile when the Federales captured the city of San Juan. Sarmiento did not return to Argentina until 1835, after the assassination of Juan Facundo Quiroga by Quiroga's political opponents.

A frenetic man, Sarmiento kept busy after his return to Argentina, founding a school for women in 1839, the Colegio de Santa Rosa de América, and establishing and editing a newspaper, *El Zonda*, also in 1839. Sarmiento's espousal of democratic ideals and his biting satire in *El Zonda* irritated Nazario Benavídez, the Federale governor of San Juan. Benavídez worried about Unitario resurgence in San Juan, so he exiled Sarmiento to Chile in 1840.[30] This exile in Chile was different: Sarmiento edited *El Mercurio* and founded *El Nacional*, two important newspapers, and continued his anti-Rosas tirades, writing perhaps the most important book published in Latin America in the nineteenth century, *Facundo: o Civilización y Barbarie* (1845).[31]

Facundo, wrote Nicolas Shumway, "defies easy categorization."[32] On its face, *Facundo* appeared to be a biography of Quiroga and Sarmiento did offer the reader a wealth of biographical information. However, given Sarmiento's strong prejudices and passions, *Facundo* ended up being much more. Sarmiento offered lengthy analysis of the conditions in Argentina necessary to produce a man like Quiroga and the result was not a flattering picture of the Federales' Argentina. As Kathleen Ross asserted, *Facundo* analyzed "the violence and evil fostered by Rosas's tyranny, which favored the countryside at the expense of the supposedly superior values of the city."[33]

Rosas, Sarmiento proclaimed, would not remain in power forever and education would play a critical role in his downfall. "Hundreds of Argentine students are sheltered in the schools of France, Chile, Brazil, North America, England, and even Spain. They will return later to realize in this country the institutions that gleam brightly in these free States; and will put their might behind overthrowing this semi-barbarous tyrant."[34] Sarmiento, who had spent large portions of his life in exile, not only understood that the exile experience could shelter and protect enemies of Rosas, but saw the connections between Argentina and the rest of the world. Even Spain, a country Sarmiento despised because it was monarchical and aristocratic, could aid in overthrowing tyranny and assist the cause of democracy.

Sarmiento saw in the rise of Rosas the culmination of a vicious cycle. "An ignorant people will always elect a Rosas,"[35] Sarmiento asserted. Therefore, "the Dictator had arisen to power through the barbarism of the people; and the poverty and ignorance of the provinces secured him from all dangerous opposition."[36] But this was not a phenomenon limited to Rosas; Sarmiento realized that other dictators could seize power just as easily. The answer to the reign of dictators, therefore, was education. "Primary education," Sarmiento declared, "is the measure of the civilization of a village. Where it is incomplete or abandoned . . . there is a semibarbarous village without lights, customs, industry, or progress." Sarmiento saw in education a panacea;[37] education was not only a prerequisite for overthrowing Rosas, but it would prevent other dictators from gaining power.

Sarmiento's use of the language of civilization and barbarism is another indicator that he was a member of a transnational group of reformers and politicians. The civilization and barbarism rhetoric was pervasive not only in Sarmiento's writings, but also in the Atlantic World. One does not have to look particularly hard to find examples. For instance, this language appears throughout Hinton Rowan Helper's famous book, *The Impending Crisis*;[38] in the writings of abolitionists;[39] in the correspondence, speeches, and presidential proclamations of Abraham Lincoln;[40] and throughout newspapers.[41] Sarmiento, when he spoke of a fundamental conflict between a barbarous countryside and civilized cities, was fully tuned into transnational discussions about civilization and modernity.[42] Furthermore, when he used "civilization," Sarmiento meant the civilization and progress he claimed European immigrants brought to Argentina. At this stage of his life, Sarmiento had not yet met the Manns or traveled to Europe and the United States. Therefore, he had not come to these ideas by copying them from later acquaintances, but through his own reading and experiences.

Facundo was a success on a variety of levels. The stinging condemnation of everything wrong in Argentina infuriated Rosas and cheered Sarmiento's fellow Unitarios.[43] Without doubt, *Facundo* proved Sarmiento's commitment to education, but the question remained: How were these ideas to benefit Argentina? Argentina did not have a well-developed school system in the 1840s, and Sarmiento was not in a position to create one, although he gained practical experience in Chile.[44] Manuel Montt, the Chilean Minister of Justice and Public Instruction appointed Sarmiento director of the Escuela Normal de Perceptores in 1842, the first teacher training school established in Chile. In addition, Sarmiento, again at Montt's request, undertook a mission of observation for the Chilean government and spent the period 1845–47 studying schools in Europe and the United States. Although he admired European monuments and scientific achievements, and although he had long been an admirer of European civilization, Sarmiento found troubling the condition of "millions of farmers, proletarians, and workingmen, who are degraded and unworthy of being counted among men."[45] These findings disheartened Sarmiento, especially since he had long argued, particularly in *Facundo*, that "the genius of European civilization" offered many benefits for Argentina.[46]

If Europe proved a disappointment, the United States fascinated Sarmiento.[47] The principal objective of Sarmiento's trip to Boston was to see Horace Mann, "the great primary education reformer, a traveler, like myself, to Europe in search of methods and systems."[48] While in Europe, Sarmiento read one of Horace Mann's reports on primary education, which fired his ardor to speak with Mann. During his time in Massachusetts, Sarmiento spent long hours conversing with Horace and Mary Mann.[49] This fruitful meeting introduced Sarmiento to a prominent United States educational reformer and provided Sarmiento with a host of new ideas, including the employment of women as teachers.[50] Prior to this, Sarmiento had clearly been interested in female education, but he thought more about educating women—hence the formation of the Colegio de Santa Rosa de América—and had not considered women as teachers.

Sarmiento proved receptive to the Manns' ideas for several reasons. For one, they produced results. Mann established a teacher training school for women, Sarmiento wrote, and Massachusetts now had, in addition to 2,589 male teachers, 5,000 female teachers. The number of teachers in Massachusetts, Sarmiento marveled, was greater than the total size of Chile's permanent army![51] In addition, Sarmiento viewed Horace and Mary Mann as kindred spirits and stayed in contact with them. When he returned to the United States in 1865, he spent time in New England with the now-widowed Mary Mann.[52] Furthermore, Mary Mann translated *Facundo* into English in 1868 and Sarmiento translated her biography of Horace Mann into Spanish as *Vida de Horacio Mann*.[53] Sarmiento's admiration of Horace Mann ran so deep that in an 1876 toast, he asserted that Abraham Lincoln and Horace Mann "completed the Independence proclaimed in 1776, by the freedom of the slave and the education of the people."[54] This kinship was due to the similarity of their beliefs, a shared interest in educational reform, and their membership in a transnational party of reformers.

After his visit with the Manns, Sarmiento returned to Chile and published an account of his trips to Europe and the United States. He remained in Chile until 1851, at which point Sarmiento returned to Argentina and joined the army of another caudillo, Justo José de Urquiza, as an officer and a traveling newspaper correspondent. Although the army marched to overthrow Rosas, Sarmiento did not think much of Urquiza, "a poor peasant without education," or of his army, which was "nothing more than a *levee en masse* of country dwellers."[55] Sarmiento insisted on the importance of education and asserted that while Urquiza was a useful instrument to topple one dictator, he would likely supplant Rosas. Indeed, after Urquiza defeated Rosas, Sarmiento and other residents of Buenos Aires such as Bartolomé Mitre grew wary of Urquiza's desire for power. In addition, irritated about their reduced position in the Confederation, Buenos Aires seceded. For the better part of eight years, the province existed autonomously. Sarmiento served in the Buenos Aires Legislature, edited a newspaper, and worked to improve schools in Buenos Aires. "It is time," Sarmiento thundered in an 1858 speech to the Buenos Aires Legislature, "that one of the concerns of the public should be the betterment of the schools."[56] Sarmiento identified Buenos Aires's lack of buildings, lack of funds, and superannuated teachers as obstacles to progress. In addition, many parents did not want their children, particularly girls, to attend school.

Nine years after meeting the Manns and four years into Buenos Aires's autonomous existence, Sarmiento began advocating for female teachers. Sarmiento's speeches and writings from this period indicate that he argued for the employment of female teachers largely on the basis of cost, a pragmatic reason. In 1856, Sarmiento approved of the tendency to employ women as teachers "because they cost less and are more adept than men at managing small children."[57] At this point, only a few Argentine women taught, and exclusively in schools for girls. Sarmiento suggested that women, who drew smaller salaries than men, could be employed in greater numbers in the Argentine educational system and thus help offset the shortage of teachers. In 1857, Sarmiento contended that women could help realize a project of "good and cheap education for the people," and that women "can be used in creating a method of educating all children."[58] Perhaps getting caught up in the moment, Sarmiento claimed that "a day will arrive in which a school of men and women are taught exclusively by women."[59]

In advocating for female teachers, Sarmiento drew on discourses about the naturalness of gender roles and utilized the language of gender inequality. In so doing, Sarmiento echoed some of the ideas of northern reformers, including Horace Mann and the equally influential Catharine Beecher. Like Beecher, Sarmiento argued for the use of female teachers based on the very fact of their unequal pay.[60] Also like Beecher, Sarmiento placed female teachers in a public sphere and declared that women would teach in mixed classrooms and would, one day, be responsible for all of the teaching. In addition, like Horace Mann, Sarmiento argued that women were by nature better teachers than men and that female teachers would inculcate the rising generation with appropriate values.[61] That Sarmiento, Beecher, and Mann embraced similar ideas is not coincidental; these three reformers shared a common intellectual background and drew on the same ideas and concepts, including about gender. Furthermore, in his conversation with the Manns, Sarmiento had likely learned about many of Horace Mann's ideas. Critically, at this juncture, Sarmiento never spoke of recruiting teachers from the United States, but of employing Argentine women as teachers.

In 1865, President Bartolomé Mitre, one of Sarmiento's rivals, appointed him Argentine Minister Plenipotentiary and Envoy Extraordinary to the United States, which gave him the opportunity to visit Mary Mann and observe life in the United States during Reconstruction. Although Horace Mann had died, Mary Mann introduced Sarmiento to the New England literary elite, educational reformers, and politicians.[62] While Mary Mann did not publish an English-language translation of *Facundo* until 1868, many New Englanders were familiar with the book.[63] Sarmiento described his heady experiences in a letter to his friend Aurelia Velez Sarsfield: "The next day I ate with Waldo Emerson, whom I had sent *Facundo*. This book serves as a method of introduction. If being Minister does not matter to everyone, being an educator is here a great title in this town of teachers; but I always have *Facundo* in reserve, it is my Parrott gun. No one can resist it."[64] Emerson, according to Michael Rockland, thanked Sarmiento for the copy of *Facundo*, and "encouraged Mary Mann to continue with her translation of the book."[65] Sarmiento's favorable reception undoubtedly influenced his opinion of New England and he was not shy about endorsing the idea that Boston was "the American Athens."[66]

While Sarmiento was being toasted by the New England literati, he kept a close eye on what was happening in the South. Sarmiento arrived in the United

States shortly after the surrender of Lee's army at Appomattox and Lincoln's assassination. Therefore, he was in the right place at the right time to observe benevolent and philanthropic efforts by Northerners during the early years of Reconstruction.[67] Sarmiento's correspondence from this time is filled with favorable comments about the actions of Northern men and women. Northerners, Sarmiento observed to Juana Manso, an Argentine educator and long-time collaborator, "have appointed superintendents of the aid societies in the South, and calculated that they need immediately fifteen thousand schools and fifteen thousand teachers, and all the societies have moved to obtain them. . . . they contracted eight hundred teachers, one hundred fifty paid for and contracted by New York alone."[68] Sarmiento greatly admired "a girl" who "moved to South Carolina" and who "was placed alone at the head of a cotton plantation of three hundred negroes, whom she not only educated, but taught the exercise of arms, all without losing the prestige of womanhood."[69] Sarmiento argued that these teachers would effect a beneficial and startling transformation of the South: "Fifteen thousand schools that on Sundays will be schools for adults, will, in few years, erase the original sin of absolute ignorance in the South, and the freedmen will be more advanced than us whites."[70] Sarmiento's prejudices dictated his analysis: what would happen to Argentina when African Americans in the South surpassed the Argentine elite? There was, however, an easy answer: Recruit white female teachers from the United States.

Sarmiento drew on what he saw in the United States to reformulate his own ideas about class, race, gender, and the employment of female teachers and was hardly in the United States a few weeks before he sent a letter to Juana Manso that avidly promoted the recruitment of teachers from the United States. Sarmiento's language merits careful examination. "One hundred Boston girls," Sarmiento wrote excitedly, "at the head of the schools in Buenos Aires, or in the Provinces, would replicate the system of education in Massachusetts, with its efficiency, its extension, and its reality."[71] Enthused about the potential for this project, Sarmiento continued, "would it not be a beautiful sight . . . to see arriving at Buenos Aires . . . forty blond girls, modest without affectation of modesty, virtuous, of that practical virtue, useful, social, that prepares a mother for a future family, school teachers, Bostonians, colonizers of education and of republicanism."[72] His language mirrored similar language in the United States and Britain about the cult of domesticity and republican motherhood, another indication that Sarmiento was in dialogue with transatlantic concepts and part of a broader community. Gone was Sarmiento's advocacy of women based on lower salaries. Sarmiento now spoke of blond girls, not women, and the positive impact these blond girls would have on Argentina. Clearly Sarmiento had a certain racial type in mind when he spoke of teachers. Despite the contingent of African American teachers, both male and female, in the South, Sarmiento did not want Charlotte Forten or Susie King Taylor; he wanted blond, elite or middle class, white New Englanders.

This is not an inconsequential point. The question of Sarmiento's racism has long been the subject of debate. In *Facundo*, Sarmiento argued that one of the causes of Argentina's failure was the fusion of Spanish, Amerindian, and African "races." He denigrated the "savage" and "barbarous" descendants of indigenous peoples, especially in comparison to "civilized" Europeans. These attitudes appeared again and again throughout Sarmiento's writings. Some scholars have contended that Sarmiento's attitudes provided a justification for the campaign of extermination, "La campaña del desierto" (1878–85), waged against the indigenous people of Argentina. As Kristine L. Jones explained, "Although not anti-Indian, Sarmiento's ideas contributed in an important way to a public discourse that equated civilization with the conquest of the Indians."[73] Not only was this ideology frequently espoused by northern Republicans after the Civil War, but Sarmiento held views sympathetic to those of some moderate and conservative Republicans insofar as he detested slavery, but did not support black equality.

The similarity of Sarmiento's writings and ideas to Europeans such as Joseph Arthur Gobineau suggest that Sarmiento was a member of an international circle of reformers as well as an international group of racial theorists that included thinkers like Confederate propagandist Henry Hotze.[74] Just as the "great liberal party of the world" agreed on many points, albeit with regional variation in ideas, the same phenomenon is evident in the thought of this international group of racial thinkers. Both Hotze and Sarmiento, for example, adhered to scientific racism, but for strikingly different reasons. For Hotze, racism bolstered the legitimacy of slavery. Conversely, Sarmiento wanted nothing to do with the proslavery argument and praised Lincoln for destroying the peculiar institution. Sarmiento's embrace of scientific racism led him to advocate "civilization" first from Europe and later from the United States and a massive influx of immigrants. If nothing else, Hotze and Sarmiento demonstrate the ambiguous relationship between racism and proslavery thought throughout the Atlantic World in the mid-nineteenth century. Finally, Sarmiento's lack of attention to African American teachers meant that he missed important lessons about how to build an educational system and grass roots education reform.[75]

Sarmiento's assertion to a Chilean correspondent that "seven hundred North American teachers in the Argentine Republic, or in Chile, would repair in ten years the stagnation of three centuries" is an excellent window into the program he hoped to enact as president.[76] In four years, 1870–74, Sarmiento built nearly eight hundred new schools in Argentina; increased the number of teachers in the schools from 1,778 to 2,868; and oversaw an expansion in the number of children attending school by 233 percent (from approximately 30,000 students to approximately 100,000).[77] A critical part of Sarmiento's program was his recruitment of teachers from the United States. Alice Houston Luiggi found that sixty-five teachers "went to Argentina from 1869 to 1898 to establish, reorganize, or head eighteen normal schools."[78] These sixty-five teachers did not arrive all at once, but in fits and starts over a period of years. Although Sarmiento was not able to interview and select the candidates, he relied on friends in New England, particularly Mary Mann, to help him select qualified women and to promote his educational project. Sarmiento's membership in a hemispheric party of reformers and politicians paid dividends and highlights an important example of pan-American cooperation.

When the teachers arrived, Sarmiento modified his ideas in another way: He did not, as he suggested in the 1850s, put women in charge of teaching children. Rather, Sarmiento placed the women in charge of teacher training schools in the provinces, perhaps remembering the success of Horace Mann's teacher training school in Massachusetts. Therefore, the teachers trained many Argentines as teachers and helped, in this way, to reduce the illiteracy rate in Argentina greatly.[79] When one considers the impressive increases in pupils, schools, and teachers during Sarmiento's presidency, the number of women who came might seem a pittance. But these women had a tremendous impact in the training of teachers.

Sarmiento's recruitment of teachers from the United States and his navigation of the intertwined issues of religion, education, and the state demonstrate affinities with his fellow hemispheric liberals. On the surface, the United States and Argentina, as well as Mexico, look quite different. Where Argentina and Mexico were Catholic countries, many in the Protestant United States were fervently anti-Catholic. But the reality was more complicated. In Mexico, for example, the Liberals and Conservatives argued over, among other things, a "Church question." The Liberals took a strong anti-clerical position, attacked the privileges of the Catholic Church, and expropriated Church property.[80] This led to the War of the Reform and later to a group of Catholics and Conservatives inviting Archduke Ferdinand Maximilian of Austria to assume the throne of a new Mexican empire. Although there was no "Church question" either in Argentina or in the United States, comparable to that in Mexico, anti-Catholicism in the

United States was strong.[81] The classic expression of this sentiment is Thomas Nast's cartoon "The American River Ganges," wherein Catholic priests, whom Nast depicted as crocodiles, menaced a group of children huddled on the bank of a river. Nast tapped into a potent sentiment; during this period, many Protestants feared that Catholics were attempting to subvert democracy, infiltrate the public schools, catechize young Protestant children, and enslave the United States to the Pope in Rome.[82]

But what about Sarmiento's Argentina? Mónica Szurmuk's observation that "Sarmiento could have saved himself many problems if he had selected Catholic teachers instead of Protestant ones" suggests a different situation.[83] Sarmiento, however, did not want to bring in Catholics from the United States; he wanted the Protestant New Englanders he saw go south during Reconstruction. Indeed, one United States newspaper commented that the work of the teachers in Sarmiento's Argentina "was for a time very discouraging, and they needed the enthusiastic support of President Sarmiento and his friends to overcome the conservative opposition of the priests to the attendance of the children."[84] Sarmiento had to fight against priests, who objected to the recruitment of Protestant teachers, in his quest to educate the population.[85] Furthermore, as C. A. Bayly noted, in the 1870s, "the Vatican turned to the offensive and sent large numbers of European priests to the spiritual war fronts in Brazil and Argentina."[86] Thus, Sarmiento faced attacks from internal and external foes.

Some of Sarmiento's preference for Protestants from the United States was attributable to his own religious attitudes. Although nominally a Catholic, Sarmiento, by this point in his life, espoused separation of church and state and did not care for the idea of priests in charge of schools.[87] In addition, Sarmiento admired the Puritans because, he claimed, they introduced universal education to the United States.[88] But some of Sarmiento's opposition to Catholic teachers came from his membership in the hemispheric liberal party. Sarmiento, like many people in the United States, Mexico, and elsewhere, thought that the Catholic Church was backwards, anti-modern, and a bulwark of reaction. Furthermore, his anti-Catholicism found echoes in Germany when Otto von Bismarck attacked the Catholic Church during the Kulturkampf. Sarmiento, therefore, tapped currents of anti-Catholicism circulating around the Atlantic World.[89] Although this decision did not make him popular with some of his fellow Argentines, it marked him as part of an international group of reformers and politicians.

Sarmiento and his fellow liberals advocated similar programs of state-building and nation-making. Sarmiento's recruitment of teachers from the United States was one plan among many that he implemented when he became President of

Argentina. Historian Robert Crassweller labeled Sarmiento's presidency a "crescendo of works initiated and pursued," a characterization that rings true and makes Sarmiento sound very much like a northern Republican.[90] As president, Sarmiento not only presided over the development of Argentina's schools, but also founded a military college, built libraries, established national academies, erected a national observatory with the help of Benjamin Apthorp Gould, and funded the construction of hundreds of miles of roads and railroad lines and 5,000 kilometers of telegraph wires.[91] Sarmiento's flurry of activity in Argentina was not surprising to those who knew him. Historians have long understood Sarmiento, along with Bartolomé Mitre and Nicolás Avellaneda, presidents of the Argentine Republic from 1862 to 1880, as the consolidators of the nation-state.[92]

While Sarmiento developed Argentina's infrastructure, the same sort of internal improvement occurred throughout the Americas. In the United States, secession gave Republicans strong majorities in both houses of Congress and they lost no time in seizing the opportunity to enact their economic program including the Morrill Tariff, the Homestead Act, the Morrill Act, and the Pacific Railroad Acts. During Reconstruction, Republicans attempted to remake the South in their free labor image and sought to transform the region by building railroads, schools, and other internal improvements.[93] A similar process occurred in Mexico. After the Liberals expelled the French and defeated the Imperialists, railroad promoters swarmed to Mexico City and beseeched Benito Juárez for land grants and other favors. The governments of Juárez, Sebastián Lerdo de Tejada, and, later, Porfirio Díaz, like that of Sarmiento, moved to construct roads and other internal improvements in order to knit the country together.[94] That political parties argued for government sponsorship of internal improvements suggests much common ground between Whigs and Republicans in the United States, Unitarios and Liberals in Argentina, and Liberals in Mexico. These parties shared an ideology of state-sponsored economic development explainable because they lived through a global transportation revolution.[95] This shared ideology reinforces the notion of a hemispheric liberal party. It also suggests how profoundly transformative the mid–nineteenth century was for peoples' expectations about what was possible in the world and highlights the fact that the United States, Mexico, and Argentina, among other countries, were following the same paths, interacting with each other, and attempting to create a common destiny.

The ties and connections between the United States and Argentina did not flow in one direction only. Sarmiento was certainly interested in the United States but he also intrigued people in the United States. The reception of Sarmiento's biography of Lincoln, not to mention the assistance Sarmiento received in recruiting teachers from the United States and promoting his programs, offers additional evidence of pan-American cooperation. Published in 1866, Sarmiento's *Vida de Lincoln* copied large sections from other Lincoln biographies, included many of Lincoln's speeches, and a lengthy introduction written by Sarmiento himself. Although some historians have dismissed *Vida*, others have argued for the importance of the work in shaping Latin American perceptions of Lincoln and creating a usable Lincoln for Latin America.[96] Sarmiento fashioned Lincoln into a champion of education, celebrated Lincoln as a specimen of natural genius, emphasized Lincoln's opposition to the Mexican War, and made Lincoln a crusader for Mexican rights and liberties who retained his popularity with the people![97] This depiction of Lincoln did not always match reality, but would have appealed to Latin Americans who saw the war with Mexico as an appalling and unjust land-grab by the United States.[98] Sarmiento not only created a usable Lincoln, but used Lincoln to justify some of his own actions, including invoking Lincoln's suspension of habeas corpus to justify his controversial use of "estado de sitio" in Argentina.[99]

Sarmiento had intended *Vida de Lincoln* to be read by his fellow Argentines and wrote to José Posse, the Governor of Tucumán, "I will send [*Vida*] to you in quantities sufficient to satisfy the hunger to read of some of your people."[100] *Harper's Weekly* believed that *Vida de Lincoln* and *Vida de Horacio Mann*, Sarmiento's translation of Mary Mann's biography of Horace Mann, would be extensively read, but there is little evidence that Argentines took much notice of *Vida de Lincoln*.[101] Later in life, Sarmiento vented his spleen about the reception of *Vida de Lincoln* in Argentina. After noting that a writer in the United States found the book worthy of being translated into English, Sarmiento delivered a blistering attack against Argentine statesmen: "In the Argentine Republic, where public men do not need examples to dictate or abolish laws, they did not trouble to read [*Vida*], as it was unworthy of attention, and the Government of Buenos Aires donated to school children, for a reading book, one that grown men cannot easily digest."[102] Sarmiento's sarcasm is puzzling; one could be excused for supposing he would have been happy to see *Vida de Lincoln* in the hands of schoolchildren. Sarmiento also commented that a citizen of the United States translated *Vida* into English for use in United States classrooms.[103] Therefore, although *Vida* was intended for an Argentine audience, it was embraced more enthusiastically by people in the United States.[104]

For much of the nineteenth century, many citizens of the United States did not have a favorable picture of Latin America. Consider, for instance, how the *New York Tribune* analyzed one South American country: "Venezuela is reported to be quiet. We doubt whether the quiet will last a whole year. Of all the disorganized republics of Spanish America, Venezuela is by far the worst."[105] This pervasive anti–Latin American sentiment has been emphasized by numerous scholars, most recently by Gregory P. Downs, who discussed the "problem of Mexicanization," or a fear that the United States would become as disordered and anarchical as Mexico allegedly was.[106] There were certainly Hispanophiles in the United States but anti–Latin Americanism was pervasive, if not universal.

Anti–Latin American rhetoric only describes part of the story. Immediately after insulting Venezuela and the "disorganized republics of South America," the *Tribune* praised Sarmiento and Argentina! Sarmiento, the paper wrote, "promises to be unusually successful, and is likely to place this country, in every respect, among the most prosperous of the South American republics."[107] While it would be incorrect to state that everyone in the United States knew of Sarmiento, he frequently appeared in newspapers and the literate public knew Sarmiento was President of Argentina, an author, educator, and leading Argentine statesman.[108] We can ask the question: Did people in the United States like Sarmiento because he was a critic of Latin American society and exalted the United States? Sarmiento's popularity in the United States clearly owed something to his appreciation for the United States. Still, this point can be taken too far.[109] Sarmiento was a fierce critic of caudillos and the rule of dictators, but he did not criticize every aspect of Latin American society. Indeed, in the preface to *Vida de Lincoln*, Sarmiento wrote that Latin Americans were interested in the life of Lincoln and the development of the United States precisely because, due to the similarity of their colonial origins, the United States could serve as a model for Argentina's development.[110]

Just because the United States could be a model, however, did not mean Sarmiento advocated slavish adherence to the United States. He clearly imported only what he thought would strengthen Argentina. For that matter, the people who aided Sarmiento, who corresponded and cooperated with him, and who praised his efforts, did not do so because he was a critic of Latin America. Rather, they liked Sarmiento—and he liked them—because they were part of a pan-American moment. People saw much to appreciate in Sarmiento's vision of Argentina's future—a vision that the United States was also working to achieve during Reconstruction. They admired the champion of education who did not recoil from criticizing tyrants. Sarmiento, in short, was not popular because he affirmed stereotypes about Latin American, but because his ideas resonated with northern reformers and Republicans and because of a desire among a hemispheric group of liberals to embrace pan-Americanism. The favorable opinion of Sarmiento, incidentally, endured long after he was dead.[111]

Feelings of acclaim for Sarmiento and the connections people felt with Latin America coexisted alongside anti–Latin American sentiment. But this should not come as a surprise. Even in the traditionally acknowledged pan-American periods—the 1810s to the 1820s and the 1880s to the 1890s—there were many people, both in the United States as well as Latin America, who were unsure that they wanted to knit their destinies together. This legacy of uncertainty is evident today: Many people welcome immigrants from Latin America while others denigrate them as rapists and drug dealers and argue for building walls on the United States–Mexico border. This combination of pan-Americanism and anti–Latin Americanism offers a counterpoint to the historiography, which tends to overemphasize anti–Latin Americanism. Sarmiento helped many in the United States connect themselves to Latin America and helped create and sustain a forgotten, but nevertheless important, pan-American moment.

Alexis de Tocqueville did not admire the new nations of South America. According to the famous French traveler, South Americans were "stubbornly determined to tear out each other's entrails." Tocqueville even wondered whether "despotism would be a blessing for them." These two worlds, Tocqueville flatly declared, "will never be linked in my mind."[112] Many people in the United States, who considered Latin Americans backward, disordered, and barbaric, and many people in Latin America, who considered the United States greedy and imperialistic, would have agreed with Tocqueville.[113] However, this is not the entire story. The life of Domingo F. Sarmiento, a largely forgotten observer of Reconstruction, reveals much about the period. Sarmiento's strategic importation of specific practices and institutions from the United States, suggests the need to continue to think about the internationalization of Reconstruction, focusing not only on the ways that people in the United States attempted to export their own values and practices, but also on ways that people in other countries imported and modified elements.

Sarmiento's dual memberships—in both the "great liberal party of the world," as well as the great liberal party of the Western Hemisphere, demonstrate that the Atlantic World was awash with ideas and that reformers drew on common intellectual backgrounds and were steeped in common intellectual currents. Sarmiento came to some of these ideas through his own reading and ambition, and others by collaborating with members of these groups. The links between the members of these groups, particularly Sarmiento's fruitful relationship with his friend Mary Mann, facilitated Sarmiento's projects: from recruiting teachers to help build Argentina's educational system to securing the services of an astronomer.[114] This community of like-minded reformers helped counteract prevailing negative impressions of Latin America. Sarmiento was popular in the United

States largely because his ideas found a sympathetic audience among reformers and Republicans, who considered him a kindred spirit.[115] In turn, Sarmiento translated some of their writings and helped popularize them in Argentina. This community existed despite significant differences in opinion about the city/country question as well as the effect of centralization. Liberalism, in other words, should be understood as a transnational and hemispheric phenomenon. While some people in the United States found much to appreciate in Europe, others found more to appreciate in their own hemisphere. Argentines and Mexicans, among others, shared these sentiments.

Sarmiento's relationship with people like Horace and Mary Mann reveals a moment of pan-American cooperation. After bursts of pan-Americanism in the 1810s and 1820s, the idea seemed to fade from view until the late 1880s and early 1890s. Reconstruction, despite a growing wave of literature highlighting its international elements, is still conceived of as a time when people in the United States looked inward. Overemphasizing the inward focus overlooks the outward gaze of many people and their strenuous efforts to bring the nations of the New World into closer alignment. Analyzing this episode of pan-Americanism suggests revisions in how historians should deal with this topic. The United States government did not use teachers as a soft power strategy to further United States domination. Rather, Sarmiento and his fellow liberals genuinely sought to engage with each other, share ideas, borrow programs, judge successes and failures, and create what they believed to be a better world. When he proclaimed that the United States and Argentina were traveling on similar paths, Sarmiento was correct. All three countries—the United States, Argentina, and Mexico—looked to each other, especially as they strove to figure out how to reassemble their countries after violent conflicts, how to consolidate nation-states, how to spur modernization and internal improvement, and how to encourage literacy and create educated publics. Understanding Sarmiento, reformers, and Republicans, as part of a larger world of liberalism and reform and as instigators of a unique moment of pan-Americanism provides a deeper understanding of the world in which Reconstruction came about, a more nuanced assessment of the nations of the New World, and less provincial historiographies.

Notes

I would like to thank Mark E. Neely, Jr., William A. Blair, Lori D. Ginzberg, Amy S. Greenberg, Matthew D. Norman, David Prior, and Matthew Hetrick for suggestions. I presented versions of this paper at the 2012 Society of Civil War Historians Conference, the 2012 Southern Historical Association Annual Meeting, and the 2015 Society for U.S.

Intellectual History Conference. Paul A. Cimbala, Enrico Dal Lago, Peter Kolchin, and Leslie Butler have my thanks for their comments. The title riffs on William Taylor, *Our South American Cousins* (New York: Nelson and Phillips, 1879).

1. Eric Foner, "Andrew Johnson and Reconstruction: A British View," *The Journal of Southern History* 41, no. 3 (August 1975), 381. For analysis of a Mexican diplomat see Thomas D. Schoonover, *Mexican Lobby: Matías Romero in Washington, 1861–1867* (Lexington: University Press of Kentucky, 1986).

2. Sarmiento spent much of his time in Washington but traveled throughout New England and the northern states.

3. Edward L. Ayers, "Exporting Reconstruction," in *What Caused the Civil War: Reflections on the South and Southern History* (New York: Norton, 2005), 148.

4. This chapter joins a growing body of literature interested in the internationalization of Reconstruction. See David Prior's discussion in the introduction to this volume. For an early discussion of South Americans and Reconstruction, see Harry Bernstein, "South America Looks at North American Reconstruction," in Harold M. Hyman, ed., *New Frontiers of the American Reconstruction* (Urbana: University of Illinois Press, 1966): 87–104.

5. For another, rather different, discussion of this topic, see Karen Leroux, "Sarmiento's Self-Strengthening Experiment: Americanizing Schools for Argentine Nation-Building," in *Teaching America to the World and the World to America*, eds. Richard Garlitz and Lisa Jarvinen (New York: Palgrave Macmillan, 2012), 51–71. Leroux spends very little time analyzing the teachers. She argues that Sarmiento's project to Americanize Argentine schools represented "a strategy of defensive, national self-strengthening" rather than the imposition of "U.S. values and practices on a less powerful society to foster relations of dependency"; both quotes on page 66.

6. See "AHR Conversation: On Transnational History," *The American Historical Review* 111, no. 5 (December 2006): 1441–64; Ian Tyrrell, "Reflections on the transnational turn in United States history: theory and practice," *Journal of Global History* 4, no. 3 (November 2009): 453–74; and Andrew Zimmerman, *Alabama in Africa: Booker T. Washington, the German Empire, and the Globalization of the New South* (Princeton: Princeton University Press, 2010).

7. *Harper's Weekly* quoted in Leslie Butler, *Critical Americans: Victorian Intellectuals and Transatlantic Liberal Reform* (Chapel Hill: University of North Carolina Press, 2007), 89.

8. See Butler, *Critical Americans*; Robert Kelley, *The Transatlantic Persuasion: The Liberal Democratic Mind in the Age of Gladstone* (New York: Knopf, 1969); Daniel T. Rodgers, *Atlantic Crossings: Social Politics in a Progressive Age* (Cambridge: Harvard University Press, 1998); and Mitchell Snay's chapter in this volume.

9. Thomas Bender, *A Nation Among Nations: America's Place in World History* (New York: Hill and Wang, 2006), 246–95.

10. Philip D. Morgan and Jack P. Greene, "Introduction: The Present State of Atlantic History," in *Atlantic History: A Critical Appraisal*, ed., Jack P. Greene and Philip D. Morgan (Oxford: Oxford University Press, 2009), 9. There are many studies of liberalism in nineteenth-century Latin America. See, for example, Charles A. Hale, *Mexican Liberal-*

ism in the Age of Mora, 1821–1853 (New Haven: Yale University Press, 1968); Nicolas Shumway, *The Invention of Argentina* (Berkeley: University of California Press, 1991); Florencia E. Mallon, *Peasant and Nation: The Making of Postcolonial Mexico and Peru* (Berkeley: University of California Press 1995); Vincent C. Peloso and Barbara A. Tenenbaum. *Liberals, Politics, and Power: State Formation in Nineteenth-Century Latin America* (Athens: University of Georgia Press, 1996); and David Rock, *State Building and Political Movements in Argentina, 1860–1916* (Stanford: Stanford University Press, 2002).

11. Sarmiento had a radically different perspective on the city/country question than many northern reformers and Republicans. Many people in the United States agreed with Thomas Jefferson that the countryside and virtuous yeoman farmers were the foundation of democracy, in contrast to the threatening specter of urban life. Sarmiento, on the other hand, advanced the idea of a barbaric countryside and civilized cities. With the exception of Boston and Philadelphia, the Republican Party derived most of its support from the prosperous regions of the rural North, and the Democratic Party was usually stronger in the cities. See William R. Brock, *An American Crisis: Congress and Reconstruction, 1865–1867* (New York: Harper and Row, 1963), 242–48; Eric Foner, *Free Soil, Free Labor, Free Men: The Ideology of the Republican Party Before the Civil War* (Oxford: Oxford University Press, 1970); and Adam Wesley Dean, *An Agrarian Republic: Farming, Antislavery Politics, and Nature Parks in the Civil War Era* (Chapel Hill: University of North Carolina Press, 2015).

12. See Snay's chapter in this volume.

13. See Efford's chapter in this volume.

14. I agree with historian John E. Hodge that historians should "seek out and preserve" instances of pan-Americanism "rather than fastening on examples of big stick diplomacy on the part of the 'Colossus of the North,'" John E. Hodge, "Benjamin Apthorp Gould and the Founding of the Argentine National Observatory," *The Americas* 28, no. 2 (October 1971), 175.

15. Leroux, "Sarmiento's Self-Strengthening Experiment," 66.

16. "Educar la masa de la población suramericana, es mi empresa" and "á la educación de los americanos he consagrado toda mi existencia," Domingo Faustino Sarmiento [hereafter DFS], "Estado de las Repúblicas Sudamericanas á Mediados del Siglo," *Obras de D. F. Sarmiento* [hereafter *Obras*], ed. A. Belin Sarmiento (Buenos Aires: Imprenta y Litografía Mariano Moreno, 1897), 16:92, 91. Unless otherwise noted, all translations are my own. I provide the original quote in each note for reference.

17. "Editor's Table," *The Standard*, February 23, 1881.

18. "In Buenos Ayres," *Morning Oregonian*, October 1, 1885.

19. Lewis Hanke, *South America* (Princeton: D. Van Nostrand Company, Inc., 1967), 76. Although the scholarly literature concerning Sarmiento is vast, his biographers have yet to appreciate the ways that a specific pattern of developments in the United States influenced him. See J. Guillermo Guerra, *Sarmiento: Sus Vidas i sus Obras* (Santiago de Chile: Imprenta Elzeviriana, 1901); Ricardo Rojas, *El Profeta de la Pampa* (Buenos Aires: Editorial Losada, 1945), 525; Edmundo Correas, *Sarmiento and the United States* (Gainesville: University of Florida Press, 1961); Allison Williams Bunkley, *Vida de Sarmiento* (Buenos Aires: Editorial Universitaria de Buenos Aires, 1966); and José Campobassi,

Sarmiento y Su Época, 2 volumes (Buenos Aires: Editorial Losada, 1975). Two exceptions are J. Fred Rippy, "Yankee Teachers and the Founding of Argentina's Elementary School System," *The Hispanic American Historical Review* 24, no. 1 (February 1944), 166–69 and Georgette Magassy Dorn, "Sarmiento, the United States, and Public Education," in *Sarmiento and His Argentina*, ed. Joseph T Criscenti (Boulder, Co.: Lynne Rienner Publishers, Inc., 1993), 77–89.

20. See *Obras*, 3:1–346.

21. See David Rock, *Argentina 1516–1987: From Spanish Colonization to Alfonsín* (Berkeley: University of California Press, 1987).

22. See Hale, *Mexican Liberalism in the Age of Mora*.

23. See Bender's discussion of the United States in *A Nation Among Nations*, 116–81. Where Sarmiento favored a centralized state that would enhance freedom, many people in the U.S. feared centralization. People often resorted to cries of "Caesarism" and charges that Andrew Jackson, Abraham Lincoln, Andrew Johnson, and Ulysses S. Grant were setting themselves up as dictators. See Eric Foner, *Reconstruction: America's Unfinished Revolution, 1863–1867* (New York: Harper & Row, 1988), 551–55 for a discussion of the heavy political price President Grant paid for interfering in the Louisiana elections of 1874. For analysis of fears of despotism, see Mark Wahlgren Summers, *A Dangerous Stir: Fear, Paranoia, and the Making of Reconstruction* (Chapel Hill: University of North Carolina Press, 2009) and Mark Summers, *The Ordeal of the Reunion: A New History of Reconstruction* (Chapel Hill: University of North Carolina Press, 2014).

24. See John Lynch, *Argentine Dictator: Juan Manuel de Rosas 1829-1852* (Oxford: Clarendon Press, 1981).

25. Most Argentine historians contend that, after 1861, the old labels (Unitarios and Federales) fell into disfavor. Ariel de la Fuente, *Children of Facundo: Caudillo and Gaucho Insurgency During the Argentine State-Formation Process (La Rioja, 1853–1870)* (Durham: Duke University Press, 2000) argues that the old labels persisted.

26. "El mas bárbaro representante de la barbarie," "Edificios y fondos de Escuelas," *Obras*, 24:173.

27. As a young man in San Juan, Sarmiento wrote that he devoured every book he could lay his hand on, "cuanto libro pudo caer en mis manos," *Obras*, 3:162.

28. Not that Sarmiento agreed with Mill on every point. In *On Liberty*, Mill argued for mandatory education, but also wrote that "If the government would make up its mind to *require* for every child a good education, it might save itself the trouble of *providing* one," Mill, *On Liberty* (London: John W. Parker and Son, 1859), 190. Sarmiento firmly believed that the government should play an active role in providing education and creating good citizens.

29. Sarmiento vaguely mentioned reading "European magazines," "revistas europeas," *Obras*, 3:10.

30. Characterizing the political ideology of the Federales is not an easy task. E. Bradford Burns, *The Poverty of Progress: Latin America in the Nineteenth Century* (Berkeley: University of California Press, 1980) calls them populists and folk leaders. Lynch, *Argentine Dictator*, argues the opposite. Shumway, *The Invention of Argentina*, argues that there were many varieties of Federalism.

31. See José A. Oria, "La literatura argentina durante la epoca de Rosas (1829–1852)" in *Historia de la nación Argentina*, ed. Ricardo Levene (Buenos Aires: Liberia Y Editorial "El Ateneo," 1951), 7:377 and William H. Katra, *The Argentine Generation of 1837: Echeverría, Alberdi, Sarmiento, Mitre* (Madison: Fairleigh Dickinson University Press, 1996).

32. Nicolas Shumway, "Andrés Bello, Domingo Faustino Sarmiento, Manuel González Prada, and Teresa de la Parra: Four Writers and Four Concepts of Nationhood" in *A Companion to Latin American Literature and Culture*, ed. Sara Castro-Klaren (Malden, Mass.: Blackwell Publishing, Ltd., 2013), 296.

33. Domingo F. Sarmiento, *Facundo: Civilization and Barbarism*, trans. Kathleen Ross (Berkeley: University of California Press, 2003), 18.

34. "Centenares de alumnos arjentinos cuentan en su seno los colejios de Francia, Chile, Brasil, Norte-América, Inglaterra, i aun España. Ellos volverán luego a realizar en su patria las instituciones que ven brillar en todos esos Estados libres; i pondrán su hombro para derrocar al tirano semi-bárbaro," *Obras*, 7:224.

35. Sarmiento quoted in Helen Miller Bailey and Abraham P. Nasatir, *Latin America: The Development of Its Civilization* (Englewood Cliffs, N.J.: Prentice-Hall, Inc., 1960), 394–95.

36. *Life in the Argentine Republic in the Days of Tyrants; or Civilization and Barbarism*, trans., Mary Tyler Peabody Mann (New York: Hurd and Houghton, 1868), 272.

37. "La instrucción primaria es la medida de la civilización de un pueblo. Donde es incompleta, donde yace abandonada . . . hay un pueblo semi bárbaro, sin luces, sin costumbres, sin industria, sin progresos," *Obras*, 28:28. See also *Obras*, 28:69, 215, 283, 372, and 367.

38. Hinton Rowan Helper, *The Impending Crisis of the South: How to Meet It* (1857; repr., Cambridge: Harvard University Press, 1968).

39. Charles Sumner, *The Barbarism of Slavery: Speech of Hon. Charles Sumner, on the Bill for the Admission of Kansas as a Free State* (Washington, D.C.: Buell & Blanchard, Printers, 1860) and Thomas Wentworth Higginson, *Out-Door Papers* (Boston: Ticknor and Fields, 1863) 108–9.

40. See *The Collected Works of Abraham Lincoln*, ed. Roy P. Basler (New Brunswick: Rutgers University Press, 1953), 2:121–32; 3:1–37; 5:198 and 518–37; 6:537; and 8:183–84.

41. See "Civilization and Barbarism," *Baltimore Gazette and Daily Advertiser*, January 1, 1831; "The Barbarism of the Day," *Albany Evening Journal*, July 28, 1857; *Public Ledger*, August 13, 1861; and *New York Herald*, December 5, 1861.

42. For useful discussions see Bruce Mazlish, *Civilization and its Contents* (Stanford: Stanford University Press, 2004) and Brett Bowden, *The Empire of Civilization: The Evolution of an Imperial Idea* (Chicago: The University of Chicago Press, 2009).

43. Many people assume that, because *Facundo* was published in 1845 and not translated into English until 1868, people in the United States did not know about it. However, David T. Haberly argues that an article about gauchos published in the *Atlantic Monthly* in 1858 communicated the gist of Facundo to the reading public in the United States. See David T. Haberly, "Facundo in the United States: An Unknown Reading," *Ciberletras: Revista de crítica literaria y de cultura* 14 (2005): n.p.

44. See "Chile," *El Siglo Diez y Nueve*, July 28, 1844; and "Ortografia Chilena," *El Comercio*, August 31, 1844. See also Mark D. Szuchman, "Childhood Education and Politics in

Nineteenth-Century Argentina: The Case of Buenos Aires," *Hispanic American Historical Review* 70, no. 1 (February 1990): 109–38.

45. "He visto sus millones de campesinos, proletarios i artesanos viles, degradados, indignos de ser contados entre los hombres," *Obras*, 5:384.

46. "¿Por qué no vemos levantarse de nuevo el jenio de la civilizacion europea, que brillaba ántes," *Obras*, 7:167. Rosas, Sarmiento contended, destroyed the civilization that Bernardino Rivadavia's government had embodied.

47. See Domingo F. Sarmiento, *Travels in the United States in 1847*, trans. and ed., Michael Aaron Rockland (Princeton: Princeton University Press, 1970).

48. "El gran reformador de la educacion primaria. Viajero como yo en busca de métodos i sistemas por Europa." *Obras*, 5:446–48.

49. Mary Mann noted, years later, that Sarmiento "could not speak English then and I talked with him in French one whole day." See Mary Mann to Henry Barnard, July 21, 1865 in Alice Houston Luiggi, "Some Letters of Sarmiento and Mary Mann 1865–1876, Part I," *Hispanic American Historical Review* 32, no. 2 (May 1952): 189.

50. *Obras*, 29:446–50.

51. *Obras*, 5:446.

52. By this point, Sarmiento spoke English and did not have to converse in French. See "He spoke English *beautifully*—not that he did not 'suffer' for he ardently did—but his pronunciation, accent, and language are almost flawless," Mary Mann to Henry Barnard, September 18, 1866, Luiggi, "Some Letters of Sarmiento and Mary Mann 1865–1876, Part I," 198.

53. Thomas Genova, "Sarmiento's *Vida de Horacio Mann*: Translation, Importation, and Entanglement," *Hispanic Review* 82, no. 1 (Winter 2014): 21–41, discusses entanglements between Sarmiento and Mary Mann.

54. "Que completaron la Independencia proclamada en 1776, por la libertad del esclavo y la educacion del pueblo," *Obras*, 22:20.

55. Sarmiento cited in Lynch, *Argentine Dictator*, 322.

56. "Hace tiempo que una de las preocupaciones del público es la mejora de las escuelas," "Edificios de escuelas," *Obras*, 18:162.

57. "La tendencia de las reformas modernas en el sistema de escuelas se dirige á ocupar mas mujeres que hombres en la enseñanza porque cuestan menos y son mas aptas que los hombres para manejar niños pequeños," "Beneficencia Pública," July 16, 1856, *Obras*, 24:373.

58. "Educar á los pueblos bien y barato es hacerlo por medio de la mujer" and "Se puede utilizar creando un medio de educación para todos los niños en general," "La caridad y el estado," October 19, 1857, *Obras*, 18:128.

59. "Un día ha de llegar en que en una escuela de varones y de mujeres se enseñe todo por mujeres," October 19, 1857, *Obras*, 18:128.

60. See Kathryn Kish Sklar, *Catharine Beecher: A Study in American Domesticity* (New Haven: Yale University Press, 1973) and Jeanne Boydston, Mary Kelley, and Anne Margolis, *The Limits of Sisterhood: The Beecher Sisters on Women's Rights and Woman's Sphere* (Chapel Hill: University of North Carolina Press, 1988).

61. See Horace Mann, *A Few Thoughts on the Powers and Duties of Women. Two Lectures* (Syracuse: Hall, Mills, and Company, 1853), 65 and Mary Tyler Peabody Mann, *Life of Horace Mann* (Boston: Walker, Fuller, and Company, 1865), 1:424.

62. See, for example, Mary Mann to Henry Barnard, July 21, 1865, and Mary Mann to Henry Barnard, July 21, 1865, in Luiggi, "Some Letters of Sarmiento and Mary Mann 1865–1876, Part I," 188–89 and 189.

63. Sarmiento sent Henry Barnard a copy of *Facundo* published in French. See Domingo F. Sarmiento to Henry Barnard, July 28, 1865, in Luiggi, "Some Letters of Sarmiento and Mary Mann 1865–1876, Part I," 190–91.

64. "Al día siguiente comí con Waldo Emerson, á quien había mandado el *Facundo*. Este libro me sirve de medio de introducción. Si ser Ministro no vale para todos, ser educacionista es ya un gran título á la benevolencia de este pueblo de maestros; pero todavía me queda en reserva el *Facundo* que es mi cañon Parrot. Nada le resiste." DFS to Señora Aurelia Velez, October 15, 1865, *Obras*, 29:67.

65. See Rockland, *Travels in the United States in 1847*, 51. Mary Mann commented, in the preface to her translation of *Facundo* that "when R. W. Emerson read the book, he told Colonel Sarmiento that if he would write thus for our public, he would be read," Mann, *Life in the Argentine Republic*, xii.

66. "La Atenas americana," DFS to Señora doña Juana Manso, June 10, 1865, *Obras*, 29:36. This phrase was not unique to Sarmiento. See "Miscellany," *The Farmer's Cabinet*, November 14, 1844 and "The Great New England Wide Awake Demonstration," *Providence Evening Press*, October 17, 1860. See also Caroline Winterer, *The Culture of Classicism: Ancient Greece and Rome in American Intellectual Life, 1780–1910* (Baltimore: Johns Hopkins University Press, 2001).

67. Sarmiento was interested in other elements of Reconstruction. See "Reconstruccion del Sur" and "Irradiacion de Civilizacion," *Obras*, 29: 120–27, 128–37, two articles Sarmiento wrote for *El Zonda* in 1866.

68. "Han nombrado *superintendentes* de la *aid societies* en el Sud, y estos calculado que se necesitan por lo pronto *quince mil escuelas* y *quince mil maestras*, y todas las sociedades se han puesto en movimiento para obtenerlas. . . . Ya se han contratado *ochocientas maestras*, ciento cincuenta de ellas costeadas y contratadas por la de New York solamente," DFS to Señora doña Juana Manso, June 10, 1865, *Obras*, 29:35–36. For more on Juana Manso, see César H. Guerrero, *Mujeres de Sarmiento* (Buenos Aires: Artes Gráficas, 1960), 75–105 and Lea Fletcher, "Juana Manso: una voz en el desierto," in *Mujeres y cultura en la Argentina del siglo XIX*, ed., Lea Fletcher (Buenos Aires: Feminaria Editora, 1994), 108–20.

69. "Una niña se trasladó á la Carolina del Sur y se puso ella sola al frente de una plantación de algodón de trescientos negros á quienes no solamente educaba sino que les enseñaba el ejercicio de las armas sin perder nunca su prestigio de señorita," DFS to Señora Juana Manso, October 15, 1867, *Obras*, 29:220.

70. "Mientras se debate esta cuestión, *quince mil escuelas*, que los domingos serán dominicales para adultos, habrán en pocos años borrados el pecado original de la absoluta ignorancia en el Sur, y los negros libertos estarán luego más adelantados que nosotros blancos," *Obras*, 29:37

71. "Cien niñas bostonianas, á la cabeza de otras tantas escuelas en Buenos Aires, ó en las Provincias, crearían todo el sistema de enseñanza de Massachusetts, con su eficiencia, su extensión y su realidad," DFS to Señora Doña María Manso, April 21, 1865, *Obras*, 29:23.

72. "No sería hermoso espectáculo . . . ver llegar á Buenos Aires . . . cuarenta mucha-chas rubias, modestas sin gazmoñería, virtuosas, de esa virtud práctica, útil, social, que prepara una madre á una familia futura, maestras de escuela, bostonianas, colonas de educación y de republicanismo," DFS to Señora Doña María Manso, April 21, 1865, *Obras*, 29:25.

73. Kristine L. Jones, "Civilization and Barbarism and Sarmiento's Indian Policy," in *Sarmiento and His Argentina*, 41.

74. Robert E. Bonner, "Slavery, Confederate Diplomacy, and the Racialist Mission of Henry Hotze," *Civil War History* 51, no. 3 (2005): 288–316.

75. See Heather Andrea Williams, *Self-Taught: African American Education in Slavery and Freedom* (Chapel Hill: University of North Carolina Press, 2005). See also Mat-thew J. Hetrick's chapter in this volume for some discussion of this theme.

76. "Setecientas maestras norte americanas en la República Argentina ó en Chile, repararían en diez años el estrago de tres siglos," DFS to Señor Redactor de "La Patria" de Valparaíso, October 1, 1865, *Obras*, 30:78–79.

77. Nerio Rojas, "Presidencia Sarmiento. Vicepresidencia Adolfo Alsina (1868–1874)" in *Historia Argentina*, ed. Roberto Levillier (Buenos Aires: Plaza & Janés S. A. 1968), 4:2873–2922.

78. Alice Houston Luiggi, *65 Valiants* (Gainesville: University of Florida Press, 1965), 17. See also "Compulsory Education," *Springfield Globe-Republic*, November 13, 1886; "South American Women," *New York Tribune*, April 14, 1901; "Many School Teachers," *El Paso Herald*, May 1, 1915; and "Teachers' Exploit of '80s Is Recalled," *New York Times*, August 6, 1933. This number did not match Sarmiento's optimistic estimate of seven hundred teachers because Sarmiento had high standards and wanted a certain type of woman to teach (blond, white, and young). In addition, some women decided, upon further reflection, that teaching in Argentina would not work for them.

79. See Table 1.4, "Literacy Rates in the Americas, 1850–1950," in Stanley L. Engerman and Kenneth L. Sokoloff, *Economic Development in the Americas Since 1500: Endowments and Institutions* (Cambridge: Cambridge University Press, 2012), 28–29. In 1869, the literacy rate for people ages 6+ in Argentina was 23.8 percent. By 1925, the literacy rate for people ages 10+ in Argentina was 73.0 percent. Clearly Sarmiento's methods and the continued commitment of the government, after his presidency, to education, had an impressive impact.

80. For a good overview, see Richard N. Sinkin, *The Mexican Reform, 1855–1876: A Study in Liberal Nation-Building* (Austin: University of Texas Press, 1979).

81. For a good recent discussion, see William B. Kurtz, *Excommunicated from the Union: How the Civil War Created a Separate Catholic America* (Fordham: Fordham University Press, 2016).

82. Republicans used anti-Catholicism and a fear of Catholics taking over the public schools during the 1875 Ohio gubernatorial election and the election of 1876.

See Michael F. Holt, *By One Vote: The Disputed Presidential Election of 1876* (Lawrence: University Press of Kansas, 2008), 50–53 and 140–42.

83. Mónica Szurmuk, *Women in Argentina: Early Travel Narratives* (Gainesville: University Press of Florida, 2000), 128n2.

84. "Argentine Schools," *New York-Herald Tribune*, July 30, 1889.

85. Teachers in the United States who went south to teach the freedpeople encountered fierce opposition because of objectives, not religious background. See Willie Lee Rose, *Rehearsal for Reconstruction: The Port Royal Experiment* (1964; repr., Athens: University of Georgia Press, 1999) and Richard Zuczek, *State of Rebellion: Reconstruction in South Carolina* (Columbia: University of South Carolina Press, 1996).

86. C. A. Bayly, *The Birth of the Modern World: 1780–1914* (Malden, Mass.: Blackwell Publishing, 2004), 317. See also "A Sacrilegious Act in Buenos Ayres Holy Week," *Irish World and American Industrial Laborer*, June 2, 1894.

87. Frances G. Crowley, *Domingo Faustino Sarmiento* (New York: Twayne Publishers, Inc., 1972).

88. "La Base de la Democracia," *Obras*, 29:232.

89. See Timothy Verhoeven, *Transnational Anti-Catholicism: France and the United States in the Nineteenth Century* (New York: Palgrave Macmillan, 2010).

90. Robert D. Crassweller, *Perón and the Enigmas of Argentina* (New York: Norton, 1987), 42.

91. See Hodge, "Benjamin Apthorp Gould," 152–75.

92. Oscar Oszlak, *La Formacion del Estado Argentino* (Buenos Aires: Del Carril Impresores, 1982). See also Bender, *A Nation Among Nations*, 116–81.

93. Heather Cox Richardson, *The Greatest Nation of the Earth: Republican Economic Policies during the Civil War* (Cambridge: Harvard University Press, 1997).

94. Mark Wasserman, *Everyday Life and Politics in Nineteenth Century Mexico: Men, Women, and War* (Albuquerque: University of New Mexico Press, 2000).

95. Eric Hobsbawm, *The Age of Capital: 1848–1875* (London: Weidenfeld and Nicolson: 1975), 29–68.

96. For the first view, see Crowley, *Sarmiento*, 147. For the second, see Nicola Miller, "'That Great and Gentle Soul' Images of Lincoln in Latin America," in *The Global Lincoln*, ed. Richard Carwardine and Jay Sexton (Oxford: Oxford University Press, 2011), 206–22, and Robert E. May, *Slavery, Race, and Conquest in the Tropics: Lincoln, Douglas, and the Future of Latin America* (Cambridge: Cambridge University Press, 2013), 278–79.

97. Domingo Faustino Sarmiento, *Vida de Abran Lincoln, Décimo Sesto Presidente de los Estados Unidos* (New York: D.A. Appleton, 1866). Subsequent references to this work will be cited as *Vida*.

98. Paul Simon, *Lincoln's Preparation for Greatness: The Illinois Legislative Years* (Norman: University of Oklahoma Press, 1965), 65, contends that Lincoln had a mixed record on education in the Illinois Legislature. Lincoln's stand on the Mexican War was not particularly popular with many of his constituents.

99. "Estado de sitio" translates as "state of siege." For Sarmiento's comparison of "estado de sitio" and the suspension of habeas corpus, see *Obras*, 31: 65. The Argentine Constitution discussed "estado de sitio" in Primera Parte, Capítulo Único, Art. 23; Segunda

Parte, Sección Primera, Capítulo Segundo, Art. 53; Segunda Parte, Sección Primera, Capítulo Cuarto, Art. 67; and Segunda Parte, Sección Segunda, Capítulo Tercero, Art. 86, http://pdba.georgetown.edu/Constitutions/Argentina/arg1853.html#seccionsegundacap3.

100. "Te enviaré [*Vida*] en cantidad suficiente para satisfacer el poco hambre de leer de tus jentes," DFS to Excelentísimo señor Gobernador de Tucumán José Posse, August 1865, *Obras*, 29:65.

101. "H. E. Domingo F. Sarmiento, Minister of the Argentine Republic," *Harper's Weekly*, December 2, 1865. Sarmiento's correspondence for 1865–66 was filled with comments about *Vida de Lincoln*. See *Obras*, 29:109, 119, and *Obras*, 30:220–21. Sarmiento soon stopped mentioning *Vida de Lincoln*.

102. "En la República Argentina, donde los hombres públicos no necesitan de ejemplos para dictar leyes ó abolirlas, no se tomaron el trabajo de leer, como cosa indigna de atención, donando el Gobierno de Buenos Aires á los niños de las escuelas para libro de lectura, uno que los hombres hechos no pueden digerir fácilmente," "La Horca," *Obras*, 31:185.

103. "Un escritor norte-americano halló digno de ser traducida al inglés para edificación de jóvenes norte-americanos," ibid.

104. See DFS to Mary Mann, December 6, 1882, *Obras*, 37:320.

105. *New York Herald-Tribune*, November 23, 1868. See also Fletcher Webster, *An Oration Delivered Before the Authorities of the City of Boston, in the Tremont Temple, July 4, 1846* (Boston: J. H. Eastburn, 1846), 32.

106. Gregory P. Downs, "The Mexicanization of American Politics: The United States' Transnational Path from Civil War to Stabilization," *The American Historical Review* 117, no. 2 (April 2012): 387–409. See also Frederick B. Pike, *The United States and Latin America: Myths and Stereotypes of Civilization and Nature* (Austin: University of Texas Press, 1992).

107. *New York Herald-Tribune*, November 23, 1868. See also "Minor Topics," *New York Times*, July 29, 1869. See also "Washington," *Chicago Tribune*, January 16, 1871 and *The Troy Weekly Times*, December 5, 1868.

108. For a sample, see "National Teacher's Association," *The Evansville Journal*, August 17, 1866; *The Daily Phoenix*, August 2, 1868; "Exalted Character of Sarmiento, The New President," *Memphis Daily Appeal*, September 20, 1868; "The Argentine Confederation," *Public Ledger*, June 26, 1869; "Brazil and the Argentine Republic," *New York Tribune*, July 15, 1870; *Tri-Weekly Astorian*, September 25, 1873; *The Wheeling Daily Intelligencer*, October 23, 1873; and "Teachers' Institute," *Los Angeles Daily Herald*, November 14, 1874.

109. Although not royalty, some of Sarmiento's popularity may have been because he was a foreign observer of the United States. For a discussion of Dom Pedro II, see Teresa Cribelli, "A Modern Monarch: Dom Pedro II's visit to the United States in 1876," *The Journal of the Historical Society* 9, no. 2 (June 2009): 223–54.

110. Sarmiento, *Vida*, xiii–xiv.

111. "Root Pledges America to the Drago Doctrine," *New York Times*, August 19, 1906 and "Brumbaugh Urges Study of Spanish," *The Philadelphia Inquirer*, December 20, 1914.

112. Alexis de Tocqueville, *Democracy in America and Two Essays on America*, trans., Gerald E. Bevan (London: Penguin Books, 2003), 264.

113. The chronological period covered by this chapter is before U.S. big business arrived in Latin America in the 1880s–1910s. Nevertheless, many Latin Americans, looking at the U.S. War with Mexico and the long history of filibustering attempts, saw the United States as imperialistic. For excellent analysis of Latin American distrust of the United States, see May, *Slavery, Race, and Conquest*, 230–76.

114. See Hodge, "Benjamin Apthorp Gould and the Founding of the Argentine National Observatory."

115. See Luiggi, "Some Letters of Sarmiento and Mary Mann 1865–1876, Part I," 187–211.

2

Liberia College and Transatlantic Ideologies of Race and Education, 1860–1880

Matthew J. Hetrick

The connection between education in Liberia and education in the post–Civil War southern states is important but not obvious. Liberia, a former colony established by white philanthropists, began as an attempt to solve the perceived problem of the presence of free African Americans in the United States by sending them to Africa. Some supporters hoped it would lead to the end of slavery but others thought the removal of free African Americans would help to secure their property in slaves. By the 1860s, Liberia was an independent nation, but one that still relied on white American supporters for funding. That same moment revealed the inherent fallacy of colonization; not only was the removal of millions of Americans an impossibility, but the slave owners also proved their recalcitrance by seceding from the Union. The cascading emancipation of the entire slave population of the United States proceeded through the activism of local African Americans on to Union military victories and culminated with the passage of the 13th Amendment in 1865.

Despite the seeming incongruities of their contemporaneous situations, a closer examination reveals many striking connections between Liberia and the United States, especially regarding attitudes toward the newly free and toward education. In many ways the issues and debates in Liberia prefigured and reflected the issues in the Reconstruction-era United States. Arguments over who was to be in charge of the schools and who should attend them can be found in Liberia as well as the South. Similarly, fundamental debates about the purpose and goal of education, whether it should be to educate the most promising students or to uplift the masses, were an issue in Liberia long before they were a matter of contention between Booker T. Washington and W. E. B. Du Bois.

In Liberia these issues only arose in a piecemeal, gradual fashion with the slow accretion of settlers. It was only after formal Liberian independence in 1847 that a group of philanthropically-minded men met in Boston to establish "a well endowed College, or University" in Liberia. With independence assured, northern white benefactors considered education the next item on the agenda, a pattern that would continue in America during Reconstruction. These men, many of whom also served on the board on the Massachusetts Colonization Society, created the Trustees of Donations for Education in Liberia (henceforward the Boston Trustees) and spent the next decade gathering monies, securing a location, and hiring faculty for Liberia College.[1] One of the overarching motives that these men shared with the later efforts during American Reconstruction was the question of what to do with former slaves. To these northern reformers and colonizationists, the answer was the same in 1848 as it would be in 1865: Educate them. They believed that only by teaching the former slaves the basic tenets of western civilization could they be made truly free and independent. In effect, only Christianity and civilization could uplift the lowly. With Liberia, white philanthropists originally directed this effort toward the Liberians, but some of those same Liberians would then seek to apply this logic to the local native populations. In the American South, white philanthropists and educated African Americans would direct a similar agenda toward the freedpeople. The founding of Liberia College represents a much neglected episode that highlights connections between the Reconstruction-era United States and the tenuous position of Americo-Liberian society in Liberia.

In early 1863, Reverends Alexander Crummell and Edward Wilmot Blyden returned to Liberia and assumed their positions at Liberia College. They had personally interviewed with the Trustees in Boston in 1861 and, after being hired, traveled to speak in support of the newly created institution. Liberia College opened in January of 1862 with three faculty members: Crummell, Professor of Intellectual and Moral Philosophy as well as English Language and Literature; Blyden, Professor of Greek and Latin Languages and Literature; and J. J. Roberts, President of the College and Professor of Jurisprudence and International Law. During the first year a local tutor prepared the students while the faculty traveled to raise interest in and funds for the College. All three spoke in England, which had a long history of philanthropic support for African Americans, while Blyden also spoke across his home territory in the Caribbean and Crummell spoke in fifteen American cities in seven different states, all to generate support for the new college. Just how much money they raised remains uncertain, but it was not enough to spare the College ongoing financial difficulties.[2]

The creation of Liberia College reflected, in part, the rapidly evolving politics of race and slavery in the United States. The 1850s had seen a resurgence of interest in African emigration. The formal independence of Liberia in 1847 made the country more attractive to African Americans just as the situation in America seemed to be worsening. The Compromise of 1850 and accompanying Fugitive Slave Law, bloodshed in Kansas, and the 1857 Dred Scott decision all challenged the place of free African Americans in the United States. In the midst of this ferment and interest in Africa, the African American author and activist Martin Delany traveled to Liberia in 1859. While his declared purpose was to seek a new place for free black settlement, he also spoke in Liberia and met with local leaders there, including Alexander Crummell. Delany recommended his friend and fellow emigration enthusiast, Martin Freeman, for a position at Liberia College.[3]

The creation of Liberia College brought together some of the leading figures of the mid–nineteenth-century black Atlantic—figures whose lives attest to their personal achievements and growing disillusionment with the United States. We know much about Crummell from Wilson Jeremiah Moses's 1989 biography of him.[4] Alexander Crummell was born into a vibrant free black community. His father, Boston, reportedly came from the Temne tribe in what would eventually become Sierra Leone. This personal link to Africa played a strong role in his empathy with Africa and in his growing interest in traveling to Africa. The Crummells' New York City home hosted the organizational meeting for *Freedom's Journal* and their pastor, Peter Williams, was integral in supporting John Russwurm's emigration to Liberia in the 1830s. Boston Crummell evidently opposed colonization during this period.[5] He also served alongside Williams, Samuel Cornish, and white abolitionist Arthur Tappan on the board of the Phoenix Society, a local society for the support and education of free blacks.

The politics of race made a deep imprint on Alexander Crummell from early in his life, confronting him with white supremacist violence and illustrating the tenuous place of African Americans in the United States. Alongside his friend and neighbor Henry Highland Garnet, he faced the rising white supremacist violence of antebellum New York City. The Garnets were not legally free like the Crummells, and when slavehunters arrived at the Garnets' door in 1829, the family narrowly escaped. White riots in 1834, principally over fears of amalgamation and in opposition to radical abolition, destroyed Peter Williams's church. When riots recurred the next year, Crummell was out of the city studying at the Noyes Academy in New Hampshire with Garnet. Crummell and Garnet's involvement with abolition was unpopular there as well. When a mob dragged the school building away with a team of oxen, Garnet led a group of boys who forged bullets and returned fire to drive away the approaching riders. Local authorities ordered the two friends out of the state.

Although Crummell followed the example of Peter Williams and entered into the Episcopal priesthood, he was refused entry to the seminary in the United States, despite his manifest qualifications and the support of the grandson and namesake of founding father John Jay. Crummell waged a long and public campaign, including publishing his correspondence with Jay and authoring a pamphlet making his case, while he traveled throughout New England and continued his studies. He worked with Frederick Douglass in 1847 toward abolition, agreeing at this point with Douglass's critique of colonization as undermining the effort toward abolition and equality in the United States. Crummell also met W. E. B. Du Bois's grandfather, who attended a series of lectures he gave. Ultimately, however, Crummell sought the education denied him in the United States across the ocean.

Alexander Crummell arrived in England in 1848 intending to collect funds for his New York City church, but he allowed himself to be persuaded by local supporters to pursue his degree at Cambridge University. He continued to speak against the American Colonization Society (ACS) while also attacking the Compromise of 1850 and resulting Fugitive Slave Law. Garnet joined his friend in England and both spoke in support of Africa and abolition but against the ACS. Garnet professed his love for Africa, the land of both his and Crummell's fathers: "I love the country; I love its interests, and feel grateful to any one and everyone who labors to promote its welfare." However, while Liberia might do some good, the ACS would never succeed in removing all blacks from America. Crummell spoke after Garnet and stressed the importance of evangelizing and educating Africa through an educated few, something that would be a recurring theme in both his preaching and his educational philosophy.[6]

After graduating from Cambridge in 1853, Crummell decided not to return to the United States. He needed warm weather for his health and his family, and there was inadequate support from the New York African American community for his endeavors. Liberia looked like a more appealing home and afforded him the best opportunity to both advance his own fortunes and uplift his people. Like Russwurm before him, Crummell's commitment to Liberia was seen as apostasy by much of the free black community, and he wrote lengthy letters justifying his actions.[7] Under the auspices of the Protestant Episcopal Church of America, Alexander Crummell left England for West Africa in May of 1853 with his wife, Sarah; three children; a servant; and a well-stocked library. They arrived ten days later, depressed by the setting but impressed with the height and the blackness of the local people. Unfortunately, the family's youngest child died of fever and they faced ongoing financial difficulties and tensions with the white bishop at Cape

Palmas. One difference between Crummell and his bishop, aside from simple prejudice and a clash of personalities, was the bishop's desire to focus on the natives and Crummell's wish to focus on the colonists, who Crummell believed could in turn evangelize native Africans. It is no surprise that a man with Crummell's personal history would emphasize the need to educate the elite before focusing on the masses.

Shortly after Martin Delany's visit in 1859, Crummell wrote "The Relations and Duties of Free Colored Men in America to Africa," in which he argued that they had a duty to assist and to uplift their brethren in Africa, but mainly through the actions of an educated and civilized few. Crummell returned to America in 1861 where the essay was published as part of his book, *The Future of Africa*, the following year.[8]

Crummell arrived in the United States for his 1861 speaking tour just as the possibility of total emancipation diminished popular interest in African colonization among the free African American population. As he traveled on behalf of the ACS and Liberia College, at times accompanied by Edward Blyden and at times on his own, Crummell spoke about Liberia's prospects. The settlers were making money from coffee and sugar while "men who not long since were heathen, but having been brought in[to] American families, are now civilized men."[9] In fact, he insisted, the interests of the settlers and "our uncivilized kin in Africa" were overlapping and mutually reinforcing. The language that Crummell used for the people of Liberia was telling. He averred that "for every *American* citizen, you may safely put down another, either *native* or *Congo*, who has been trained in our families or schools."[10] What they needed were "educated free colored men" who were "*the* fit agents to effect the regeneration of Africa." Crummell was calling for a cadre of educated African Americans to uplift and civilize their African brethren, rhetoric that prefigured similar efforts in the postwar South. Yet, African Americans should emigrate not just for the betterment of Africa but also for the opportunities that the United States denied them: "We have been deprived of many of our rights in this country. We have been debarred from many of those privileges and prerogatives which develop character into manhood, and mastery, and greatness."[11] Here the obvious personal connection to being denied the schooling and education he sought in America became clear. Liberia, and its new College, offered the only hope for those elite few to get the education they so richly deserved. Only then could they civilize and uplift their "native brethren" in Africa. Sounding much like his acquaintance Martin Delany, Crummell believed that the "freed black man of America is . . . a superior man . . . to the Russian, to the Polander, to the Hungarian, to the Italian," in potential as well as historical achievement. They were, in fact, "Black Yankees," and the best suited to uplift Africa.[12] A similar missionary impulse would push other "Yankees" to move south after the Civil War in order to uplift the freedpeople. Crummell sought to put his call into action; arriving in Liberia in the fall of 1862 with some 4,000 volumes for the library, Crummell began classes at the College alongside President Roberts, Edward Blyden, and Martin Freeman.

Martin Freeman, recommended by Martin Delany to Alexander Crummell for his position, was born in Rutland, Vermont on September 11, 1826 to free black parents; his father's father had won his freedom through military service in the American Revolution.[13] Freeman was tutored by a local Congregational minister and, thanks to his recommendation, entered Middlebury College in 1845 at age 19. After being unanimously selected to give Middlebury's commencement address, in 1850 Freeman was recruited to the faculty of the first black college in America, Allegheny Institute in Pittsburgh, soon to be renamed Avery College after its founder, white abolitionists Charles Avery. The contrast to New England was striking; racism was more virulent in Pittsburgh but the African American community was more engaged as well. Freeman soon became an active member of that community, publishing letters in black newspapers and traveling to conventions.

In a letter to *Frederick Douglass' Paper* in 1854, Freeman acknowledged tension within the black community about color and appearance: The claim "that every one of African descent values himself in proportion to the degree of white blood in his veins is too near the truth to admit of cavil."[14] Although this concern with complexion was not then widely acknowledged within the published works of African Americans, it would come up soon after freedom in both Liberia and America. The important overlap that skin color had with status in both places was mirrored in the role that status played in education. In fact, the conflation of lighter skin color, higher status, and better education was a recurring theme and challenge, and all of these issues were tied up with the debate about the competing benefits of liberal arts and practical education. Freeman would find these concerns about color, status, and education only amplified within Liberia.

In his letter, Martin Freeman then went on to challenge his African American audience to pride and self-respect: "To illustrate, the white man believes his race to be the race par excellence; the colored man believes his race naturally inferior." African Americans must take pride and not stoop to imitation, Freeman declared. "Ah! sir, the colored man is sadly mistaken if he thinks to become just like a white man by merely acquiring, honorably or dishonorably, sharp features and straight hair. Let the man of whatever hue, respect himself, and be true to the instincts of his manhood; then and not till then, will he be the co-equal, and compeer of the haughty Anglo-Saxon."[15] Freeman was more right than he knew. Many Liberians would come to regard themselves as not only the equal of the Anglo-Saxon, but as the haughty superiors of the native Africans, often in much the same language as other imperialists.

It is no coincidence that Freeman's call for pride and self-respect mirrored the language of Martin Delany. In the midst of the tumult of the 1850s, Delany had called his own convention to challenge the anti-emigration ideology of Frederick Douglass. One result of the convention was an African expedition, the same expedition where Delany met Crummell in 1859. When Delany emigrated to Canada in 1856, Freeman asked him to look for a suitable plot of land to purchase on his behalf. Later that year, Freeman became President of Avery College and then married Louisa Eleanor Peck, daughter and sister of leaders in the local free black community. He also sent Delany $400 to purchase a 50 acre plot, evidently as a safety measure in case things continued to worsen in America. Following the death of his young daughter in 1858, Freeman wrote Delany that "I am more and more convinced that Africa is the country to which all colored men who wish to attain the full stature of manhood, and bring up their children to be men and not creeping things, should turn their steps; and I feel more and more everyday, that I made a great mistake in not going there, when I was untrammeled by family ties and had the opportunity."[16] The next year, 1859, Freeman published an article in the *Anglo-African Magazine* entitled "The Educational Wants of the Free Colored People." Freeman saw education as physical, mental, and moral, but believed that racial oppression prevented blacks from equaling white achievement. He advocated going to the countryside and engaging in agricultural work: "select some little country town and there wield the implements of your craft, be honest, be industrious and economical and you will secure a position in [the] community for which you might strive in vain in the crowded city."[17] Here again is a foreshadowing of the much more well-known debate about what to do with the freedpeople following freedom. Questions of whether to live in the city or the country and whether to work in the field or gain an education came to matter a great deal. When Crummell met with Freeman in 1862, his offer of a position at Liberia College fell on fertile ground and, despite his father-in-law's opposition, Freeman gratefully accepted. Freeman wrote to the Trustees in the fall of 1863 that he awaited "with impatience the time of departure for my Fatherland."[18] Freeman was committed: "Come life or death, to me or mine, I must go to Liberia."[19] This commitment allowed him to join his desire for self-determination with education.

Despite Freeman's dedication, problems soon arose. Freeman traveled across New England trying to raise money and buying supplies for the college, but the Emancipation Proclamation and Union victories made it difficult to find much interest in Liberia. When one of the Boston Trustees suggested that Freeman try to find enough settlers to fill a ship, he was aggrieved and outraged. "Now this may be *sport* to the Managers of the Col. Society, but it is *death* to a poor Emigrant who has given up his all, and risked his reputation in the expectation of going to Liberia." But Freeman had not given up. "I do not despair," he declared, "and I will not give up the idea of going. God willing I shall yet go if not this year, the next, or failing in that the next."[20] After being reassured of his passage, Freeman wrote somewhat apologetically, that the "idea in regard to my raising a company was perhaps not an unnatural one, considering the almost universal tendency of the Negro of this country to be at the head of something." Freeman did not blame the white supporter who raised the idea, for the idea "showed at once but little knowledge of me as individual and a thorough acquaintance with my race." Instead, Freeman placed the blame on his "own people" who "are alone culpable in this matter, or rather slavery that terrible system that has crushed the manhood and manly aspirations almost completely out of the American Negro, is to be blamed for it all."[21] And yet even after slavery ended Freeman still found the best place to educate and uplift "the Negro" was in Africa.

Although a fractured leg again delayed his sailing, Freeman reassured the Boston Trustees that despite the fact that "My people are all going crazy over the good time coming in this country," to him Liberia was still "land of the *free*, and land of my *hope!*"[22] By the summer of 1864, Freeman wrote that his four-year old daughter was "imbibing ideas in regard to color, race, &c which I did hope she never learn."[23] He was therefore grateful that in September they could "start for the land of Ham."[24] Freeman, 37 years old, sailed with his wife Louisa, age 30, daughter Cora, age 4, and son Edwin, age 2. Upon arrival, he was impressed with the college faculty in Monrovia and wrote that, "I am not the same misanthropic, miserable mortal that I was two months ago. I am a man for the first time in my life, invested with all the rights, privileges, duties and immunities that pertain to manhood."[25]

From before its opening and into its early years, Liberia College was plagued with problems: insufficient funds, lackluster attendance by students, divided loyalties and competing rivalries within the faculty, even disagreement over the mission of the college. Crummell and Blyden refused to live in the college building and were frequently absent from class due to speaking and traveling in both England and the Americas. President Roberts was increasingly dissatisfied with

Crummell's attendance and believed that Blyden's new position as Secretary of State of Liberia detracted from his college duties. Crummell had traveled to visit his daughters at Oberlin College and questions concerning his absence and his salary would prove a point of contention for the Boston Trustees. Crummell also sought to open the college to women, both from his belief that educated women were needed to civilize and uplift the country and to give his eldest daughter an educational opportunity following some ill-defined difficulties at Oberlin.

Blyden, Crummell, and Freeman all vowed that "as Negroes" they would "uphold the honor of the race" against those who had "no confidence in the African" and who were "ever at work in Liberia to humble and disgrace *black men*."[26] Here is a marked difference with efforts at education and uplift between Liberia and the United States. While the overt distinction within America was between "white" and "black," in Liberia similar concerns with color manifested themselves in the differing shades and hues of blackness. For many Liberians, the lighter one's skin, the higher one's status. Blyden, Crummell, and Freeman dissented from this view, often reversing the argument, and there was an implicit critique in their language about Roberts, who was of mixed heritage. Their experience in Liberia seemed to radicalize both Blyden and Freeman so that they became increasingly concerned with racial purity. Despite the Faculty's protestations, President Roberts had the backing of the Boston Trustees and they controlled the purse strings. In April of 1866, Crummell wrote to the Trustees in Boston seeking his salary[27] and, when it was not forthcoming, he inveighed against the mulatto clique, led by Roberts, who were "as Negro hating as the voters of Memphis."[28] Crummell resigned that fall. Blyden kept his position after apologizing and vowing to improve, but his dissatisfaction with the light-skinned Roberts would only increase. Meanwhile, Freeman had injured his eyes, possibly in viewing a solar eclipse with his students in August 1865. Seeking medical treatment, he returned to America in October 1867 and was in Pittsburgh when the President of Avery College resigned, reopening Freeman's old position.[29]

Before leaving Liberia, Freeman had written to reassure the Trustees that he would not be staying in America: "You are probably aware that my family are now in America, and I wish the Board to believe that it is with no intention of joining them and remaining there that I now go." Hinting at some familial discord, Freeman made his position clear. In spite of the hopeful events in the United States, "I shall not see things with the eyes of those colored people over there, and hence shall not adopt their views of life, or duty, or interest. I never was very like them, and three years of life in Liberia, under influences and circumstances such as they *never had, have not and never can have* in the U.S. have made me still more unlike."[30] Despite the end of slavery and the expansion of African American rights throughout the South, this teacher could still see no place for himself in America.

Whether the Trustees had expressed these fears or whether Freeman was acting preemptively, they were certainly not unfounded. In October of 1867, tremendous pressure was applied to keep Freeman in America, likely by both the Avery College trustees and his wife, but he advised that "they will most assuredly fail, nothing but death, or blindness will prevent my seeking again my chosen field of labor."[31]

In the midst of Reconstruction, most African Americans sought to build their future in a new America. Despite the widespread rejection of African colonization, Freeman remained unimpressed with America and the possibilities for African Americans: "As for the scattered remnant of the Negro in this country he will never achieve much, and what he does will be of no benefit to the Negro. My mission is to the Negro, pure and simple as he exists in his Native Land, the best specimen of his race now to be found." In this passage, Freeman made clear that his pride, his identification as a Negro and as an African, could only be satisfied in Africa: "I have never been happy until I made Liberia my home, not even in my childhood, for my recollection does not recall a time when I was not aware of my true status as a Negro in this country." Even during this brief period he "suffered more during the week past in this country than all the horrors of the African fever and the discomforts of poverty, in a word than all that sickness and hunger and all the manifold ills of Africa can inflict." While Freeman had only faced "one or two direct insults," he explained that "the very presence of this mighty civilization in which the Negro is so completely hidden, is oppressive."[32] It was this lack of opportunity in America that Liberia had come to remedy. Even his position as the head of Avery College in Pittsburgh was inferior to his position at Liberia College. In Liberia, he could direct the education and exert his influence in a way that was still not possible in America.[33]

Although it is possible that Freeman was only tailoring his message to his white benefactors in Boston, the consistency and vehemence of his views belie this interpretation. Also, the mention of more personal objections to returning to Liberia reinforced his honesty: "I very much regret that I had to come to this country as I am aware that I shall have much trouble to get away again. My wife does not openly oppose our return, but harps constantly on our deprivations of luxuries and comforts there, which we have always had and might have again if I would only stay here."[34] To Freeman, the oppressive atmosphere, including in matters of education, far outstripped any possible material benefits. It was a matter of principle and racial pride.

Freeman requested that the Boston Trustees find information on life insurance in Boston. He required the life insurance because unless he could show Louisa "that she runs no risk of a destitute widowhood in Liberia, she will not *willingly* go, if at all. My highest convictions of duty point to Africa, and *there* I shall go. And if the dearest ties of earth are sundered or my children are prematurely orphaned, God must take care of them." Despite a large offer to return as President of Avery College, $1,500 per annum plus a furnished house, Freeman could think of "no greater earthly punishment meted out to me, than to be compelled to remain here."[35]

Throughout the fall of 1867, Freeman sought to placate his wife and to sell his plot of land in Canada, but Louisa refused to return without greater financial security. Freeman wrote, "though I would rather my little ones would be left to starve in Liberia than be brought back here to be clothed in purple and fine linen and fare sumptuously every day, I cannot make her see the matter in that light."[36] Despite Louisa's pregnancy, Freeman was resolved to return: "come death or life, famine or feasting; the worst conditions in Liberia are (to me) preferable to the best here."[37] Although his friends and family in Pittsburgh advised that Louisa remain, their belief that this would force Freeman to stay as well was "a slight mistake."[38] Freeman sailed for Liberia later that month. He would not see his wife and children for three years.

Upon Freeman's return, Edward Blyden was serving as President of Liberia College, but his frequent absences and ongoing involvement in politics meant that Freeman was often President pro tem. In July of 1868, Freeman wrote to the Trustees in Boston as acting President to update them on the college. There were ten students in the college and twenty in the preparatory department. Freeman continued to serve as needed, including covering Professor Blyden's classes during his frequent absences.[39] During this period, Freeman communicated with his wife Louisa by mail, often through the Boston Trustees. Louisa wrote to Boston as well, passing along a message from her husband as well as news about the illness of their daughter.[40] This no doubt helped explain her absence from Liberia, and two weeks later she wrote to Boston that she would "wait with as much patience as possible until Mr. Freeman comes or sends sufficient money to take us to Liberia."[41] In March of 1870, Freeman explained that he would not need to go to America to collect his children because Louisa had recovered from her illness: "As my wife has recovered, I do not wish to come, as she must come to me. I have not any, the least desire, to ever set foot in your country again. There is but one locality, that I ever yet heard of, to which I would not rather go." One year later, Louisa and their three children—Cora, Edwin, and Clarence—returned to Liberia. Martin Freeman's only concern was that he would die without saving enough money and his children would "have to return to the States, and thus be lost to the Negro Race. Rather than this, may they die young before I do."[42]

After Alexander Crummell left his post at Liberia College, he returned full-time to his calling as an Episcopal minister in Liberia. Crummell strenuously and frequently advocated for an "indigenous" church led by educated Africans from the diaspora, something the local white bishop did not look kindly on. In addition, Crummell saw his primary purpose as working among the Liberian settlers, but the bishop remonstrated that Crummell's work among the local tribes and natives was lacking. Again, the difference in attitude and emphasis regarding outreach and education is striking. The white bishop believed efforts should be directed toward uneducated natives while Crummell believed his time was better spent on the higher status, English-speaking settlers. Unlike his erstwhile colleague Edward Blyden, Alexander Crummell never developed an interest in Islam or local languages.[43] However, like Blyden, Crummell had difficulties with some local Liberians that he blamed on color, referring to one mulatto minister as "a bastard child; with the blood of both races in his veins and with the virtues of neither."[44] Despite his lack of interest in local culture, he did value the natives' eternal souls. Crummell worked in some villages and settlements in the interior, but he noted that among the recent converts to Methodism he found "noise, hysterias, and shrieking" and "leaping, hallowing, and gesticulating most violently," behavior he explicitly linked with the freedpeople in the South.[45] His observations not only reinforced his reputation among his contemporaries as a conservative churchman, but also clearly demonstrated his awareness of events in America and his belief that he was part of a broader community. Throughout his efforts to raise and uplift his African brethren, Crummell's sense of intellectual superiority remained paramount.

In January of 1870, Crummell's friend Edward James Roye became the fifth president of the Republic. Despite Crummell's prior reluctance to evangelize among the natives, he had always favored incorporating them into the nation. Roye ended his inaugural speech by reiterating the notion, common to earlier pamphlets and publications and similar to nationalist sentiments in the United States, that providence had "set Liberia, as it were upon a Hill."[46]

On July 26, 1870, Alexander Crummell gave a speech on the anniversary of Liberian Independence.[47] His message was clear from the very first line: "*One great mistake of the people of Liberia has been neglect of our native population.*"[48] This marked a stark departure from his earlier efforts and writings. On this day of national celebration, Crummell chastised the Liberians for the task left unfinished.

"In a little more than a monthly change of the moon, we were metamorphosed from the position of underlings to one of mastery; with a vast population of degraded subjects around us," Crummell declared. "It has blinded too many of us to the fact that we are but a few generations removed from the condition and the benightedness of the heathen around us."[49] While the "native African" may be "a barbarian,"[50] Liberians must work with them. We "have not the ability, to destroy the native"[51] and are obligated to them as fellow members of the race: "If we neglect them, then they will surely drag us down to their rude condition and their deadly superstitions; and our children at some future day, will have cast aside the habiliments of civilized life, and lost the fine harmonies and grand thoughts of the English tongue."[52] Crummell's words reveal not simply a Christian duty to convert and civilize the natives, but the ongoing fear common to many settlers that their children could sink back into barbarism. At the same moment in the U.S. South, black and white teachers were educating the freedpeople to uplift them out of the barbarism of slavery. This concern was especially important to black teachers, who were keenly aware of white Americans tendency to paint all African American with the wide brush of barbarism and low expectations. The direct connection can be seen with Crummell's earlier comments on religion. Also keenly aware of the burgeoning European imperialism, Crummell noted that "the negro races of Africa still retain, for the most part, their original birthright" and it was up to Liberians to civilize the natives and to improve the position of "the African race."[53] Again, the implicit connection to the missionary impulse found in many teachers of the freedpeople seems clear, to uplift the race they needed to educate and uplift the lowliest among them.

Crummell and his compatriots, like Freeman and Blyden, were interested in incorporating the natives into the body politic. After a suitable period of education and civilizing they could be equal members of Liberian society. The fact that Crummell entitled his call to action "Our National Mistake" acknowledged some measure of personal culpability through his earlier neglect of the natives in both his education and evangelization efforts.[54] There was, of course, an ancillary benefit. Both Crummell and, especially, Blyden were interested in Liberian politics. By reaching out to the natives, whether from altruistic of selfish motives, they could finally break the power of the mulatto class, which had ruled Liberia from the beginning.

One year after the election of President Roye, things had not gone as well as they might have hoped. Roye had secured a $500,000 loan from bankers in London, but the usurious terms had outraged the Liberian populace and occasioned accusations of corruption. Soon after the reunification of Martin Freeman's family in 1871, Edward Blyden resigned as President of Liberia College.[55] Blyden's political disputes and rough handling by a mob likely contributed to his quick exit to Sierra Leone. There is evidence that he was nearly lynched on the streets of Monrovia. It is unclear how much of the outcry was genuine public outrage over the perception that the government had made a bad deal with London bankers for their personal benefit or simply that the ruling classes wanted to re-take power. Mob violence was frequent throughout the fall of 1871; Freeman and either Crummell or Crummell's eldest son were also assaulted. President Roye was arrested and there is still some dispute as to whether he drowned in an escape attempt or was murdered. By 1872, Crummell also fled to Sierra Leone and the "mulatto" group was back in power.[56]

While in Sierra Leone, Blyden encouraged the British to become more active in civilizing Africa and he also returned to his early Liberian days by founding and editing a newspaper in Freetown, *The Negro*. That name was not accidental. Blyden's biographer sees his antipathy towards "mulattoes," by which Blyden seemed to mean anyone with an apparent infusion of white "blood," and his corresponding celebration of the "pure" Negro as central to his thinking.[57] Despite the importance he placed on race membership, Blyden saw no superiority between races, only difference. The races each had something to contribute to history, but only if kept "pure." Those of a mixed-race background only clouded the issue and should be kept out of Africa. There is no evidence of his antipathy towards mulattoes before 1862, when he revealed his feelings at a speech in Maine as he traveled in support of the newly opened Liberia College. Blyden married the niece of Liberia's Vice President, a member of the mulatto class, and there are hints that the difficulty of the marriage contributed to the growing vehemence of his views. He also seemed to regard the mental retardation of one daughter as his penalty for marrying outside of the race.[58] Following his flight from Monrovia in 1871, his attitudes became more entrenched and more pronounced. Blyden went to great lengths to justify his views in his correspondence with influential white Americans.

In September of 1871, Martin Freeman wrote to Blyden and congratulated him upon his safe arrival in Sierra Leone. There he could "labor for the Negro more effectually," away from the "Negrophobists here" in Liberia.[59] Freeman had continued their correspondence and, as Blyden recounted, "he [Freeman] expresses great desire to leave Liberia on account of the distressing political condition. He says he has no hopes of doing anything for Africa there." Not only would this be beneficial for Freeman but, according to Blyden, the "people here [in Sierra Leone] need a little intercourse with Negroes of foreign training and culture."

Thankfully, "Prof. Freeman is a pure Negro." Blyden hoped to open a competing "Collegiate Institution" in Sierra Leone, although this did not come to pass.[60]

By 1874 Edward Blyden had returned to Liberia, but he documented his continuing disenchantment with the local mulatto ruling class and his desire to improve the natives in both word and action. In October of 1874, Blyden wrote to William Coppinger, the longtime Secretary of the ACS and his longstanding correspondent, that Liberia College was in disarray, but he had a plan. He would draw students from around the region, not simply Monrovia, and "make the College a place of learning for Africa and the race." This plan seemed to prefigure the later ambitions of Booker T. Washington and the Tuskegee Institute. Blyden sought to draw many students, both from the settlers and the natives, and to educate them in practical, manual trades. So far Liberia College had been "a conspiracy against the Negro race," but Blyden implied it was not the only conspiracy against their interests. He demanded that the ACS stop sending mixed race settlers: "By continuing to send such a people to this country, you are really doing more damage to Africa than the slave trade did. You are planting here a nest of vipers who hate the country and the race." Again, according to Blyden, they could not be part of the race, only traitors to it. He acknowledged that in "the days of slavery you could not help the kind of emigrants you sent out. You were obliged to send such as the south offered, but now you have the power of selection and you should exercise a discrimination." Blyden even cited recent "scientific" studies by Dr. William Draper and Prof. Joseph Henry supporting his points about the inherent inferiority of mixed blood.[61]

Demonstrating a strong familiarity with leading African Americans and their thinking, Blyden admonished: "Keep the Douglasses, Langstons, Purvises with you—where they prefer to remain . . . Send us if you can, the Garnets, the Reeves, the Wilsons and in a few years we will show you an African nation of some power and usefulness." Not coincidentally, the former were against settling in Liberia and were of mixed descent. The latter were in favor of settling in Africa and were, according to Blyden, pure Negroes. Of course the accuracy of Blyden's racial purity test is a matter of conjecture. Blyden's first proposal was to rescue Liberia College from "the hands of mongrels" by abolishing the local Board of Trustees and giving sole power to a Negro President of the College; he graciously agreed to return to the position if offered.[62]

In a lengthy postscript, he detailed what Martin Freeman, still a Professor at the College, thought of his ideas. Blyden could cite Freeman's thinking as supporting his own because while Blyden had only traveled in the United States, Freeman was born there: "Prof. Freeman reminds me of the bitterness which prevails in America between the *colored* and *black*, which he says only a few white men understand." The "colored" sought advantage by calling himself a Negro whenever a question arises involving the whole class "and pretends to be proud of the name, while his contempt for the Negro is supreme." Although there were tensions within the Reconstruction South along these lines, notably within the older freed, lighter-skinned communities of Charleston and New Orleans, it seems more likely that Blyden and Freeman were projecting the problems of Liberia onto the United States. Of course, in both Liberia and these free black communities this color component mirrored class divisions as well. In Blyden and Freeman's view, this moral failing seemed to apply to the wealthier African Americans. These pernicious habits continued in Africa, even among the Negro immigrants. "When they come here, the poor blacks accustomed to the rule of white men in America, very soon allow the mulattoes to acquire an unnatural and mischievous ascendancy, thinking as they always pretend, that they love Africa." Linking his racial thinking to events in the United States, Blyden compared the Liberian Legislature, "a farce and a drag upon the country," to the Reconstruction governments of "South Carolina and Louisiana." As he explained, "You have an example in your own country of what we have in Liberia on a small scale." Closing his letter with a reminder of both of the unpopularity of his opinions and his past difficulties, Blyden noted, "Now, if you want me shot you have only to let it be known here that I have written you such a letter."[63]

The next year Blyden returned to his former position as principal of Alexander High School in Liberia. He used the opportunity to put some of his plans into action by moving the high school away from Monrovia to Harrisburg, along the St. Paul River in the interior. He also instituted the teaching of Arabic, manual crafts, and new methods of agriculture, a melding of what would become competing philosophies of manual and liberal arts education, most famously embodied in later debates between Washington and Du Bois. By 1877, Blyden was serving as Liberia's first ambassador to Great Britain and enjoying great success on the London social scene, something widely and admiringly reported in the West African press.[64]

Freeman continued to serve at Liberia College as needed, with the next decade a contentious one for the college. In 1873, there were only ten students in the college and thirty-three in the preparatory department. Throughout the 1870s, there was discussion about moving the college away from Monrovia and to the interior, a discussion led by politicians from that area.[65] In 1876, a letter from recent graduates to the Boston Trustees helped convince the Trustees to continue paying the professors' salaries.[66] Two years later, J. B. Pinney, who had been a missionary and President of Liberia before independence, was selected by the Boston Trustees as President of the College.[67] The only white President's tenure was short-lived. During it, General Armstrong of the Hampton Institute in Virginia advised him to open a manual or industrial school as part of Liberia College, an idea that would well outlast Pinney's tenure as college president.[68]

Following the tumultuous events of 1871, Alexander Crummell ended his long African sojourn and returned to the United States in 1872. After spending a few months in New York City, he settled in Washington, D.C as rector of St. Luke's Episcopal Church. Crummell had returned to an America very different from the one he left some eighteen years earlier. A few of the notable changes were that slavery no longer existed and African Americans were now, legally at least, equal citizens. Following the outbreak of the Civil War, and accelerating with the Emancipation Proclamation in 1863, African Americans had weakened the Confederacy. From the first rumors of the election of Abraham Lincoln, but especially with the arrival of Union troops in their neighborhood, African Americans fled their masters. While the first arrivals to the Union forces were single young men, whole families and multiple generations seeking freedom soon followed them, many with all of their possessions that they could carry. When the federal government confronted this reality, government officials classified them as contrabands and put them to work for the Union war effort. Following the Emancipation Proclamation in January 1863, many of these young men fought in the Union blue. Even those enslaved people who did not flee their homes frequently either renegotiated their terms of service or ignored their putative masters all together. Others began farming for their own benefit and some masters resorted to cash payments or a share of the crop to keep the farms functioning at all.[69]

Even during the early banner years of Reconstruction, from the fall of 1865 to the spring of 1868, some heads of families in Alabama, Georgia, and the Carolinas were corresponding with the ACS about the possibility of leaving for Liberia,[70] but the volume of correspondence increased dramatically with the rise in white violence and terrorism. White violence targeted an emerging black and white Republican leadership, mainly members of the Union leagues, leaders of the black churches, and teachers in the new schools. Not coincidentally, the same people were often the nexus and organizing force of all three. Although the toll is impossible to calculate, some sense of its scope can be seen in the tremendous drop in Republican voting. In one Louisiana parish, the Republican vote dropped from 2,987 in April of 1868 to 1 that fall.[71] Many hundreds, if not thousands, were killed or driven off. They were organizers, ministers, teachers, and property owners; anyone with ambition or courage would be targeted.

The importance of teachers and education, as both a source of African American pride and a target for white violence, cannot be overstated. Much like in Liberia, now that freedom was at hand, the first goal of sympathetic white supporters and, especially, the newly freedpeople themselves was education. Long denied to them through both law and custom throughout the South, as soon as they could they sought out the basics of literacy and arithmetic. While some of the first schools were staffed by those select few freedpeople who had managed to achieve some measure of education, these quickly gave way to more formal schools staffed by white and black, northerner and southerner alike.

Less than two years after the war's end, the Freedmen's Bureau was running 1,207 schools with 1,430 teachers and 77,998 students. By 1869, there were 3,000 schools and 180,000 students and these numbers exclude informal night schools and adult students.[72] When Republicans passed the authorization bill for the Freedmen's Bureau over President Johnson's veto in July 1866, they allocated $521,000 for education and salaries, which explains some of the complaints from the faculty at Liberia College regarding the allocation of those funds. In 1884, Martin Freeman was still bemoaning that "If a tithe of the interest and pecuniary aid could be expended for education in Africa that is poured out like water for the education of the Freedman of the U.S. then indeed Liberia College would become the beacon light of West Africa."[73] Here is evidence that, at least to those in Liberia, the connection between education in America and education in Africa could not be clearer.

What those in Liberia missed was the way that the possibility of education galvanized the entire African-American community in America. The newly freedpeople pooled what little resources they had to augment these funds and there are countless heartwarming stories of community collective action to keep schools open, well-lit, and warm. As John Alvord, superintendent of education within the Freedmen's Bureau, noted, their "chains are no sooner broken than they spring to their feet and start up an exceeding great army, clothing themselves with intelligence. What other people on earth have ever shown, while in their ignorance, such a passion for education?"[74] One white, northern teacher, demonstrating an awareness of the missionary impulse wrote, "It requires less courage to go as a missionary to Burmah than to teach colored children in Georgia."[75] Indeed, most traditional accounts of the teachers emphasize that northern teachers followed fast on the heels of the liberating Union army, funded by the American Missionary Association. However, the idea that these schools were staffed by devoted New England radicals, most of them women, has recently been overturned.

Recent scholarship has revealed a much more complicated and diverse population of teachers during Reconstruction. More than one-third of all teachers were African American and over half of the teachers who can be identified were from the South. White teachers, as a whole, were not particularly abolitionist or radical and were often sponsored by various philanthropic groups. Those who were especially committed spent many years teaching, but most teachers served less than two years. As one scholar has put it, "The small group of women and men who spoke clearly of their abolitionism when they went into the South and who went on to devote entire lifetimes to the freed people, then, were not merely abolitionists. They were race radicals."[76] Most white teachers did not express an interest in black freedom; their goal was "the spiritual and moral regeneration of the freed people; and the problem was the freed people themselves."[77] Their mean age was 30, not the youthful idealists as often depicted, while white men and women taught in almost equal numbers.

While the interest and faith in education among the freedpeople remained constant, there was a vast discrepancy among the different groups of teachers. Surely the most closely aligned and sympathetic were the African-American teachers. They seemed to share the freedpeoples' understanding of education as a fundamental emancipatory force. Northern whites seemed mainly concerned with literacy for salvation's sake, to ensure the triumph of their students in the next life, not this one. Farthest away from black goals were white southern teachers, many of whom were only teachers for one or two years and seemed most concerned with preserving the social order or collecting a meager paycheck.[78] Along this spectrum, elite Liberian attitudes toward education fit comfortably between African-American teachers and white northern ones: more concerned with civilization, evangelization, and uplift than with true equality and emancipation, especially as it concerned the local native population.

As white national support for federal intervention on the behalf of African-American rights waned, the new black schools were some of the most obvious and frequent targets of white terror and violence. Not only did they represent one of the largest local changes, from education being illegal to becoming a right, but they stood for black activism and autonomy. The presumptions of African Americans to a place above their station seemed manifest in the schoolhouse and the teacher. In the words of one scholar, "Literate African Americans undermined a belief in racial inferiority that was essential to the psychic health of postbellum whites."[79] Therefore, they had to go.

The creation of Liberia College mirrored the larger colonization project; it began under the auspices of white supporters but was co-opted by African Americans in Liberia. In this way, it foreshadowed the efforts toward education that followed emancipation. However, as this examination has shown, the overlap between the two efforts was not limited to a similar narrative trajectory. In both cases, important African-American actors took a leading role in shaping and fashioning their own futures. While they may have agreed with the broader ideas about the importance of education for racial uplift, they sought to apply education under their own power and for their own ends. Men like Martin Freeman, Alexander Crummell, and Edward Blyden sought a better future for themselves and their people through their actions at Liberia College.

Of course, they were not alone in their efforts toward education and uplift of African Americans. Brave men and women across the post–Civil War South sought a similar means of education and uplift toward ultimate racial equality. That they did so with limited white support and in the face of rising white violence only reinforces their claims to our admiration. However, their attitudes toward those they taught are more complicated than a narrative of simple heroism can allow. In both American and Liberia, students sought out education as a means of personal advancement, but their teachers were not always admiring of their abilities. It is no small irony that the description of the African natives by Americo-Liberians sounds remarkably like the description of racist whites toward the freedpeople in America. Both groups were allegedly uncivilized, almost savages, who could only be redeemed through proper education and decorous Christianity.

Despite these contrasts and congruities, one of the overwhelming revelations of this study is the importance of race. The social construction of race may be dependent on local conditions, but its historical importance transcends national boundaries. Martin Freeman fled across the Atlantic to seek a home of equality and opportunity yet found that color was no less important in Liberia, just different. It was only by arriving in Africa that these African Americans realized just how American they were, especially given their emphasis on Christian values and education in English. A close examination of their thoughts and ideas, as well as the reality of their lived experience, illustrates how much a comparison of education in Liberia and America has to tell us about the immediate period following freedom.

Juxtaposed in this way, the history of the education of the freedpeople seems not so much unique as emblematic. The shared concerns, about education and uplift, and the need for individual education in order to achieve collective uplift, were shared across the Atlantic in both Liberia and the Reconstruction-era American South. In fact, the much more famous African-American educational debates about practical versus academic education, famously embodied by Booker T. Washington and W. E. B. Du Bois, echoed the much less known arguments and debates surrounding Liberia College. Ideologies about race and education criss-crossed the ocean, carried in the hearts and minds of the people and embodied in their letters. The ideologies operated in two related but distinctive contexts, and a close comparison helps to illuminate them both.

By the 1880s, the similarities between the ideologies of race and education in Africa and America had become even more obvious. In both locations, ideologies of race and education began developing in the immediate aftermath of freedom, on a small scale with the settlers in Liberia and on a much larger scale with the emancipation following the Civil War. In both locations, the ideologies started with the premise that the first object after freedom was education, to civilize the newly free and to uplift the collective race. In both locations, proponents of education grappled with ideas about skin color and class, over who would lead the efforts toward education, and just what exactly that education should consist of. During the 1880s, Liberia College engaged in a decades-long debate about opening a trade or manual school modeled on the Hampton Institute in Virginia. They also brought in new teachers from America to engage in the education of and outreach to the local native population, usually with the express purpose of evangelizing and uplifting them. Their goal was to create an educated Christian cadre of natives who could go among the natives and uplift them, a goal that would have seemed remarkably similar to many of those educators arriving in the South twenty years earlier.

Notes

The author would like to thank the contributors to this volume for their input on earlier drafts as well as the Massachusetts Historical Society for financial support and feedback during the early stages of research.

1. For the only account of the Trustees and the creation of Liberia College see Gardner W. Allen, *The Trustees of Donations for Education in Liberia: A Story of Philanthropic Endeavor, 1850–1923* (Boston: Thomas Todd Company, 1923).

2. The scope and sequence of their travels can be deduced from the records and correspondence of the main supporting organization, the Trustees for Donations to Education at Liberia, Massachusetts Historical Society (hereafter TDEL). See also: Wilson Jeremiah Moses, *Alexander Crummell: A Study of Civilization and Discontent* (New York: Oxford University Press, 1989), and Hollis R. Lynch, *Edward Wilmot Blyden: Pan-Negro Patriot, 1832–1912* (London: Oxford University Press, 1967).

3. For an account of Delany's activities and thinking during this period see Robert S. Levine, *Martin Delany, Frederick Douglass, and the Politics of Representative Identity* (Chapel Hill, N.C.: University of North Carolina Press, 1997).

4. The following summary is principally drawn from Moses, *Alexander Crummell*.

5. *The Liberator*, July 25, 1835, mentioned him by name.

6. *Anti-Slavery Reporter*, June 2, 1851, 86–87.

7. Moses, *Alexander Crummell*, 80–90.

8. Alexander Crummell, *The Future of Africa* (New York: Charles Scribner, 1862). Unsurprisingly, Frederick Douglass admired the author but disagreed with his sentiments: *Douglass' Monthly*, July 1862.

9. Alexander Crummell, "The Progress and Prospects of the Republic of Liberia," Delivered at the Annual Meeting of the New York State Colonization Society, May 9. 1861, reprinted in *Destiny and Race: Selected Writings, 1840–1898, Alexander Crummell*, edited by Wilson Jeremiah Moses (Amherst: University of Massachusetts Press, 1992), 168.

10. Ibid., 171.

11. Ibid., 172–23.

12. Ibid., 173–24.

13. The only account of any length about Freeman is Russell W. Irvine, "Martin H. Freeman of Rutland: America's First Black College Professor and Pioneering Black Social Activist," *Rutland Historical Society Quarterly* 26, no. 3, 1996, 71–96; the discussion that follows is based on the same.

14. *Frederick Douglass' Paper*, September 8, 1854.

15. Ibid.

16. Quoted in Irvine, "Freeman," 79.

17. Quoted in Irvine, "Freeman," 80.

18. Freeman to Tracy, September 3, 1863, Trustees for Donations to Education at Liberia, Massachusetts Historical Society (hereafter TDEL).

19. Freeman to Tracy, October 12, 1863, TDEL.

20. Freeman to Tracy, November 7, 1863, TDEL.

21. Freeman to Tracy, December 1, 1863, TDEL.

22. Freeman to Tracy, January 30, 1864, TDEL.

23. Freeman to Tracy, August 1, 1864, TDEL.

24. Freeman to Tracy, September 3, 1864, TDEL.

25. Freeman to Tracy, November 30, 1864, TDEL.

26. Minutes of the Faculty of Liberia College, April 12, 1866, TDEL.

27. Crummell to Fearing, April 1866, TDEL.

28. Crummell to Tracy, August 24, 1866, TDEL.

29. Irvine, "Freeman," 88.

30. Freeman to Tracy, August 9, 1867, TDEL.

31. Freeman to Tracy, October 17, 1867, TDEL.

32. Ibid.

33. There is an apparent contradiction in Freeman's thinking here; he left Avery College, with its white trustees, to teach at Liberia College, with its white trustees. However, Freeman's letters make clear that it was the overall racist and oppressive environment in America he sought to escape, not simply the oversight of white trustees. In addition, the geographical distance meant that while the Boston Trustees controlled the purse strings, they had no direct oversight or control over the daily operations. This may have been the best measure of autonomy that Freeman could hope to attain.

34. Freeman to Tracy, October 17, 1867, TDEL.

35. Freeman to Tracy, October 24, 1867, TDEL.

36. Freeman to Tracy, November 25, 1867, TDEL.

37. Freeman to Board of Trustees, March 2, 1868, TDEL.

38. Freeman to Tracy, April 6, 1868, TDEL.

39. Official Report, Freeman to Tracy and Board, July 15, 1868, TDEL.

40. Louisa Freeman to Tracy, May 25, 1869, TDEL.

41. Louisa Freeman to Tracy, June 9, 1869, TDEL.

42. Martin Freeman to Tracy, April 5, 1871, TDEL.

43. Moses, *Alexander Crummell*.

44. Crummell to Denison, August 11, 1869, Papers of the Domestic and Foreign Missionary Society, quoted in Moses, *Alexander Crummell*, 102.

45. Crummell to Denison, February 1, 1869, Papers of the Domestic and Foreign Missionary Society, quoted in Moses, *Alexander Crummell*, 172.

46. Quoted in Moses, *Alexander Crummell*, 190.

47. Alexander Crummell, "Our National Mistakes and the Remedy for Them," in *Destiny and Race*.

48. Crummell, "National Mistake," 176–77.

49. Crummell, "National Mistake," 177.

50. Crummell, "National Mistake," 180.

51. Crummell, "National Mistake," 184.

52. Crummell, "National Mistake," 191.

53. Crummell, "National Mistake," 193–200.

54. Crummell's biographer sees a marked change in his attitude toward the natives during his last two years in Liberia. See Moses, *Alexander Crummell*, Chapter 10.

55. Letter from William Fray to Emory Washburn, May 20, 1871, TDEL.

56. The basic story is recounted in both Moses, *Alexander Crummell* and Hollis R. Lynch, *Edward Wilmot Blyden: Pan-Negro Patriot, 1832–1912* (London: Oxford University Press, 1967).

57. See the introduction to *Selected Letters of Edward Wilmot Blyden*.

58. Lynch, *Selected Letters*, 15.

59. Blyden to the Rev. Henry Venn, September 16, 1871 in Lynch, *Selected Letters*, 93. Blyden extensively quotes from a letter from Freeman dated September 6.

60. Blyden to Venn, April 17, 1872 in Lynch, *Selected Letters*, 112.

61. Blyden to William Coppinger, October 19, 1874, ACS.

62. Blyden to Coppinger, ACS.

63. Blyden to Coppinger, ACS.

64. Lynch, *Blyden*.

65. Allen, *Trustees*, 30–50.

66. Letter from Graduates to Board, July 4, 1876 and the vote taken on August 20, 1876, TDEL.

67. Flier for lecture in New York, November 18, 1878, TDEL.

68. Though it falls beyond the time span of this chapter, the ongoing example of Hampton Institute would have a lasting influence on Liberia College. The Boston Trustees sent out two new professors to teach and investigate the college. T. McCants Stewart

and Hugh M. Browne were not impressed with what they found in Liberia, advocating instead a manual college modeled on Hampton. This caused a heated correspondence across the Atlantic between themselves, the Boston Trustees, and Edward Blyden. See Stewart and Browne to Trustees, October 1, 1883; Blyden to Braman, October 25, 1883; Blyden to Davemport, October 25, 1883; Blyden to Braman, January 16, 1884; Stewart to Samson, January 16, 1884; Browne to Samson, January 19, 1884; and many others.

69. For a good overview of the transition from slavery to freedom in the South see: Steven Hahn, *A Nation Under Our Feet: Black Political Struggles in the Rural South from Slavery to the Great Migration* (Cambridge: Harvard University Press, 2003); Eric Foner, *Reconstruction: America's Unfinished Revolution, 1863-1877* (New York: Harper, 2002); and Leon Litwack, *Been in the Storm so Long: The Aftermath of Slavery* (New York: Vintage, 1980). The number of soldiers is taken from Chapter 1 in Hahn.

70. Hahn, *A Nation*, 167.

71. Ibid., 268.

72. Douglas R. Egerton, *The Wars of Reconstruction: The Brief, Violent History of America's Most Progressive Era* (New York: Bloomsbury Press, 2014), 137.

73. Freeman to G. W. Samson, October 22, 1884, TDEL.

74. John W. Alvord, *First Semi-Annual Report* (January 1866), 10.

75. Quoted in Egerton, *The Wars of Reconstruction*, 154.

76. Ronald E. Butchart, *Schooling the Freed People: Teaching, Learning, and the Struggle for Black Freedom, 1861-1876* (Chapel Hill: University of North Carolina Press, 2010), xiii.

77. Ibid., xiv.

78. For a summary of these views, see Chapters 2–4 in Butchart, *Schooling the Freed People*.

79. Ibid., 176.

3

Transatlantic Liberalism

Radical Republicans and the British Reform Act of 1867

Mitchell Snay

In March 1867, Republicans in the United States Congress passed a series of Reconstruction Acts that divided the former states of the Confederacy into five military districts, mandated the convening of constitutional conventions in the South, and enfranchised newly emancipated African-American men to vote for delegates to those conventions. Over the course of that same year, the British Parliament debated and ultimately passed a Reform Act that broadened the franchise for British workingmen. Republican leaders in America noted the similarities between and simultaneity of these two events. "The controversy is quite analogous to that going on with us on the same subject," observed the Springfield *Republican* in April 1867.[1] The Hartford *Courant* expanded on this: "This extension of the right of suffrage to half a million of English workingmen is paralleled in our country by the recent admission to the privileges of the ballot-box of nearly equal number of colored workingmen. The great principle involved in these two just acts is the same . . ."[2]

There are concrete grounds for comparing Republican policies for reconstructing the Union and the English Reform Bill. Obviously, both occurred in 1867. Both involved an extension of suffrage. Both were part of compromises within a party system—among Republican factions in the United States, between Republicans and Democrats, and between Liberals and Tories in England. Both involved dynamic party competition over basic ideologies. (Here the British Liberals were more like Democrats.) The British Reform Act of 1867 and the expansion of voting rights in the United States also shared an interest in women's suffrage.

In America, the female vote was a logical consequence of the debate over extending the franchise for African-American males. "It is remarkable that in England, as in America," the Boston *Commonwealth* noted, "the agitation for the enfranchisement of woman has been chiefly produced by those who have been interested in the rights of the negro in America and in the English colonies."[3] The more radical Republican press in the United States, exemplified by the Boston *Commonwealth*, tended to support women's suffrage.[4] An Equal Rights Association meeting in New York in 1867 resolved that "as republican institutions are based on individual rights, the first question for the American people to determine is not the rights of races or of sex, but the rights of individuals."[5] In Great Britain, a National Society for Women's Suffrage operated in London, Manchester, and Edinburgh.[6] Both events suggest the existence of a "transatlantic liberalism" that stressed civil liberty, toleration, individual freedom, progress, and laissez-faire.[7]

Pairing Radical Reconstruction and the British Reform Act of 1867 involves several themes of historical inquiry. The first is *comparative history*, a well-trodden path in Reconstruction historiography. With the advent of Post-Revisionism in the 1960s and 1970s, historians began comparing emancipation in the United States to other New World slave societies to show both the commonalities of the transition from slavery to freedom and to highlight the unique features of the American experience. Recent scholars have followed the lead of historians such as Frank Thistlethwaite and Robert Kelley in creating a new *Anglo-American history*.[8] As historian Mark Summers has recently suggested: "Parliament's passage in 1867 of the Second Reform Act owed some debt to those who gave America its new birth of freedom."[9] During the 1860s, British reformer Thomas Perronet Thompson was in close touch with *Chicago Tribune* editor Horace White.[10]

A second historiographical theme that can be usefully employed in bringing together American Reconstruction and British Reform is what historians are now labeling *transnational, global, "entangled,"* and *"histoire croisee"* history. They have subjected these terms to serious scrutiny, recognizing their complexity and the difficulties of definition. Obviously, the boundaries between these new approaches and comparative history are highly permeable. Nonetheless, the general thrust of these current trends is to place developments and events in America within a larger global framework. A large part of the goal of transnational history is to ascertain more precisely what was distinctly *exceptional* about the United States and about American history. The Civil War era has become a particular area of interest in transnational history. Contemporaries at the time viewed the American war as part of a larger global history. Historians have increasingly adopted this perspective and now tend to see the Civil War in an international context of wars of national consolidation, as in Italy and Germany in the mid–nineteenth century.[11] From this same perspective, Southerners during the 1860s considered the Civil War another example of wars of nationalist self-determination.[12]

Most relevant to this essay has been the effort to embed the Civil War in a larger history of liberalism. The American war, according to historian Don H. Doyle, "was at the time understood by many as an epic battle in a prolonged struggle between liberal republican ideas and the 'monarchic principle.'"[13] With these new approaches provided by transnational and global history, historians can now turn their gaze to the framing of Radical Reconstruction in the context of the British Reform Bill of 1867.[14]

This essay will focus on how the Radical Republican press viewed the progress and meaning of franchise reform in Great Britain. More than anything else, Radical Republicans saw the struggle over the Reform Bill as a contest between aristocracy and democracy. This perception mirrored and was largely shaped by Republican views of the South, the sectional conflict over slavery, the Civil War, and the current process of Reconstruction. The Radical Republican representation of the English Reform Bill sharpened a Republican vision of the role of the United States in a globalizing world that helped lay an ideological foundation for American expansionism in the late nineteenth century.[15]

The liberal reform tradition begun in post-Napoleonic western Europe continued through the 1860s and 1870s, providing the context for the Great Reform Act of 1867. In the aftermath of the revolutions of 1848, European states experimented with measures aimed at stabilizing society in the midst of industrialization. At stake was the viability of institutions in containing domestic conflict. England had a Parliamentary system that simultaneously valued traditions of freedom and stability. William Ewart Gladstone was a classical liberal who believed in free enterprise and laissez faire government. Gladstone's first ministry (1867–74) was a high point of British liberalism that witnessed attacks on institutions like the Anglican Church that stood as bulwarks of the aristocracy. It abolished Anglican religious requirements for faculties of Oxford and Cambridge. The Ballot Act of 1872 introduced voting by secret ballot. Gladstone further eliminated tariffs, advanced state supported public education, legalized labor unions, and reformed the military and government administration by merit.[16]

Reconstruction in the United States bore many similarities to European liberal reform. At the state level, Republicans engaged in a series of reforms aimed at strengthening the ability of institutions to cope with domestic problems. In New York, Pennsylvania, and other northern states, Republicans attempted to reform institutions like schools, prisons, and asylums.[17] In the newly reconstructed states in the South, Radical Republicans sought to create these institutions in former slaveholding societies with a weak institutional base. In brief, Radical

Republicans attempted to "republicanize" American institutions. The Hartford *Courant* described the extension of suffrage in the Reconstructed South as "steps to republicanize their institutions."[18] During the late 1860s, Republicans spoke in terms of the "progress of republicanism," "the demand of populations for their rights," and the "progress of civilization and the improvement of the race."[19]

At the same time, agitation for the extension of the suffrage and reform in the representational system grew in England. In 1866, Lord Russell introduced a reform bill that was defeated by a coalition of antidemocratic Liberals and Conservatives. Russell resigned and was replaced by the Conservative Lord Derby. Conservatives, led in the House of Commons by Benjamin Disraeli, introduced their own reform bill, hoping to take credit among what were to be the newly enfranchised voters. Disraeli, with a newly placed faith in the working class took over leadership of the reform bill.[20] In the United States, the Republican editors affirmed his strong position. "The general belief in England," reported the *Philadelphia Press*, "seems to be that Mr. DISRAELI laid the heads of a new Reform Bill before the Cabinet."[21] The Springfield *Republican* opined that Disraeli "takes rank at once as the great politician of the age. Our Congress never saw his equal, our politicians never conceived of such riding the storm, and making the whirlwind serve their own glory and power."[22] In England, the working class and the middle class had come together to demand the suffrage. Republican editors in the United States also gave great credit to the reformer and agitator John Bright and his Reform League. The *New-York Tribune* labeled Bright "the master spirit, and the Reform League the organized power."[23] As it passed during the fall of 1867, the Reform Bill doubled the electorate and gave suffrage to a new urban population of shopkeepers, clerks, and workers. The act expanded the electorate from approximately 1,430,000 to 2,470,000. It added 938,000 to an electorate of 1,056,000 in England and Wales; working class voters were now a majority in towns, while the new country voters were from the middle classes.[24]

The Republican press noted the oddity that it was the Tory party rather than the Liberal Party that was largely responsible for the Reform Bill of 1867. "Instead of adhering to tradition, and manfully struggling 'to stem the tide of democracy,'" commented the *Chicago Tribune*, "the tories of England are endeavoring [not] only to float along with it, but to direct its course."[25] The Boston *Commonwealth* argued similarly that "it is certainly a more liberal measure that the Tories are now offering than the Liberals introduced last year—a change entirely attributable to *fear*."[26]

Throughout 1867, the Republican press in the United States paid close attention to party and policy developments in England. This was in keeping with the journalistic custom of following events in Europe. They created their own narrative of English Reform politics that closely mirrored developments in England. In their account, the debate over the Reform Bill was a contest between the forces of aristocracy and democracy. "To break the power and the influence of the aristocracy," argued the *New-York Tribune*, "is the main object of the English party of progress."[27] It was a narrative that often explicitly contrasted the two nations with the invidious comparisons directed against England.[28]

American Republicans viewed Britain as a country ruled by an outmoded, corrupt, and ineffectual aristocracy. The Springfield *Republican* insisted that "the ruling classes of that country are too tenacious of power; they do not yield readily enough to the growing capacity and desire of the people to share in the government. They cling to ancient prerogative and privilege and resist popular progress at every point." In contrast, the Massachusetts editor continued, "Our constitution embraces all that is best in that of England, and is a century in advance of it in its adaptation to the ideas of liberty and justice now universally recognized among men of thought in all nations."[29] The "vice" of English statesmanship, the *Republican* argued further, is "that it estimates men by classes and not as individuals." In addition, the British press had made "little effort" to keep the public informed about acts of the government.[30] In contrast, noted the *Hartford Courant*: "So important a document as the new Reform Bill would, in the United States, have been made public in the columns of every newspaper between the Atlantic and the Pacific."[31]

As the debate over the Reform Bill unfolded, Republican leaders placed the onus of aristocracy on the Tory Party. According to the Springfield *Republican*, the Tories "are the real blue blood of the kingdom, who think there are great differences in the quality of the class that mankind are made of."[32] The Tories were also condemned for their anti-democratic inclinations. They "are fighting hard for every link in the chain that holds down the republic," insisted the Boston *Commonwealth*, "—believing firmly . . . that the public is a beast."[33] Even though the Tory Party eventually passed the Reform Bill of 1867, American Republicans were unconvinced. "The people instinctively feel," stated the *New-York Tribune*, "that a party habitually pledged to reactionary principles, traditionally opposed to the increase of democratic power, traditionally jealous to a degree of the classes below their own order, cannot possibly be sincere in their professions of a desire to secure the extension of popular privileges."[34] The House of Lords joined the Tory Party as a bastion of conservatism and political incompetency. "Certainly a lazier and more incapable assemblage of legislators is not to be found in the world than the Upper House of the British Parliament," noted the *New-York Tribune*.[35] Peers were allowed to vote by proxy, the House did not require any quorum, and debates were meaningless. According to the *Hartford Courant*, efforts to reform and reinvigorate House of Lords were opposed by the "aristocracy . . . tooth and nail."[36]

The contrast between English aristocracy and American democracy was also evident outside the political arena. Conscious of their heritage of homesteading and free land, Republicans noted the closed economic system of British land-holding. "There can be no liberty, no peace, no contentment," insisted the *Chicago Tribune*, "among any people who are excluded by law for the ownership of the soil they inhabit."[37] Republicans attacked the ancient English practice of primogeniture "whereby the land of England, Ireland, Scotland, and Wales is owned by a handful of bloated aristocrats, while thirty millions of Britons and Irishmen toil and pay rent to support the aforesaid Lords in wasteful luxury and vicious idleness."[38] The British system of landholding meant that the English laborer "lives in a mean and sordid style that our working classes would not endure for a day . . ."[39] Republicans were boastful about their own free labor ideology that had characterized their party since the 1850s. "Labor is honored and rewarded as Republicanism flourishes," insisted the *Philadelphia Press*.[40] The Springfield *Republican* explained further that in the American free labor system is "the free exchange of their own products by free laborers."[41] The *New-York Tribune*, edited by Horace Greeley, neatly summed up the contrasting labor systems of England and America: "It is not simply that ours is a new country, presenting in its widespread territory and immense resources every inducement and encouragement to the industriously inclined—although this consideration must necessarily form an important element in any comparison instituted between Great Britain and America; but it is that the rights of labor, the honorableness of industry, lie at the very root of our whole system, political and social."[42]

Along with its political structure and system of land tenure, Republicans in the United States attacked England for its established church. The *Chicago Tribune* chose the value-laden term "peculiar institution," long used to refer to southern slavery, to describe a system whereby a majority of Englishmen and Irishmen support a church "to which they do not belong, and to whose dogmas they do not subscribe."[43] The *Chicago Tribune* newspaper noted further "the anomaly of a nation being taxed for the support of the Church which numbers among its members a minority of the people."[44] The *New-York Tribune* again contrasted British monopoly with American freedom, this time in terms of religion: "In this country religion thrives without state support, and churches regulate their affairs without the aid of the magistrate's sword. The English people have yet to learn what religious freedom means, from a practical experience of its power and its benefits."[45]

From the perspective of Republicans, England was a nation deeply flawed and troubled by its aristocratic institutions. Throughout 1867, they suggested that England was suffering an irrepressible conflict between aristocracy and democracy and reaction and reform. In May, the *New-York Tribune* editorialized that "the spirit of revolution is abroad in England. The people are resolved upon having their rights."[46] If English and Irish reformers can unite, the Springfield *Republican* reasoned, "British toryism and aristocracy must soon bend or break."[47] Republican editors even hinted that revolution in England was not a distant impossibility. "The English people deserve a better fate than to be forever the slaves of their aristocracy," argued the *New-York Tribune*, "and we hope that if their rights should be withheld from them much longer, they will know how to conquer them."[48]

For Republicans, the plight of a conflicted Britain contrasted sharply with the stability and progress of a United States now free from slavery. Republicans believed that the Republican-sponsored war had purified and democratized American institutions. "The one idea above all others underlying our form of government," explained the Boston *Commonwealth*, "and which should claim defense from every magistrate and citizen, is that this is a government of all, by all, and for the good of all. The theory of our civil polity is that of a pure democracy—the entire power resting with the people."[49] The greatest victory of the Civil War, noted Republican Senator Charles Sumner of Massachusetts, "was the definition of a republican government according to the principles of the Declaration of Independence."[50]

The essence of American democracy, now that slavery had been destroyed, was universal suffrage. "We are in favor of universal suffrage," proclaimed the *Chicago Tribune*. It explained in greater detail: "Universal suffrage is in accordance with the genius of our institutions as re-moulded by the war. It is the destiny of this nation, as inevitable as was the war itself, the seeds of which existed in the fruitful soil of two systems perpetually hostile in the nature of things. It is not only the destiny of the country, but of the Europe. It is to-day the great question of the world."[51] The *New-York Tribune* agreed: "Universal Suffrage is the watchword of the progressive party in every country of the world."[52] New Jersey Republicans, when forming a state auxiliary of the American Equal Rights Association, declared that the purpose of the organization was "the exercise of the right of suffrage to every adult citizen of the United States, and generally to spread and enforce the principle of the liberty of all, limited only by the like liberty of each."[53]

In this spirit, Republican editors generally hailed the Reform bill as a harbinger of democracy for the English people. The reality remained, however, that the Reform bill did not bring universal suffrage. "It may be styled with truth a democratic measure," noted the *Hartford Courant*.[54] The *New-York Tribune* called British Reform "an important advance toward manhood suffrage."[55] "It almost inaugurates universal suffrage," opined the *Chicago Tribune*, "and places it wholly within the power of the Radical party to abolish all class privileges of the aristocracy, divorce the church from the State, repeal of the laws of primogeniture and entail and thus secure a subdivision of the landed states among the people, and to establish the American system of equal, representative districts and vote by ballot."[56] The Reform bill moved England in the direction of American governmental ideals. The Springfield *Republican* described the reform bill as it was taking shape as "an enormous stride towards republicanism."[57] The *New-York Tribune* significantly labeled the change in representation as the "Americanization" of English institutions.[58] "Revolutions never go backwards," explained the *Chicago Tribune*, "and our English radical friends will never stop until they have secured all the rights and principles enjoyed by their brethren in America."[59]

Republicans of the Civil War era believed firmly that the extension of suffrage had to be accompanied by education, echoing the Revolutionary belief in the necessity of an informed citizenry. "The forefathers recognized the great fact that popular intelligence and virtue are essential to the full success of free institutions," declared the Springfield *Republican*.[60] The Massachusetts newspaper explained further that popular education must be placed on a broad basis "or it cannot meet the wants of the people, and make popular suffrage consistent with good government."[61] Not surprisingly, the emphasis on education as a requisite for universal suffrage had special relevance for Republicans supporting the vote for newly emancipated African-American males in the South. They noted the similar situations of England and the United States in 1867. "As a result of the extension of the elective franchise in England," wrote a Philadelphia Republican editor, "the first minds and leading statesmen of that land are turning their attention and bending all their energies to the question of popular education." The freedmen of the South must be similarly educated. "Enfranchisement and enlightenment walk hand in hand. They mutually stimulate and develop each other. In a free country the ballot box is the schoolmaster."[62] Another Republican paper noted the connection between the education of the English working classes and the newly enfranchised freedmen. "England is thus confronted, as a chief duty," noted the Springfield *Republican*, "with the necessity of educating her voters. What we have to do with the millions of blacks at the South, England has to do with her new hundreds of thousands of voters and their families.[63]

The Republican narrative of the British Reform Bill of 1867 thus reflected the Radical ideology of the Republican Party. The language used to describe the progress of English reform was similar to how Republicans were defining their own struggles against President Johnson and the Democrats. But Radical Republican spokesmen went even further. The presentation of history as it was unfolding in England served as a kind of allegory for the recent history of both the United States and the Republican Party. American Republicans tended to see in the current crisis in England a mirror of their own fight against slavery and "aristocracy."

The Republicans portrayed themselves as the party of democracy in a kind of Manichean struggle against the forces of aristocracy. "We have always been the party of the common people as against the landed interested and aristocratic or financial combinations," wrote the *Philadelphia Press*. ". . . In our late war the Democracy [meaning the Democratic Party] had the sympathy of the aristocratic capitalists of England. We had their enmity."[64] The struggle occurring in England was similar. A democratic movement, according to the *New-York Tribune*, "confronts that proud aristocracy of birth and privilege which has hitherto guided the destinies of England, and shaped legislation for its own selfish ends."[65] The battle between democracy and the landed aristocracy in England resembled the contest between the free labor North and the slaveholding aristocracy of the South. In a refrain familiar from the late 1850s, the Boston *Commonwealth* attacked the monopoly of land in the South: ". . . with almost the entire land of a country in the hands of a few persons, there will necessarily be aristocratic privileges, a repression of all enterprise, and the denial of equal rights to the mass of the people."[66]

Following these analogies, Republicans likened the British aristocracy to their own political opponents. In speculating on the future of English politics, the *Chicago Tribune* wrote that "the Republican party of England will have the Tories as firmly by the throat as the Republicans of America have the Copper-rebels by the wind pipe."[67] The English aristocracy was also likened to former slaveholders. "The Tories in England," explained the *Chicago Tribune*, "who have opposed the Reform Bill deplore it as the death, not only of the monarchy, but of the aristocracy, and shudderingly point out the awful things that will happen when the newly-enfranchised voters shall send a butcher, or a baker, or a laborer, or an artisan, without education or refinement, to Parliament and our American Tories equally lament the awful calamity of permitting negroes to vote, and affect to shrink with horror from the self-drawn pictures of Negroes sitting in Congress, and in the State Legislatures."[68] In discussing the post–Civil War South, Republicans compared the English people with the Southern yeomanry. The *Philadelphia Press* urged that a new order of things must come—"a new society must be created. The domination of a class must be swept away forever."[69]

The manner in which Republicans characterized the party dynamics in English politics hinted at the recent history of party politics in America. In particular, the split in Liberal Party in England recalled the rift in the Democracy between antislavery and proslavery factions and the division between Northern and Southern Democrats in 1860. "The Liberal party has been composed all along of inharmonious elements," explained the *New-York Tribune*, "for it has embraced at once the Radicalism that verges on Democracy, and the Conservatism that inclines to Toryism."[70]

The *Tribune* detected another aspect of intra-party conflict in America when it described a split among English liberals between "that portion of the party which looks more for the purity of principles quarrels with the portion that looks more for the preservation of power."[71] The recent history of both England and America pointed out the dangers of political compromise to deeply held and cherished principles. "The thoughtful observer of today," remarked the Boston *Commonwealth*, "will not fail to see that the finest schemes of compromise, policy, and State-craft, are, throughout the earth, ending in dismay and ruin, and that society is forced to turn its reluctant steps in the direction of ideas and humanity."[72] The *New-York Tribune* also believed ". . . there are periods and occasions when nothing in political action can be more dangerous than compromise." It explained that compromise "will never answer in revolutionary periods, when men's passions are stirred to their very depths, and political excitement assumes the character of the storm."[73]

The narrative arc of the rise of the Republican Party in the fight against slavery can also be detected in the way in which Republican spokesmen portrayed the politics of reform in Great Britain. It suggests a self-characterization of a new party driven by a popular uprising. For instance, the *New-York Tribune*, covering the course of the English Reform Bill, wrote that "before Reform can be carried, a new party, a people's party, will have to be formed with Bright as its leader." "Appearances, then, indicate a break up of present combinations, and the formation of a new party under whose banners, sooner or later, the principle of manhood suffrage will be established."[74] As in the United States in the 1850s, a novel situation required a new party. Again, the *New-York Tribune* explained that "there is work to be done in England, in the interests of the people, requiring a new political organization resting on a foundation essentially different from the aristocratic basis of the present Liberal party, and leaders possessing greater moral robustness—so to speak—and wielding greater popular power than men of the stamp of those who have hitherto been the chiefs of the Liberals."[75] In England as in America, a successful political party would arise on the mobilization of the people. "If a righteous Reform bill should be carried this session of Parliament," Greeley's *Tribune* believed, "the work will have been the achievement of the people, who are beginning to feel their power, and learning how to use it with the best effect."[76]

These similarities in the politics of reform between England and the United States were mostly allusions, though revealing ones at that. At other times, however, the likeness between the expansion of suffrage in the United States and the English Reform Bill were made explicit. The *Chicago Tribune*, for instance, wrote that despotism in Ireland "seems likely to be extended through another generation—unless the republican party of Great Britain break their chains and set those white slaves free, as the Republican party of the United States liberated the black slaves from a more endurable bondage."[77] While discussing the Reform Bill, this influential Midwestern Republican journal wrote: "Enough is known to verify the belief that the new voters will swamp the old tory constituencies, just as the new Radical voters to South Carolina and Louisiana will swamp the old element in these States."[78]

Republican leaders in America thus tended to view the Great Reform Act of 1867 in light of their own political ideologies. While they applauded the direction of democratic change in England, they assumed the superiority of American ideals and institutions. One result was the expressions of what well might be termed "American exceptionalism." Simply, the United States represented the fate of popular government in the world. Such statements are worth quoting at length. "The Republic of the United States," declared the *Chicago Tribune*, "has demonstrated the great truth that 'God *has* given to men the power to govern themselves well and to improve their position upon this earth.' It has also demonstrated that neither monarchs nor peers, nor titled lords of any sort, are necessary to aid them in governing themselves well, or in maintaining the integrity of their soil and upholding their free institutions on the battle-field."[79] The Springfield *Republican* assumed that the United States can "furnish to the fatherland a model and an example of the best form of government ideally and practically, for civilized men everywhere."[80] It was the American mission "to furnish to the world the first successful experiment in self-government," proclaimed the Springfield *Republican*. The United States is "about to prove our faith in the fundamental idea of free government by giving the suffrage to all citizens without distinction of class or race. When we have fully completed this work we shall have a right to claim the respect of the world as a true republic; and we shall receive it, and our example will be, more than ever before, the inspiration and hope of the friends of liberty throughout the world."[81] These sentiments of self-righteous exceptionalism, forged in the crucible of Reconstruction and the British Reform Bill of 1867, would help create the ideological foundation for American imperialism in the late nineteenth century.[82]

In 1867, during the launch of Radical Reconstruction, Republican leaders presented their own interpretation of the Second Reform Act in England. In contrast to their own free and democratic order, England was an aristocratic society where privilege dominated and the common people were oppressed. It was witnessing an irrepressible conflict between aristocracy and democracy, one that threatened revolution if not resolved. The Reform Act represented this kind of resolution, part of a global trend away from caste and autocracy toward a freer government. American Republicans urged further reforms to end the power of the established church and break up the privileges of the landed aristocracy. Paradoxically, Radical Republicans applauded and perhaps even exaggerated the democratic achievements of the Second Reform Act while insisting that Britain was an aristocratic social order unlike the United States.

The evidence for this essay has come largely from the Radical Republican press. It has been assumed that the Radicals embodied the most egalitarian approach to Reconstruction in the South and would thus have been most interested in democratic experiments in England. Yet this assumption of the uniqueness of Radical views, informed by their radicalism, needs to be cautiously qualified. A very brief survey of newspaper opinion across party lines lies might be helpful to indicate what such lines of inquiry might produce.

During Reconstruction, the Republican Party was divided into Radical and Moderate factions (some historians might also posit a Conservative group). The Radicals were veterans of the antebellum antislavery crusade and sought to extend civil equality to blacks in both the North and South. The Moderates advocated less extreme measures that were more in tune with Northern public opinion.[83] The views of moderate Republicans are well illustrated in the *New York Times* whose editors followed events in England closely. There were a number of similarities between the views of the Radicals and the *Times* on the Second

Reform Act. Like the Radical press, the *Times* believed in the revolutionary nature of the suffrage reforms embodied in the Reform bill: "The old moorings
have been cast away, the old channels destroyed."[84] They also applauded the Tory
party for carrying "a franchise scheme of a more comprehensive character than
has ever been attempted by the leaders of either of the great parties."[85] The *Times*
applauded Benjamin Disraeli as a Parliamentary leader and underscored the importance of education to the extension of suffrage whether in the United States
or Great Britain. "If we indeed are to be a model, and not an everlasting warning
to every people," the *Times* opined, "it behooves us as the most pressing national
duty, to educate those whom we have enfranchised."[86]

A fuller transnational history of the expansion of suffrage in the United States
and the British Reform Act of 1867 needs to take Democratic attitudes into account in order to see more clearly the distinctiveness of Republican responses.
Democratic leaders throughout the late 1860s fought against Radical Reconstruction, portraying it as an unwarranted expansion of national power and a military
despotism yoked on the South. Moreover, Democrats tended to be hostile to
racial equality, critical of black aspirations toward suffrage and office holding,
and suspicious of Republican motives. From their antebellum heritage, however,
Democrats might be expected to be hostile toward the aristocracy in British society but applaud the English efforts toward suffrage equality as long as it was
limited to whites.[87]

A brief survey of the reaction of northern Democratic newspapers to the British Reform Act of 1867 shows several similarities to the Republicans. First, urban
sheets like *The Boston Post*, the *New York World*, the *Cincinnati Enquirer*, and the
Cleveland *Plain Dealer* carried foreign news, often from foreign correspondents,
that included the progress of electoral reform in England. Second, they recognized and applauded the extent of democratization in the Reform Act of 1867.
The leading Democratic newspaper in Detroit called the extension of suffrage "a
remarkably liberal one."[88] Later that summer, the same paper explained: "Fragment by fragment the foundations of aristocratic privilege are crumbling to ruin
. . ."[89] *The Boston Post* explained similarly: "Power passes now from the few to the
many. Aristocracy makes way for Democracy."[90] Some Democrats, like Radical
Republicans, acknowledged the global magnitude of the Reform Act. The *Detroit
Free Press* declared it similar to "other great events in this world."[91] *The Boston
Post* affirmed this judgment. "The same wave of Reform which has taken them
off their feet," proclaimed the editor, "is rolling over all the governments of the
Old World. The people discuss popular rights in Germany, in France, in Hun-
gary, in Greece."[92]

Like Radical Republicans, Democratic editors and party leaders interpreted the British Reform Act of 1867 from their own partisan perspective. George Pendleton, a leading Ohio Democrat, saw in the Tory Party of Benjamin Disraeli a manifestation of the American Democratic exaltation of liberty and hatred of tyranny: "There is such a party in England to-day, and it wrests from Government a large reform in the matter of representation."[93] Perhaps hinting at the anxiety of their own political position after the Civil War, the editor of the Boston *Post* assured his readers that the British Reform Bill also "provides safeguards for the minority." He explained: "All are to have their rights because all will have representation."[94] Considering his party's historic commitment to giving the vote to all adult white males, one Democratic editor strangely voiced his concern over universal suffrage. In the editorial "Does a Republican Form of Government Exclude Slavery?," the editor of the Detroit *Free Press* answered that "there is absolutely nothing in a republican polity that necessarily excludes slavery." Echoing the proslavery theorists of the Old South, he went on to explain that as "a republican form of government demands that the controlling power should be placed in intelligent hands, republics have always opposed indiscriminate suffrage."[95] In the eyes of this Michigan editor, Benjamin Disraeli relied on these principles to convince his fellow Tories to consent to the Reform Act of 1867: "According to him [Disraeli], social influences invariably affect the lower classes so powerfully, that a more democratic basis may be expected to lead to a conservative reaction against the middle and truly liberal."[96] This admonition against universal suffrage, seemingly paradoxical for a nineteenth-century Democrat, might well have been only a slightly veiled attack on African-American suffrage being pushed by some Radical Republicans in 1867.

The Radical representation of the Second Reform Act helps illuminate the nature of Republican ideology during the heart of Reconstruction. It illustrates some of the crosscurrents of ideological influence after the Civil War. Simultaneously, Radical Republicans seemed to affirm American exceptionalism while maintaining a faith in the spreading democratic movements in Europe. Into this ideological mix must also be added an Anglophobia that was a heritage of the antebellum era but also reinforced during the Civil War by events such the *Trent* Affair and the *Alabama* Claims. The uniqueness of American Reconstruction, when placed beside the Second Reform Act, lies in race. The challenge in Great Britain was to broaden the suffrage to be more inclusive of class developments. The challenge in America was not only to extend the vote to the new freedmen but to create a permanent place for African-Americans in the civil polity. The crisis of Reconstruction, when seen from the vantage point of the Second Reform Act, thus brought out some of the contradictions and complexities of the merging of liberalism and nationalism during the Civil War era. Both events were part of a larger global struggle to "define the relationship between race, class, and nation."[97]

Notes

The author would like to thank the contributors to this volume for their feedback on earlier versions of this chapter.

1. Springfield *Republican*, April 2, 1867.

2. *Hartford Courant*, August 28, 1867. See also the *New-York Tribune*, May 13, 1867. According to historian Paul Quiqley: "Global connections were quite evident to actors in the period" of the Civil War era. "Interchange: Nationalism and Internationalism in the Era of the Civil War," *Journal of American History* 98, no. 2 (September 2011): 461.

3. Boston *Commonwealth*, February 9, 1867.

4. Boston *Commonwealth*, March 23, 1867.

5. Springfield *Republican*, May 11, 1867.

6. On the issue of women's suffrage, see also the *Hartford Courant*, July 12, 1867, Boston *Commonwealth*, May 11, 1867; Springfield *Daily Republican*, June 8, 1867 and June 20,1867; *New-York Tribune*, June 1, 1867. On women's suffrage in England at the time, see Catherine Hall, Keith McClelland, and Jane Rendall, eds., *Defining the Victorian Nation: Class, Race, and Gender and the British Reform Act of 1867* (Cambridge: Cambridge University Press, 2000), Chapter 3. For the United States, see Ellen C. DuBois, *Feminism and Suffrage: The Emergence of an Independent Women's Movement in America, 1848–1869* (Ithaca: Cornell University Press, 1978).

7. The huge difference, of course, between British Liberals and American Republicans would have been the tariff question. Republicans were generally protectionist, though the party contained various opinions on the tariff. A political and cultural history of the tariff during Reconstruction is one of the great lacunas in Reconstruction historiography. The recent publication of Nicolas Barreyre, *Gold and Freedom: The Political Economy of Reconstruction* (Charlottesville: University of Virginia Press, 2015) should help fill it.

8. The idea for this essay was initially inspired by re-reading Robert Kelley's *Transatlantic Persuasion: The Liberal Democratic Mind in the Age of Gladstone* (New York: Knopf, 1969). Other important books in Anglo-American history include Leslie Butler, *Critical Americans: Victorian Intellectuals and Transatlantic Liberal Reform* (Chapel Hill: University of North Carolina Press, 2007); Christopher Leslie Brown, *Moral Capital: Foundations of British Abolitionism* (Chapel Hill: University of North Carolina Press, 2006); Jamie L. Bronstein, *Land Reform and Working Class Experience in Britain and the United States, 1800–1862* (Stanford: Stanford University Press, 1999); Andrew Robertson, *The Language of Democracy: Political Rhetoric in the United States and Britain, 1790–1900* (Ithaca: Cornell University Press, 1995); R. J. M. Blackett, *Building an Antislavery Wall: Black Americans in the Atlantic Abolitionist Movement, 1830–1860* (Baton Rouge: Louisiana State University Press, 1983); and Betty Fladeland, *Men and Brothers: Anglo-American Antislavery Cooperation* (Urbana: University of Illinois Press, 1972).

It is worth revisiting some of the pioneering essays in C. Vann Woodward, ed., *The Comparative Approach to American History* (New York: Basic Books, 1968) and Eric Foner, *Nothing But Freedom: Emancipation and Its Legacy* (Baton Rouge: Louisiana State University Press, 1983). Many of these works either implicitly or explicitly write in the context of an "Age of Capital" pioneered by Eric Hobsbawm's *The Age of Capital, 1848–1875* (London: Scribner's, 1975).

9. Mark Wahlgren Summers, *The Ordeal of the Reunion: A New History of Reconstruction* (Chapel Hill: University of North Carolina Press, 2014), 205.

10. Michael J. Turner, "Perceptions of America and British Reform during the 1860s," *Civil War History* 59, no. 3 (2013): 320–57. Turner's footnotes provide a guide to the more recent literature on Anglo-American history.

Historian Jörg Nagler argues that for this period, "there was a direct transatlantic exchange of people, information, and ideas that mutually influenced each other." "Interchange: Nationalism and Internationalism in the Era of the Civil War," 463.

11. "Interchange," 464. A brief introduction to comparative and transnational approaches to the Civil War era is W. Caleb McDaniel and Bethany L. Johnson, "New Approaches to Internationalizing the History of the Civil War Era: An Introduction," *Journal of the Civil War Era* 2, no. 2 (May 2012): 145–59. A fuller and richer discussion can be found in "Interchange" cited earlier. The literature that places the American Civil War in a global context has grown enormously in the past few years. An early and highly influential book in the "transnational turn" in American history is Thomas Bender, *A Nation Among Nations: America's Place in World History* (New York: Hill & Wang, 2006). More recent works following this trend include Don H. Doyle, *The Cause of All Nations: An International History of the American Civil War* (New York: Basic Books, 2015) and Andre M. Fleche, *The Revolution of 1861: The American Civil War in the Age of Nationalist Conflict* (Chapel Hill: University of North Carolina Press, 2012).

12. "Interchange," 467.

13. Ibid., 458, 463.

14. Perhaps the inquiry pursued here offers "historian-defined questions and answers perhaps unimaginable by the historical actors," although the comments in the first paragraph suggest that some kind of linkage was indeed imagined. Ibid., 467.

15. My emphasis on the importance of democracy to an understanding of Reconstruction draws from my earlier *Fenians, Freedmen, and Southern Whites: Race and Nationality in the Era of Reconstruction* (Baton Rouge and London: Louisiana State University Press, 2007). James Allen, *Reconstruction: The Battle for Democracy* (New York: International Press, 1937) and W. E. B. Du Bois, *Black Reconstruction in America* (1935; New York: Oxford University Press, 2007) are earlier works that stress the centrality of the struggle for democracy during Reconstruction.

Democracy and its dangers were a central theme in the nineteenth-century history of other European nations such as Great Britain, France, and Germany. Margaret Lavinia Anderson, *Practicing Democracy: Elections and Political Culture in Imperial Germany* (Princeton: Princeton University Press, 2000), 4. Transnational and global historians might want to explore the rise of universal suffrage (France in 1852 and Germany in 1867) in their narratives of nation building, national self-determination, and republican attacks on aristocratic rule in the mid-nineteenth century. Ibid., 4–5. The political scientist

Dankwart Rustow suggests the notion that "the transition to democracy" can be seen as a distinctive historical period, adding weight to the idea that Republican Reconstruction and the Second Reform Act should be viewed in an Anglo-American context. Ibid., 3.

16. Among many works on British liberalism, see Hall, et al., *Defining the Victorian Nation*; Eugenio F. Biagini, *Liberty, Retrenchment, and Reform: Popular Liberalism in the Age of Gladstone, 1860–1880* (Cambridge: Cambridge University Press, 1992); Jonathan Parry, *The Politics of Patriotism: English Liberalism, National Identity and Europe, 1830–1886* (Cambridge: Cambridge University Press, 2006); and Robert Saunders, *Democracy and the Vote in British Politics, 1848–1867: The Making of the Second Reform Act* (Farnham: Ashgate, 2011).

17. For reform of the treatment of the insane, see Springfield *Republican*, December 2, 1867, and for the hearing impaired, ibid., February 15, 1867. On prisons, see the Philadelphia *Press*, December 24, 1867. On Reconstruction Republicanism as reform, see Summers, *Ordeal of the Reunion*, Chapter 10; James C. Mohr, *Radical Republicans and Reform in New York During Reconstruction* (Ithaca: Cornell University Press, 1973); and Edwin Stanley Bradley *The Triumph of Militant Republicanism: A Study of Pennsylvania and Presidential Politics, 1860–1872* (Philadelphia: University of Pennsylvania Press, 1964). This broader process of Reconstruction in the northern states deserves further exploration.

18. *Hartford Courant*, July 17, 1867.

19. *Chicago Tribune*, August 9, 1867; ibid., January 1, 1867; Springfield *Republican*, November 12, 1867.

20. See F. B. Smith, *The Making of the Second Reform Bill* (Cambridge: Cambridge University Press, 1966); Maurice Cowling, *1867: Disraeli, Gladstone and Revolution: The Passing of the Second Reform Bill* (Cambridge: Cambridge University Press, 1967); and E. L. Woodward, *The Age of Reform, 1815–1870* (Oxford: Clarendon Press, 1938). More recent is Hall, et al., *Defining the Victorian State*.

21. *Philadelphia Press*, January 2, 1867.

22. Springfield *Republican*, June 26, 1867

23. *New-York Tribune*, May 13, 1867 and February 2, 1867.

24. George Macaulay Trevelyan, *British History in the Nineteenth Century and After: 1782–1919* (1922; New York: Harper & Row, 1966), 343–47.

25. *Chicago Tribune*, November 20, 1867.

26. Boston *Commonwealth*, May 18, 1867.

27. *New-York Tribune*, March 14, 1867; ibid., April 29, 1867.

28. Historian Thomas Bender has suggested: "Certain 'liberal' nationalist ideas of the nation were circulating around the Atlantic world at this time. The clearest point, I suspect, was the opposite of monarchy/aristocracy." "Interchange," 470. In his recent study of the international significance of the American Civil War, Don H. Doyle notes similarly that Europeans perceived in that struggle "a decisive showdown" between democracy and aristocracy. Doyle, *The Cause of All Nations*, 7.

29. Springfield *Republican*, January 16, 1867.

30. Springfield *Republican*, April 2, 1867.

31. *Hartford Courant*, August 28, 1867. See also Springfield *Republican*, February 13, 1867. On the poor administration of the empire, as evidenced in the Orissa famine in India, see the comments in the *Hartford Courant*, August 27, 1867.

32. Springfield *Republican*, June 26, 1867.

33. Boston *Commonwealth*, February 23, 1867;

34. *New-York Tribune*, May 13, 1867.

35. *New-York Tribune*, June 26, 1867.

36. *Hartford Courant*, July 2, 1867. See also *Hartford Courant*, July 10, 1867.

37. *Chicago Tribune*, September 21, 1867.

38. *Chicago Tribune*, December 27, 1867.

39. Springfield *Republican*, November 18, 1867.

40. *Philadelphia Press*, November 19, 1867.

41. Springfield *Republican*, July 13, 1867.

42. *New-York Tribune*, January 7, 1867. See also the *Philadelphia Press*, December 13, 1867, and the *Chicago Tribune*, August 9, 1867.

43. *Chicago Tribune*, December 27, 1867.

44. *Chicago Tribune*, September 21, 1867.

45. *New-York Tribune*, June 3, 1867. See also Springfield *Daily Republican*, June 1, 1867.

46. *New-York Tribune*, May 13, 1867.

47. Springfield *Republican*, February 26, 1867.

48. *New-York Tribune*, May 16, 1867. See also *New-York Tribune*, May 8, 1867 and February 11, 1867.

49. Boston *Commonwealth*, January 12, 1867.

50. Boston *Commonwealth*, May 11, 1867.

51. *Chicago Tribune*, February 21, 1867.

52. *New-York Tribune*, April 23, 1867.

53. *New-York Tribune*, June 5, 1867. See also *Chicago Tribune*, November 6, 1867; Springfield *Republican*, January 4, 1867; and *Hartford Courant*, July 25, 1867.

54. *Hartford Courant*, August 27, 1867.

55. *New-York Tribune*, May 8, 1867.

56. *Chicago Tribune*, September 2, 1867.

57. Springfield *Republican*, June 26, 1867.

58. *New-York Tribune*, March 11, 1867.

59. *Chicago Tribune*, September 2, 1867. That democratization was embedded in the English reform bill was a prominent theme in Republican newspapers. For additional examples, see the *Chicago Tribune*, July 20, 1867, July 23, 1867, and September 21, 1867, and the *Hartford Courant*, August 9, 1867.

60. Springfield *Republican*, February 9, 1867.

61. Springfield *Republican*, October 17, 1867.

62. *Philadelphia Press*, November 20, 1867.

63. Springfield *Republican*, August 8, 1867. See also, the Springfield *Republican*, January 9, 1867, August 7, 1867, and August 29, 1867. On the value of popular education, see *Philadelphia Press*, October 9, 1867.

64. Philadelphia *Press*, October 5, 1867.

65. *New-York Tribune*, March 14, 1867.

66. Boston *Commonwealth*, March 30, 1867. See also, Ibid., April 6, 1867.

67. *Chicago Tribune*, September 2, 1867.

68. *Chicago Tribune*, July 30, 1867.

69. *Philadelphia Press*, November 19, 1867.

70. *New-York Tribune*, April 24, 1867.

71. *New-York Tribune*, May 16, 1867.

72. Boston *Commonwealth*, March 9, 1867.

73. *New-York Tribune*, May 13, 1867. For my purposes, it is linguistically significant that the *New-York Tribune* spoke of the coming contest in England over Reform as "the impending conflict." *New-York Tribune*, February 2, 1867.

74. *New-York Tribune*, February 23, 1867.

75. *New-York Tribune*, April 24, 1867.

76. *New-York Tribune*, May 31, 1867.

77. *Chicago Tribune*, September 25, 1867.

78. *Chicago Tribune*, September 2, 1867.

79. *Chicago Tribune*, July 12, 1867.

80. Springfield *Republican*, February 2, 1867.

81. Springfield *Republican*, January 16, 1867.

82. See also *New-York Tribune*, February 13, 1867. Here it is useful to recall Robert Penn Warren, *The Legacy of the Civil War* for the idea of the "Treasury of Virtue."

Historians David Armitage and Jay Sexton have pointed out the connection between the rise of nation-states in the mid–nineteenth century and the rise of empires. "Interchange," 478, 479. The literature on American imperialism in the late nineteenth century is extensive, but Walter LaFeber *The New Empire: American Expansionism, 1860–1898* (Ithaca: Cornell University Press, 1963) remains a valuable introduction. For the most up-to-date discussion of American expansionism in the Reconstruction era, see Summers, *Ordeal of the Reunion*, Chapter 9.

83. On Republican factionalism, see David Herbert Donald, Jean Harvey Baker, and Michael F. Holt, *The Civil War and Reconstruction* (New York: Norton, 2001), 536–43.

84. *New York Times*, July 20, 1867.

85. *New York Times*, March 19, 1867.

86. *New York Times*, August 4, 1867.

87. See, for example, "The Crisis in England" for April 16, 1867 and "Recognition of Gladstone" for April 22, 1867 in the *Cincinnati Enquirer*. For the Cleveland *Plain Dealer*, see February 7, 1867. Other examples include *The Boston Post*, May 9, 1867, May 30, 1867, and June 10, 1867. Edward L. Gambill, *Conservative Ordeal: Northern Democrats and Reconstruction, 1865–1868* (Ames: Iowa State University Press, 1981), 176–77 provides a convenient list of Democratic newspapers during Reconstruction.

88. *Detroit Free Press*, March 22, 1867.

89. *Detroit Free Press*, August 8, 1867.

90. *Boston Post*, August 19, 1867.

91. *Detroit Free Press*, July 10, 1867.

92. *Boston Post*, August 19, 1867. Although urban Democratic newspapers tended to follow political developments in England and the rest of Europe, my impression is that they gave perhaps a little less coverage than Republican ones. For example, the *Columbus Crisis*, a rabidly Copperhead sheet during the Civil War that continued publication during Reconstruction, contained hardly any mention of the British Reform Act during

1867. Similarly, the *Old Guard*, a monthly Democratic journal published in New York, made no mention of the Reform Act that year.

93. *Boston Post*, August 1, 1867.

94. *Boston Post*, August 19, 1867.

95. Ibid.

96. Ibid.

97. Fleche, *The Revolution of 1861*, 154.

4

The Arms Scandal of 1870–1872

Immigrant Liberal Republicans and America's Place in the World

Alison Clark Efford

On February 20, 1872, future president James A. Garfield wrote in his diary that Senator Carl Schurz had just made "the most brilliant senatorial speech of his life."[1] That was no small compliment, given Schurz's renown as an orator. He had begun public speaking in 1848, rousing restive Germans as a student revolutionary. When the uprisings failed the following year, he moved to the United States, where he quickly learned English and went on to much greater acclaim. Abraham Lincoln praised his work on the stump in 1860, rewarding him first with a position as United States minister to Spain and later with a commission as a brigadier general in the Union army.[2] After the Civil War, Schurz turned his rhetorical talents to the cause of black suffrage. It was as a Radical Republican as well as a leader of German Americans that Schurz was selected to represent Missouri in the Senate in 1869.

Although historians of Reconstruction are familiar with Schurz's career, the performance that caught Garfield's eye in 1872 usually escapes their attention.[3] Schurz was demanding an investigation into the War Department's sale in 1870 and 1871 of surplus rifles to E. Remington & Sons, a New York firm under contract with the French government. In anticipation of a good afternoon's entertainment, foreign diplomats, residents of the capital city, and representatives from the House crowded into the Senate chamber. With the galleries packed to capacity, senators passed a motion to allow women to listen from the cloakrooms, and when that proved insufficient, the spectators squeezed onto the floor, flanking Vice President Schuyler Colfax.[4] According to the *Chicago Tribune*, Schurz's speech elicited "an interest and an attendance almost unprecedented in the recent history of Senatorial debates."[5]

Schurz's audience listened attentively for three hours while he accused the War Department of violating American law regarding neutrality and breaching the statutes governing the drawdown of U.S. armories.[6] He exhibited a firm command of the details of a complicated case—proxy buyers and specially manufactured ammunition added to the intrigue[7]—while driving home a few main points. The neutral status of the United States was at issue because the transactions had occurred at the height of the Franco-Prussian War, which arrayed all of the German states except Austria against their longtime enemy to the west. A few days before the big speech, Schurz had quoted a petition sent to him in the winter of 1870–71 by a group of immigrants who had complained that American weapons were "killing our brothers and relatives."[8] Now he stressed that all Americans should be worried if "this great American Republic of ours understands and interprets her good faith and her neutral duties only upon a strictly cash principle!"[9] It would have been bad enough if all the profits had gone into government coffers, but Schurz suspected that bribery was behind the abuses.

The arms scandal was one of many such exposés in the era of Crédit Mobilier, "Boss" William M. Tweed, and the Whiskey Ring, but it stood apart in injecting immigrant politics and international comparisons into the Liberal Republican critique of the administration of Ulysses S. Grant.[10] Schurz's public condemnation of the arms deal drew meaning from changing patterns of German-American self-identification during the period of the Franco-Prussian War and German unification, and it represented new ideas about how the United States related to—and compared with—other countries. As essays in this volume by Caleb Richardson and Julia Brookins also show, immigrants had interests quite particular to their position in the United States, but they maintained emotional ties to their homelands and brought transnational perspectives to the often illiberal and violent project of creating, defending, and governing nation-states.[11] Schurz had previously held German governments up as negative examples, but he now accompanied his censures of American behavior with admiring descriptions of certain aspects of German administration. Simultaneously, he pushed to professionalize the American civil service along the lines of its British and Prussian counterparts. Approaching this international scandal with attention to German-American politics facilitates a recasting of the Liberal Republican movement and the political culture of the 1870s in general.

Historians agree that although the Liberal Republicans were unsuccessful in unseating Grant in 1872, their campaign to limit the federal government, reform the civil service, and reconcile northern and southern whites held profound implications.[12] Liberal Republican proposals would of course affect the status of African Americans in the South, the concern around which Reconstruction historiography has revolved. Several historians have disputed the idea that racism was the movement's driving force, observing that leading Liberal Republicans expressed no more hostility toward African Americans than their Republican adversaries and that Liberal Republicans generally appreciated the achievement of formal equality before the law.[13] The new party's leaders did, however, associate black voters with corruption and what they deemed excessive government involvement in the economy. Such prejudices were evident in their conservative misgivings about governance under Grant and their forward-looking interest in expert-led reform.[14] In reality, it is difficult to isolate racism from other motives. Explaining the Liberal Republican movement therefore requires recapturing the subtle reordering of priorities that defined a group that coalesced, briefly, in opposition to another party then identified with African American rights.

Examining the arms scandal contributes to the task of explaining the Liberal Republican shift by positioning it internationally. The reform ethos of the Liberal Republicans heralded a new style of transnational comparison in which Americans became more comfortable drawing political inspiration from European sources. It also partook of the rising interest in administration around the world. Informed by their optimism for the future of the German Empire, the immigrants whom Schurz represented took up the issue of exemplary bureaucracy with a gusto that opened the way for the subordination of black voting rights as a political priority.[15]

For scholars interested in understanding the United States in a transnational perspective, German-American Liberal Republicans help bridge the historiographical gap between the antislavery Forty-Eighters—refugees of the Revolutions of 1848—and the public intellectuals educated in German universities in large numbers after 1870. Historians have already integrated German immigrants into the bourgeoning literature that traces how foreign ideas, events, and people influenced the American antislavery impulse and connects the U.S. Civil War to efforts to consolidate nation-states around the globe.[16] Historians such as Daniel T. Rodgers and Andrew Zimmerman have also described how Germany featured in the late nineteenth century's promiscuous transnational sharing of interrelated ideas of empire, race, labor control, business regulation, and social safety nets in an industrializing world.[17] In showing that events overseas reverberated in American political culture during the intervening period of Reconstruction, this chapter builds on the work of historians such as Philip M. Katz, David Prior, and Gregory P. Downs.[18] Most ambitiously, it gestures toward the contours of Thomas Bender's sweeping argument about global connections and contexts in *A Nation Among Nations: America's Place in World History*. Although actors at the time could not know it, the arms scandal marked a moment when ambitions to secure "freedom in an age of nation-making" were yielding to struggles over how to administer government in an era of industrialization.[19]

A brief survey of the activities of the German Forty-Eighters before 1870 shows that initially their transnational politics added momentum to the Republican efforts to extend the federal protection of black rights. Settling mainly in the North, they had converted their passion for German unity and individual rights into hostility toward slavery and support for the Union war effort. As Republican politicians, the exiles aspired to lead all of the 1.3 million odd German immigrants who made the United States home by 1860, but they ran up against the diversity of their community.[20] Members of the substantial Catholic minority and residents of eastern states were especially likely to remain loyal Democrats. Nonetheless, Forty-Eighters attained standing among German Americans who were trying to define a place for themselves in a new country. At the same time, they won influence among Anglo-American Republicans who believed that immigrants were vital swing voters in tightly contested Midwestern elections.[21]

German immigrants also owed their prominence in the Republican Party to the sense that their German connections granted them special insight into the United States. Before the rise of the Liberal Republican movement, Schurz and other Forty-Eighters in the Republican Party went out of their way to compare the country favorably to European states. They used their first-hand knowledge of states under dynastic rule to reinforce the ubiquitous Republican trope that slave societies resembled backward aristocracies.[22] Although the Forty-Eighters certainly believed that slavery stood in the way of their chosen land realizing its own ideals, they held that it represented, as Schurz said in 1859, "the last depositories of the hopes of all true friends of humanity."[23]

During the 1860s, German-American Republicans used international comparison and appeals to ethnic superiority differently than Schurz would in 1872. Inspired by the spirit of 1848, they popularized the idea of the "freedom-loving German" who had been thwarted in Europe but crossed the Atlantic to stand against slavery. A St. Louis editor wrote on the eve of the Civil War that German Americans held a unique "mission" in the "present crisis" because they were "filled with more intensive concepts of freedom, with more expansive notions of humanity than most peoples of the earth."[24] While such conceits could hardly stand up to scrutiny, they were nonetheless powerful.[25] They guided moderate German Republicans toward black rights, and even German-American Democrats in the North began to embrace such ethnic claims. They were quicker than their native-born colleagues to come around to emancipation and, later, black suffrage.[26]

After the war, leading German-American Republicans used their transnational credentials to provide important encouragement to the laws and constitutional amendments that promoted African American rights. Having completed his military service by the summer of 1865, Schurz famously toured southern states and found evidence to support the enfranchisement of black men. In his *Report on the Condition of the South*, Schurz focused on the "effect of the extension of the franchise to the colored people upon the development of free labor and upon the security of human rights in the South."[27] Some of Schurz's colleagues, speaking to a narrower, German-language audience, were more explicitly transnational in their pro-suffrage arguments. In stumping for Grant in the 1868 election, Forty-Eighter August Willich described black suffrage as the capstone of German Americans' global mission, telling Cleveland Germans that they must "continue to act for the dominance of the German spirit, in accordance with complete freedom."[28] The connection he made between German-American identity and black rights sounded plausible because African-American suffrage was gaining ground among Republican politicians between 1865 and 1870. But voting returns in state referenda tell a more nuanced story. German wards, even Republican-leaning ones, frequently disappointed Republican leaders.[29] As Julia Brookins points out in Chapter 6 of this volume, German Texans cared more about national control than liberal laws. Schurz's waning interest in black suffrage after 1870 did not signify a complete reversal among his constituents.

Using immigrant experiences to compare the United States to other countries was always a limited tool for dismantling racial inequality. Important leaders constructed German-American ideals in a way that supported the interests of African Americans for the time being, but the transnational approach of the white immigrants had intrinsic weaknesses from the standpoint of Americans of color. Even at its most idealistic, the image the freedom-loving German was only ever tenuously connected to the lives of black southerners, who were far less important to Schurz than the immigrants upon whom he built a career. German Americans' self-absorption made them unreliable allies, and so too did their preoccupation with events far across the Atlantic Ocean. The energy from the Revolutions of 1848 survived with surprising vigor in late 1860s America, but conditions in Europe were always subject to change. If unsuccessful uprisings could so forcefully shape how immigrants participated in American politics, what might come of a conventional land war with a traditional adversary?

France declared war on Prussia in July of 1870, setting in motion events that would transform Europe and reconfigure German-American politics. Prussian

Prime Minister Otto von Bismarck was ready, eager even, for an armed confrontation. A military threat was just what he needed to convince smaller German states to unite under Prussian auspices, completing the complex and drawn out process of national consolidation. The German forces advanced rapidly, besieging Paris and capturing Emperor Louis Napoleon III on the battlefield by September. The French responded by declaring a republic and fighting on until their final defeat in January 1871. By that time, Wilhelm I of Prussia was emperor of the new Germany; Bismarck was its chancellor.

Schurz's arms scandal was part of the American—and especially German-American—response to the Franco-Prussian War. The recently laid Atlantic cable gave the European events an immediacy that prior conflagrations had lacked.[30] Ohio Governor Rutherford B. Hayes received a letter from an associate in New York informing him that "the war telegrams make immense excitement here[. A]s much as our own war."[31] Newspaper correspondents used the wires to dispatch updates on troop movements and sieges, while long-form descriptions of troop morale and supply networks still came by mail. Most American newspaper editors matched the stream of information with commentary. They evaluated the military strength of each side and contemplated the relative merits of the French Republic and the German Empire. Republicans, who were swayed by Prussia's Protestantism and an interest German immigrant votes, showed more sympathy toward the Germans than the Democrats. Napoleon III had earned Republican distrust when he encouraged the Confederacy with his invasion of Mexico during the Civil War.[32] (At the time, General Grant had gone as far as facilitating the covert arming of the Juárist resistance to the French-supported government, an act Schurz could have turned to his political advantage in 1872 if he had known of it.[33]) When the Franco-Prussian War began, President Grant proclaimed American neutrality but told his minister to France, Elihu B. Washburne, "Every unreconstructed rebel sympathizes with France, without exception, while the loyal element is almost as universally the other way."[34] Revealing his own sympathies, Grant charged Washburne with representing the Germans who were stranded in Paris at the outbreak of hostilities.[35] Grant's opponents in the Democratic Party, even leaders with solidly Unionist credentials, were indeed more likely to defend France. They cited its republican heritage and contributions to the American Revolution, arguments that won more support after the declaration of the Third French Republic.[36]

Among German Americans, there were few partisan divisions over the war itself. Not only did they see France as the aggressor, but they also welcomed the unification that had eluded the revolutionaries of 1848. In large cities and small towns across the United States, thousands of German immigrants attended "sympathy meetings." At these and a host of demonstrations and fundraisers, Forty-Eighters who had once fought Prussian troops thrilled at the prospect of German lands uniting under Bismarck's control.[37] German-American Catholics disagreed with the Forty-Eighters on many things, but they joined the excitement, predicting naively that Bismarck's Protestantism would not affect his administration.[38] There were only a few pockets of dissent from the general fervor. In some cities, Hanoverians and socialists warned of Bismarck's authoritarian tendencies. One radical working-class newspaper in New York, for example, was famous for its critique of German Americans' zeal for Bismarck's war. The *Arbeiter-Union* lost subscribers and folded in 1870, a fate that observers attributed to this position.[39] Schurz summed up the climate of opinion before a crowd in Chicago, stating, "The great soul of Germany, which for ages has haunted the history of the world like a specter, has finally found again a body mighty like herself."[40] At this moment of intense optimism, most German Americans were willing to place their aspirations for Germany's future in the hands of Bismarck's government.

German Americans did not endorse all of Bismarck's positions, but the euphoria of 1870–71 carried with it new priorities relevant to the arms scandal, the Liberal Republican movement, and a new kind of transnational outlook in the United States. Wishful thinking among the immigrants led them to accentuate the positive aspects of German governance. Hoping that individual rights and democratic decision-making, the two main priorities of 1848, would follow in due course, German-American leaders turned their attention to Prussia's educational success, military might, and incorruptible civil service.[41] Missouri's *St. Charles Demokrat*, for example, attributed the triumph of German troops over the French to a comprehensive system of public education superior to that of the United States.[42] The German armies won editorial praise for their training, order, and efficiency, although a few German Americans warned of the risk that such admiration could slide into an endorsement of militarism.[43] Regardless of these cautions, the exuberant war news that filled every German-American newspaper for months argued strongly for German prowess. When France became a republic, immigrants had to explain why they believed that "Germany is today, without bearing the name, closer in reality to the concept of the true essence of a free state than Paris with all its republicanism." The faith that "minor institutions" expressed German capacities formed part of the answer.[44] Cincinnati Republican J. B. Stallo told a crowd in September 1870, "No republic can be made overnight merely by proclaiming it; it must be developed slowly and gradually within a *Volk*, in its minor institutions, in its everyday actions and intentions."[45] The details of administration were as important as electoral systems. The encouraging lessons of 1870 seemed as significant to German immigrants as the cautionary tales of 1848, and the sale of American arms to the French became an opportunity to communicate them.

On October 4, 1870, reports that the French were purchasing American guns made it out of the shipping news columns and onto the front pages of the New York newspapers.[46] The *New-York Tribune* ran a dramatic description of dockworkers loading crates of small arms into a French Steamship Company vessel behind an improvised screen.[47] The following day the paper disclosed that some of the boxes had been labeled with the names of U.S. arsenals and that the deliveries had been commissioned "by the direct order" of the new republican government of France.[48] Despite the cloak-and-dagger tone of the reporting, the *Tribune* maintained that the rifle sales were consistent with American policy, which allowed individuals and companies to continue to sell arms to belligerents on a private basis.[49] The administration could have agreed, asserting that it bore no responsibility for what private traders did after they bought arms from the government. Instead, it claimed that the United States was not selling arms to the French or the Prussians either "directly or indirectly."[50] The statement sounded like an outright denial of the *Tribune* account.

Many German Americans demanded clearer answers to the questions raised by Horace Greeley's *Tribune* and other papers from late 1870 to early 1871. Immigrants in the Democratic camp naturally added aiding the French to their list of complaints against the sitting president. It provided a good rejoinder to German Republicans who capitalized on their party's rhetorical support for the German cause. Oswald Ottendorfer, New York's imposing Democratic editor and politician, sounded more incensed than Schurz ever would. In December 1870, he wrote, "The freedom-loving German people reached out the hand of brotherhood [during the Civil War], and now America delivers to their archenemy weapons with which German warriors will be destroyed and a brutal war will be prolonged. This ingratitude will be avenged sooner or later."[51] But Ottendorfer's vehemence was atypical. Although the editor of the Democratic *Cincinnati Volksfreund* was no fan of Grant, he wrote more calmly that the affair merited "serious consideration."[52] Another Democrat, Milwaukee editor and state assemblyman Peter V. Deuster, asked the Wisconsin legislature to censure the president, but his newspaper, the *Milwaukee Seebote*, devoted only a few paragraphs to the proposal.[53]

News of the shipments to France also provoked some German-American Republicans. Hermann Raster edited the *Illinois Staatszeitung* in Chicago, and his service to Grant would soon earn him a post as local collector of internal revenue. In January 1871, Raster's paper printed an editorial that stated that the administration's position was "wrong [*falsch*], and must be condemned by every true American." Yet the editor perceived a relatively lackluster response from German Americans. He complained, "It has not occurred to anyone to do anything else about the matter other than holding forth behind a beer glass."[54] Raster experienced the same sort of frustrations as the Fenain leaders trying to rouse Irish immigrants to fight the British Empire in Chapter 5. The readers of the *Illinois Staatszeitung* were not Germans but German Americans. In January 1871, some Chicago Germans did organize a public meeting, one of a flicker of protests in cities including Detroit, Cincinnati, St. Louis, and Washington, D.C., which petitioned for an end to any sales.[55]

Schurz felt the pressure by January 1870, but as he told his business partner, "raising the matter in Congress" was "a somewhat sensitive thing" in "the prevailing circumstances." The German-born freshman senator, who had already antagonized Grant, did not want to question American actions when the German Confederation had not lodged a public protest.[56] Schurz's St. Louis newspaper, the *Westliche Post*, assured readers he would act, but the action occurred behind the scenes.[57] On Saturday, January 21, after getting nowhere with Secretary of War William Belknap, he paid a call to the secretary of state, Hamilton Fish.[58] Just two days later, he received a "personal and confidential" letter from Fish. The president, Fish confirmed, had ordered Belknap to "suspend all sales."[59] German-language newspapers covered the halt, but English-language newspapers hardly mentioned it.[60] By this point, French capitulation was the main story. The shipments and the war were over.

About a year would pass—from early 1871 to early 1872—before the arms sales reemerged as the arms scandal. New suggestions of bribery meant that German-American charges were more significant to the movement gathering against the Grant administration. A twist came when a diplomat, and not a German but a French one, Charles Adolphe de Pineton, the Marquis de Chambrun, approached Senator Charles Sumner shortly before Christmas 1871 with details of a French investigation into irregularities in arms purchasing during the recent European war.[61] Although the distinguished Radical Republican from Massachusetts remained strongly committed to African-American rights, Sumner too had fallen out with Grant, and he was happy to share the new information with his friend Carl Schurz. By the end of January 1872, Schurz and Sumner were working together to sift through the evidence Chambrun had collected and the press had wind of them "smelling around."[62] It was Sumner who introduced a resolution that called for an investigation on February 12, 1872.

Thinly veiled allegations that individuals in the War Department had taken money under the table in return for violating neutrality law drove two critical weeks of Senate debate on the international standing of the United States and administrative propriety. Direct evidence of bribes never surfaced, but Sumner cited Ordnance Bureau records that failed to account for hundreds of thousands of dollars. If highly placed employees had diverted assets, perhaps bribes had induced them to make unauthorized sales. But this line of inquiry was so poorly grounded that Sumner and Schurz backed away from it within a few days. They had simply misunderstood the charts.[63] Schurz then took over, focusing on evidence that Secretary Belknap had learned that Remington & Sons was "an agent" of France in mid-October 1870, presumably shortly after his office denied trading with the country, and therefore cut off sales from the Ordnance Bureau to the firm.[64] Schurz considered indirect sales to Remington's firm using proxies between October 1870 and January 1871 just as reprehensible as the original transactions. Calling the idea that the Ordnance Bureau had exercised "reasonable diligence" in vetting dealers a "transparent farce," Schurz quoted letters indicating that Samuel Remington had personally intervened to have cartridges manufactured in order to facilitate a deal that supposedly had nothing to do with his firm.[65] Incredulous, Schurz exclaimed, "There is an impression prevailing in this country that somewhere in this Government there sits 'a military ring.'"[66]

Before Schurz's numerous opponents got to the implications of his assault, they addressed the specific charges. They said that the secretary of war had never *knowingly* sold arms to France and contended that the Ordnance Bureau bore minimal responsibility for scrutinizing arms dealers.[67] Matthew H. Carpenter of Wisconsin went so far as to argue that the United States government could trade in munitions without compromising its neutrality, but few senators agreed with his reading of international law, probably thinking of the arbitration still pending in the *Alabama* Claims.[68] The United States was pursuing damages because Britain had failed to prevent ships such the *Alabama* from being built and sold to the Confederacy during the Civil War. In a novel step, the two countries had agreed to submit the issue and other disputes between the United States and Great Britain to an international tribunal. With the *Alabama* Claims still under consideration, Schurz pointed out, Americans did not want to appear to condone the equipping of belligerents in—and especially by—neutral countries.[69]

Yet during the second half of February 1872, debate in the Senate ranged far beyond the case's specifics to touch on the American place in the world and the future of Republicans' southern policy. Senators and the public understood the scandal in the context of the Schurz's leadership of the solidifying Liberal Republican movement. During 1870 and especially 1871, his longstanding distaste for "party despotism" and preexisting inclination to treat former Confederates with magnanimity had come to dominate his politics.[70] When he first entered the Senate in December 1869, he had introduced a civil service reform bill, and his interest in such legislation increased as Grant made poor appointments, removed Schurz supporters from office, and failed to disentangle the administration of government from party politics.[71] Men such as Senator Lyman Trumbull of Illinois, E. L. Godkin at *The Nation*, and Horace White at the *Chicago Tribune* shared Schurz's belief that outright corruption was connected to both the power of unqualified voters and federal overreach in subsidizing business, enacting tariffs, and enforcing black rights. Liberal Republicans issued a call for a national convention weeks before Sumner's resolution, so the scandal communicated, advanced, and shaped their program at a critical time.[72]

In particular, the arms scandal reflected the ideas of the German-American Midwesterners who were both leading and following Schurz out of the Republican Party, away from active support for black rights, and toward new transnational comparisons. Disgruntled immigrants had been indispensable to the Liberal Republican movement from its early days in Missouri. About a third of the delegates to the Republican state convention of 1870, men mostly from St. Louis and other heavily German counties, had bolted to join a competing convention chaired by Schurz.[73] The movement's spread left Grant with few high-profile German-American backers in the Midwest by the end of 1871. Chicago's Hermann Raster and Ohio's Lieutenant Governor Jacob Müller held out, as did scattered minor leaders, but important German-speaking Republicans such as Gustav Koerner, Caspar Butz, and Friedrich Hecker of Illinois, and J. B. Stallo, Friedrich Hassaurek, and August Thieme of Ohio were preparing to leave their party.[74] Schurz later observed that German Americans "had joined [the Liberal Republicans] in Masse [*sic*]" and "in some Western states they formed the whole backbone of the movement."[75] At the national level, the proportion of Liberal Republicans among German Americans was higher than the proportion of German Americans among Liberal Republicans. But one of the reasons for Schurz's stature in the party was the belief that he represented an indispensable group of voters.[76]

Since 1870, German-American Liberal Republicans had been developing a reform sensibility that incorporated their reactions to events in Europe and the original news of the arms shipments. When Schurz became the public face of the arms scandal in February 1872, he had already been party to an eighteen-month discussion of administrative propriety that was fueled by unfavorable comparisons between the United States and other governments, especially the rising German state. In 1871, the editor of the *St. Charles Demokrat*, which had until recently supported Republican candidates, worried that corruption meant that the United States was "losing respect in the eyes of all other civilized nations."[77] The Democratic *Cincinnati Volksfreund* lamented, "Corruption, special interest legislation, and privileges, characterize our public life in such a conspicuous way that we must blush when we hold up our current state of affairs, republican in name only, as an example for other nations to imitate."[78] Also in Cincinnati, maverick Republican Friedrich Hassaurek was annoyed that Americans feigned to have "the best government under the sun."[79] Another Forty-Eighter and discontented Republican, Friedrich Hecker, delivered a speech on the German-language lecture circuit in 1871 and 1872, which Schurz's *Westliche Post* published weeks before the scandal broke. Hecker maintained, "In no civilized to half-civilized land of the world, not even in Turkey, is an unlimited administration in relation to the naming and removal of officials laid in the hands of an individual [the president] as here." He was, in fact, critical of the Prussian system, too, which made him an outlier in the German-American community. Holding the United States to a higher standard than the German Empire, he remarked that the U.S. civil service was better fitted to a "princely state" than a "people's state."[80] Like most German Americans, he preferred the United States, but Hecker presented it as an imperfect country grappling with common problems.

Standing in the Senate, Schurz built the arms scandal on the foundation of German Americans' critical comparisons, but he found it unnecessary to detail them. His underlying complaint was that American corruption had deprived Prussia of the respect it deserved in international dealings. In relatively few words, he signaled to German Americans that he shared their perspective and reassured other Americans that foreign practices were no threat. Schurz stipulated that immigrants were devoted to "liberty" and "republican principles," but also— and here lay the stress of the sentence—"honest government."[81] He notably spoke of upholding "the honor of the American name" far more frequently than he cited any German considerations.[82] When he said, "My country right or wrong; if right to be kept right; if wrong to be set right," he was talking about the United States.[83] Yet he also declared, "I certainly am not ashamed of having sprung from that great nation whose monuments stand so proudly upon all the battlefields of thought; that great nation, which having translated her mighty soul into action, seems at this moment to hold in her hands the destinies of the Old World. . . ."[84]

Schurz spoke of origins, not allegiances, but the statement demonstrated his on-going political engagement with Germany. Schurz defended the empire when Oliver P. Morton of Indiana and Roscoe Conkling of New York speculated that the allegations might "poison Prussian minds" against the United States right as Wilhelm I was about to sit on a tribunal to adjudicate one of the disputes with Britain related to the *Alabama* Claims. Schurz retorted that "mean, miserable, personal motives" did not drive the "great Government" of Germany.[85]

Schurz's rhetorical defense of Germany had a policy corollary in Liberal Re-publican initiatives to institute civil service reforms to prevent the sort of cor-ruption that they thought must have caused the arms scandal. Congress had debated several bills that included examinations and merit-based promotion standards like those that had developed in Prussia and other German states since the eighteenth century and in Britain since the Northcote-Trevelyan Report of 1854.[86] Back in 1865, Republican Congressman Thomas A. Jenckes had cited Brit-ish, French, and Prussian precedents when he introduced an unsuccessful civil service reform bill, and in 1872, Horace White at the *Chicago Tribune* described the Liberal Republicans' desired system as "English or Prussian" in a letter to Schurz.[87] Schurz and others had strong domestic arguments for reform, so they did not make foreign references the mainstay of the English-language debate.[88] It was only the beginning of a the transition from a politics of rights and represen-tation in which most Americans considered themselves frontrunners to a politics of administration with international leadership up for debate.

In February 1872, some senators made the political risks of Schurz's compari-sons clear when they equated it with disloyalty. Frederick Frelinghuysen of New Jersey said that after reading part of one of Schurz's speeches to German Ameri-cans he "could plainly see the chord of sympathy that ran and vibrated between the speaker and his auditors. I could see that the common bond of union be-tween them was their own, their native land, the fatherland as the speaker called his home." Frelinghuysen pointedly stated that Americans "have a sensitiveness in behalf of the honor of this country equal at least to the sensitiveness of Ger-mans for the national rights of Germany."[89] Senator Carpenter, who represented the very German state of Wisconsin, was more hostile. He brought up the idea of apologizing to Prussia, which no one had advocated, so that he could say that he saw "humiliation" in "voluntarily prostrating ourselves before a foreign Power." He generously "acquitted" Schurz of "want of patriotism," but warned ominously that if a senator "is not able to cast off his allegiance to his native land," perhaps naturalization law ought to be changed.[90]

Yet for all the attacks on Schurz, most senators joined their colleague in prais-
ing German Americans and the new German Empire. Carpenter aside, even
Grant's supporters accepted the idea that incorruptible German immigrants made
upstanding Americans. They flattered immigrant voters in hopes of dissuading
them from leaving the party. Morton, for example, insisted, "[T]he Germans
of this country do not belong to anybody. They cannot be carried in anybody's
breeches pockets. I do not care how capacious those pockets are. . . . They cannot
be led from one party to another at the whim or caprice of politicians."[91] No one
challenged Schurz's positive depiction of Germany. Morton, Conkling, and Frelinghuysen, three of his main opponents, all spoke respectfully of the new country, instead fretting that what they saw as Schurz's antics would alienate leaders
that Americans admired.[92] All this was in keeping with Grant's statement to Congress the previous year, which complimented the German people and compared
the German Empire to the United States.[93] Republican senators would have read
the approving accounts of Germany in their partisan newspapers and especially
in the periodicals now aligning with the Liberal Republicans.[94] Bismarck did not
beguile Republicans, but they anticipated that his empire might incorporate what
they considered the best of German traits and they treated it with a respect they
had not accorded its forerunners. The resulting impression was that the United
States and Germany belonged to a select community of states that were roughly
equal. Just as they might arbitrate each other's disputes, they would attentively
observe and evaluate each other's achievements.

No one who followed the scandal could miss the relevance of international
standing and administrative probity to the domestic issues that have occupied
scholars of the post-war United States. Liberal Republicans connected outright
malfeasance to the active—they would say unconstitutionally overzealous—enforcement of the Reconstruction acts and amendments. During 1871, Schurz had
opposed the Ku Klux Klan Act on the grounds that empowering the president to
enforce the Fifteenth Amendment might lead to abuses of executive power. He
supported rather symbolic bills to grant amnesty to the few former Confederates whom the Fourteenth Amendment still barred from holding office.[95] Right
before the arms debate, Schurz had spoken against Sumner's efforts to amend
an amnesty bill to include a provision outlawing racial discrimination in access
to various public accommodations.[96] In a substantial comment in the Senate,
Schurz said that the main question confronting Americans since the ratification
of the Fifteenth Amendment was how to "secure good and honest government

to all."[97] Schurz repeated several times that "nothing could be further from my intention than to cast a slur on the colored people of the South," but he regretted that replacing "intelligent and experienced" voters with and "ignorant and inexperienced" ones had led to what he saw as maladministration, which in his mind had exacerbated Ku Klux Klan outrages.[98]

Less than a week later, while discussing the Ordnance Bureau sales, other Liberal Republicans alluded to the link Schurz perceived between corruption and Republican actions in the South. Lyman Trumbull of Illinois believed Americans would understand his reference to "the history of the enormous frauds which have been perpetrated in nearly all the reconstructed States" without further explanation.[99] Thomas W. Tipton of Nebraska said Republicans had closed ranks ever since "the discovery was made that the President's body guard intended to make the first object of their reconstruction laws the perpetuation in power of the Republican Party in the South."[100] Discussing corruption meant discussing southern policy.

Republicans loyal to Grant argued that anything that undermined the administration would result in victories for Democrats, who intended to erode the gains African Americans had made. Morton recounted the history of Missouri, where many more Democrats than Liberal Republicans had been elected to the Missouri legislature in 1870. The Liberal Republican governor, Benjamin Gratz Brown, had begun to support unabashedly racist Democrats, while the state legislature sent Frank Blair, Jr., to the Senate. Blair was famous for running a particularly nasty anti-black campaign for the vice presidency in 1868, and Morton now dubbed him Schurz's "official offspring."[101] As if to underline the potential cost of fraternizing with Democrats, Blair dismissed Republican accounts of Klan violence as "the foulest calumny ever perpetrated or circulated upon or against a helpless people" the day before Schurz's big speech on the arms deals.[102]

Thomas Nast, the country's leading political cartoonist, illustrated the Republican interpretation of the racial import of a scandal that alleged corruption on the world stage. Nast had himself emigrated from Bavaria as a child, but the New Yorker stood aloof from German-American politics. His nativity seems to have served mostly to free him to attack Schurz with more gusto than Anglo-Americans dared display.[103] One of Nast's many cartoons about the scandal, "Mephistopheles at Work for Destruction: A Bid for the German Vote," ran in *Harper's Weekly* in March 1872. In it, Schurz plays the devil from Goethe's celebrated tragedy *Faust*, tempting a wary Charles Sumner to abandon his racially egalitarian principles. The lanky German American leans over Sumner to guide his hand as he drafts his controversial Senate resolution, and behind his bent back is a sign

Figure 4.1. Thomas Nast depicts Carl Schurz as the devil from Goethe's *Faust*, trying to tempt Charles Sumner to abandon his racial egalitarianism. *Harper's Weekly*, March 9, 1872, 185.

reading, "WANTED: NEW PLANS FOR BREAKING DOWN THE ADMINISTRATION" and "WANTED: PLANS TO STIR UP BAD FEELINGS BETWEEN EUROPEAN POWERS AND THE UNITED STATES." Sumner, whose large figure sits at the center of the page, gazes uncertainly over his shoulder at a female representation of the American republic. She is poised above large volumes entitled "Sumner's Anti-Slavery Record" and "Sumner's Rebellion Record." Nast thought the scandal baseless and Schurz's motives base, but worst of all was how it imperiled black rights.[104]

A German-American senator made a *cause célèbre* of the arms sales because they involved partisan power and national honor, but those same qualities checked the scandal's progress. Anglo-American reactions followed the predictable lines of party affiliation. Democrats and Liberal Republicans located evidence of the corruption and partisan arrogance, while Republicans saw an underhanded and potentially disloyal attempt to derail what they had gained in the South.[105] Ethnicity changed the equation somewhat for German Americans. Immigrants from around the country wrote to Schurz to thank him for bringing a "German" approach to American corruption. One Ohioan enthused: "After I read your great speech on the 'arms hagglers' in the Cin. Volksblatt through very carefully, I feel compelled & spontaneously drawn to congratulate you from the bottom of my true German heart."[106] But the exuberance of the letters contrasted with the circumspection of the German-language press. The more of a spectacle the scandal became, the more reluctant editors seemed to be to identify as Germans. The relationship between the United States and Germany had to be handled carefully. Democrat Peter Deuster had brought the arms scandal to the attention of the Wisconsin legislature in 1871, but now his *Milwaukee Seebote* commented tersely that Democrats played the most "honorable" role in the Senate debate by staying quiet.[107] Raster in Chicago, who still supported Grant, agreed with Schurz that an investigation was vital, but he disapproved of Schurz's divisive grandstanding.[108] Schurz's most enthusiastic supporters were Liberal Republicans such as Friedrich Hecker and August Thieme.[109]

Ultimately, the partisan nature of the wrangling and the imperative of national face-saving prevented the Senate investigation, and a smaller one in the House, from achieving more than adding to the general impression that Grant's administration was an imperious one. Members of the Senate committee were exclusively Republican except for one Democrat, John W. Stevenson of Kentucky. Schurz himself participated, but as a witness and an unofficial member. In a canny political move, Republican senators had given the committee the additional responsibility of investigating senators' possible entanglements with foreign powers, and Schurz could not investigate himself.[110] Committee members grilled him at length on his interactions with foreign informants, apparently to raise suspicions about his loyalty. Chairman Hannibal Hamlin of Maine was thinking of Schurz when he provocatively asked Sumner, "Would you deem it the duty of a patriotic Senator to inquire of foreign legations in relation to questions which would tend to put his own Government in the wrong with other governments . . . ?"[111] When Schurz acted as interrogator, Secretary Belknap and other witnesses from the War Department defended themselves and the Grant administration, testifying that any irregular practices only made money for the government.[112] The officials stubbornly denied knowingly selling to direct agents of foreign powers.[113] The committee took this position in its final report. Any infractions on the government's part were minor technicalities, nothing to bring "dishonor" upon the country or "officers of the Government," it concluded.[114]

Schurz fired back by reiterating his transnational framing of corruption one last time in the Senate at the end of May. Agreeing with Stevenson that the sales were "in direct violation of the letter and spirit" of the law, he described the inadequacies of the investigation.[115] The speech began by likening Grant's "defiance" of public opinion to that of "profligate European aristocracies," which clearly did not include modern Germany. He commended German immigrants for remonstrating against the sales and spoke at great length of "the honor and the international standing" of the United States. Senators again heard about the *Alabama* Claims and the importance of "favorable public opinion abroad."[116] Perhaps because it was repetitive, Schurz's speech received only perfunctory coverage in the press, and the broader issue of corruption subsumed the scandal in the fall campaign.[117] It is hard to see the scandal's conclusion as anything but anticlimactic.

Yet even if Schurz's work on the scandal did not result in prosecutions, it was, like the Liberal Republican movement more broadly, significant because it influenced American political culture. The Liberal Republican part in helping to spell the "doom of Reconstruction" bears emphasizing. Republicans began to appropriate Liberal ideas just weeks after the third party nominated Horace Greeley for the presidency. Congress finally passed an amnesty bill, and then in June, Republicans placed civil service reform and liberal economic policies on their national platform.[118] Greeley became more active in criticizing Republican support for African Americans once Democrats endorsed him, a change that also affected his opponent. Grant was reelected, but he began a slow disengagement from the South. The president gave Democrats patronage positions, backed off prosecuting violations of the Fifteenth Amendment, and withheld aid from the victims of racially motivated attacks such as those that stained Mississippi's elections in 1875.[119] In the settlement that decided the 1876 election, Rutherford B. Hayes made it known that the military would stand down from the role it had assumed in the South since the war. The new president showed his debts to Liberal Republicans by selecting Carl Schurz to serve as secretary of the interior. Once he oversaw his own department, Schurz had his chance to implement a system of efficiency reports, examinations, and merit-based promotion.[120]

The German-American Liberal Republicans who stoked the arms scandal were harbingers of the Gilded Age reform ethos of expertise and oversight that encouraged receptivity to examples overseas. Like their successors, they had an orientation that did not amount to a coherent ideology.[121] German immigrants valued the American tradition and sometimes spoke in classical republican terms. They did not think of themselves as defending centralized power or authoritarian government—the very things for which they criticized Grant. It would make no sense to see them as ambassadors for the ideas of German philosopher G. W. F. Hegel, whose work blurred the distinction between the people and the state.[122] Yet German-American Liberal Republicans implicitly believed in the practical benefits of insulating officeholders from parties and markets by inducting them into a self-regulating group with its own criteria for inclusion and advancement. Their campaign to make a scandal of the arms sales both borrowed principles from European nations and negatively compared the United States to those nations.

The immigrants who turned optimistically from the reference point of the Revolutions of 1848 to the consolidating Germany of 1871 prepared the way for a generation of public intellectuals looking for solutions to the problems of industrialization. After 1870, the number of Americans attending German universities rose dramatically to several thousand per decade, with a peak in the 1890s preceding a rapid decline.[123] Influential student sojourners such as Richard T. Ely and Henry C. Adams, and later W. E. B. Du Bois and Lincoln Steffans forged transnational bonds and exchanged political ideas. Ely, the important economist who features in Daniel Rodgers's seminal description of these developments, wrote an article in 1883 that showed how well the arms scandal augured the future.[124] Describing the Prussian civil service for California's *Overland Monthly*, Ely included a nod to the republican example of Rome and the need for "public and private virtues," but he found in Prussia the sort of procedures that he believed could institutionalize such ideals. With a judicious eye on Bismarck's recent retaliations against dissenting public servants, he set out why scholars considered "the Prussian civil service the most admirable of which we have any knowledge."[125] The piece contained nothing to surprise the immigrants involved in the arms scandal. They would have been glad to see their ideas spreading. The decade following the Civil War was not a hiatus between an era of transatlantic radicals and nationalists who criticized Europe's governments and an era of interconnected reformers and experts who were open to the lessons of Europe; it was a pivot.

Notes

The author is grateful to David Prior, Julia Brookins, and Andrew L. Slap for their encouraging and detailed criticism and to Mark Summers for his staggeringly comprehensive feedback.

1. James A. Garfield, *The Diary of James A. Garfield*, ed. Harry James Brown and Frederick D. Williams, 4 vols. (East Lansing: Michigan State University Press, 1967–81), 2:21.

2. Carl Schurz to Margarethe Schurz, October 2, 1860, in *Intimate Letters of Carl Schurz, 1841–1869*, ed. and trans. Joseph Schafer (Madison: State Historical Society of Wisconsin, 1928), 226.

3. Devoting one paragraph each to the scandal are Andrew L. Slap, *The Doom of Reconstruction: The Liberal Republicans in the Civil War Era* (New York: Fordham University Press, 2006), 123; and Mark Wahlgren Summers, *The Era of Good Stealings* (New York: Oxford University Press, 1993), 208. It is the subject of an extensive footnote in Summers, *The Ordeal of the Reunion: A New History of Reconstruction* (Chapel Hill: University of North Carolina Press, 2014), 432–33. It also receives three pages in the standard biography of Schurz; Hans L. Trefousse, *Carl Schurz: A Biography*, 2nd edition (New York: Fordham University Press, 1998), 178–81.

4. *Congressional Globe*, 42nd Cong., 2nd sess. (all *Globe* citations refer to this session unless otherwise noted), 1131 (February 21, 1872); *Chicago Tribune*, February 21, 1872; *Cincinnati Volksfreund*, February 27, 1872.

5. *Chicago Tribune*, February 21, 1872.

6. *Congressional Globe*, App. 67 (February 20, 1872).

7. Ibid., App. 72 (February 20, 1872).

8. Ibid., 1047 (February 15, 1872).

9. Ibid., App. 70 (February 20, 1872).

10. On corruption as an issue, see Summers, *Era of Good Stealings*.

11. Usefully interrogating the liberal narrative, see Gregory P. Downs and Kate Masur, eds., *The World the Civil War Made* (Chapel Hill: University of North Carolina Press, 2015).

12. Slap, *Doom of Reconstruction*, 238; Eric Foner, *Reconstruction: America's Unfinished Revolution, 1863–1877* (New York: Harper & Row, 1988), 488; Heather Cox Richardson, *The Death of Reconstruction: Race, Labor, and Politics in the Post–Civil War North, 1865–1901* (Cambridge: Harvard University Press, 2001), 119; John G. Sproat, *"The Best Men": Liberal Reformers in the Gilded Age* (New York: Oxford University Press, 1968); Nancy Cohen, *Reconstruction of American Liberalism, 1865–1914* (Chapel Hill: University of North Carolina Press, 2002), 119–22.

13. On the absence of especially pronounced racism, see Michael Les Benedict, "Reform Republicans and the Retreat from Reconstruction," in *The Facts of Reconstruction: Essays in Honor of John Hope Franklin*, ed. Alfred Moss and Eric Anderson (Baton Rouge: Louisiana State University Press, 1991), 55; Slap, *Doom of Reconstruction*, 85–86; Summers, *Ordeal of the Reunion*, 305. Additional works that downplay race include Robert W. Burg, "Amnesty, Civil Rights, and the Meaning of Liberal Republicanism," *American Nineteenth Century History* 4, no. 3 (2003): 29–60; Richard A. Gerber, "Carl Schurz's Journey from Radical to Liberal Republicanism: A Problem in Ideological Consistency," *Mid-America* 82, nos. 1–2 (Winter/Summer 2000): 71–99. On the historiographical debate, see Patrick W. Riddleberger, "The Radicals' Abandonment of the Negro during Reconstruction," *Journal of Negro History* 45, no. 2 (1960): 88–102; Richard A. Gerber, "The Liberals of 1872 in Historiographical Perspective," *Journal of American History* 62, no. 1 (June 1975): 40–75; James M. McPherson, "Grant or Greeley: The Abolitionist Dilemma in the Election of 1872," *American Historical Review* 71, no. 1 (October 1965): 43–61.

14. My framing of Liberal Republicanism owes most to Foner, *Reconstruction*, 488, 497–99, and insights in Sproat, *Best Men*; Summers, *Era of Good Stealings*, 163–65; Richardson, *Death of Reconstruction*, 83–121; and Cohen, *Reconstruction of American Liberalism*, 4–5, 119–22.

15. There is limited work on German-American Liberal Republicans. See Efford, *German Immigrants, Race, and Citizenship in the Civil War Era*, 171–98; Jörg Nagler, "Deutschamerikaner und das *Liberal Republican Movement, 1872*," *Amerikastudien/American Studies* 33 (1988): 415–38.

16. On German Americans, see Daniel Nagel, *Von republikanischen Deutschen zu deutsch-amerikanischen Republikanern: Ein Beitrag zum Identitätswandel der deutschen Achtundvierziger in den Vereinigten Staaten, 1860–1861* (St. Ingbert: Röhrig Universitätsverlag, 2012); Mischa Honeck, *We Are the Revolutionists: German-Speaking Immigrants and American Abolitionists after 1848* (Athens: University of Georgia Press, 2011); Bruce Levine, *The Spirit of 1848: German Immigrants, Labor Conflict, and the Coming of the Civil War* (Urbana: University of Illinois Press, 1992). More broadly, see Don H. Doyle, *The Cause of All Nations: An International History of the American Civil War* (New York: Basic Books, 2015); W. Caleb McDaniel, *The Problem of Democracy in the Age of Slavery: Garrisonian Abolitionists and Transatlantic Reform* (Baton Rouge: Louisiana State University Press, 2013); Andre M. Fleche, *The Revolution of 1861: The American Civil War in the Age of Nationalist Conflict* (Chapel Hill: University of North Carolina Press, 2012); Patrick J. Kelley, "The North American Crisis of the 1860s," *Journal of the Civil War Era* 2, no. 3 (September 2012): 337–68; Timothy Mason Roberts, *Distant Revolutions: 1848 and the Challenge to American Exceptionalism* (Charlottesville: University of Virginia Press, 2009); Edward Bartlett Rugemer, *The Problem of Emancipation: The Caribbean Roots of the American Civil War* (Baton Rouge: Louisiana State University Press, 2009); Paola Gemme, *Domesticating Foreign Struggles: The Italian Risorgimento and Antebellum American Identity* (Athens: University of Georgia Press, 2005); David M. Potter, "The Civil War in the History of the Modern World: A Comparative View," in *The South and the Sectional Conflict* (Baton Rouge: Louisiana State University Press, 1968), 187–99.

17. Daniel T. Rodgers, *Atlantic Crossings: Social Politics in a Progressive Age* (Cambridge: Belknap Press of Harvard University Press, 1998), 76–111; Andrew Zimmerman, *Alabama in Africa: Booker T. Washington, the German Empire, and the Globalization of the New South* (Princeton: Princeton University Press, 2010), 205–35. See also, Leslie Butler, *Critical Americans: Victorian Intellectuals and Transatlantic Liberal Reform* (Chapel Hill: University of North Carolina Press, 2007).

18. Philip M. Katz, *From Appomattox to Montmartre: Americans and the Paris Commune* (Cambridge: Harvard University Press, 1998); David Prior, "'Crete the Opening Wedge': Nationalism and International Affairs in Postbellum America," *Journal of Social History* 42, no. 4 (Summer 2009): 861–87; Gregory P. Downs, "The Mexicanization of American Politics: The United States' Transnational Path from Civil War to Stabilization," *American Historical Review* 117, no. 2 (April 2012): 387–409. For a more comparative example, see Mitchell Snay, *Fenians, Freedmen, and Southern Whites: Race and Nationality in the Era of Reconstruction* (Baton Rouge: Louisiana State University Press, 2007). My own ideas are developed further in Alison Clark Efford, *German Immigrants, Race, and Citizenship in the Civil War Era* (New York: Cambridge University Press, 2013).

19. Thomas Bender, *A Nation Among Nations: America's Place in World History* (New York: Hill and Wang, 2006).

20. U.S. Bureau of the Census, *Abstract of the Eighth Census* (Washington, D.C.: GPO, 1865), 620–23; Walter D. Kamphoefner, "German-Americans and Civil War Politics: A

Reconsideration of the Ethnocultural Thesis," *Civil War History* 37, no. 3 (September 1991): 232–45.

21. Eric Foner, *Free Soil, Free Labor, Free Men: The Ideology of the Republican Party before the Civil War* (Oxford: Oxford University Press, 1970), 259.

22. Fleche, *Revolutions of 1861*, 40–43.

23. Carl Schurz, "True Americanism," April 18, 1859, in *Speeches, Correspondence and Political Papers of Carl Schurz*, ed. Frederic Bancroft, 6 vols. (New York: G. P. Putnam's Sons, 1913), 1:50.

24. *St. Louis Anzeiger des Westens*, April 17, 1859, quoted and trans. in Kamphoefner, "St. Louis Germans and the Republican Party, 1848–1860," *Mid-America: An Historical Review* 57, no. 2 (April 1975): 82.

25. Kristen Layne Anderson, *Abolitionizing Missouri: German Immigrants and Racial Ideology in Nineteenth-Century America* (Baton Rouge: Louisiana State University Press, 2016).

26. Alison Clark Efford, "The Appeal of Racial Neutrality in the Civil War–Era North: German Americans and the Democratic New Departure," *Journal of the Civil War Era* 5, no. 1 (March 2015): 68–96.

27. Carl Schurz, *Report on the Condition of the South* (Senate Executive Documents, 39th Cong., 1st sess., no. 2, 1865; reprint, New York: Arno Press, 1969), 44.

28. *Cleveland Wächter am Erie*, September 29, 1868.

29. Efford, *German Immigrants, Race, and Citizenship*, 120–42.

30. *St. Louis Westliche Post*, September 16, 1870.

31. J. A. Joel to Rutherford B. Hayes, Aug. 25, 1870, reel 19, Rutherford B. Hayes Papers (microfilm), Library of Rutherford B. Hayes Presidential Center (hereafter HPC), Fremont, Ohio.

32. Katz, *From Appomattox to Montmartre*, 86–93; John G. Gazley, *American Opinion of German Unification, 1848–1871* (New York: Columbia University, 1926; reprint, New York: AMS Press, 1970), 322–58, 380–422.

33. U.S. Grant to Andrew Johnson, Washington, D.C., July 15, 1865 and U.S. Grant to Philip H. Sheridan, West Point, July 25, 1865 in *The Papers of Ulysses S. Grant*, ed. John Y. Simon, 32 vols. (Carbondale: Southern Illinois University Press, 1967–2012), 15:164–65, 285–86.

34. U.S. Grant to Elihu B. Washburne, Long Branch, N.J., Aug. 22, 1870 in *Papers of Ulysses S. Grant*, ed. Simon, 20:254.

35. E. B. Washburne, *Recollections of a Minister to France, 1869–1877* (New York: C. Scribner's Sons, 1889), 39.

36. *Cincinnati Enquirer*, July 30, 1870; *New York World*, July 16, 17, 1870; Gazley, *American Opinion of German Unification*, 358–75.

37. America's largest German-language newspaper claimed from New York that it would be impossible to report all the sympathy meetings. *Wochenblatt der New-Yorker Staats-Zeitung*, July 23, 1870. There were elaborately planned gatherings in cities from New Orleans to Boston, spontaneous neighborhood celebrations, and smaller events in towns such as Toledo and Dayton in Ohio, Jefferson City, LaGrange, and St. Joseph in Missouri, and Wausau in Wisconsin. *Westliche Post*, August 1, 2, 8, 9, October 19, 1870; *Cincinnati Commercial*, July 20, 1870; *Milwaukee Seebote Wöchentliche Ausgabe*,

August 22, 1870; *Wisconsin Banner und Volksfreund*, August 28, 19, 1870. See also Heike Bungert, "Der Deutsch-Französische Krieg im Spiegel der Wohltätigkeitsbazare und Feiern deutscher und französischer Migranten in den USA, 1870/71," in *Deutschland— Frankreich—Nordamerika: Transfers, Imaginationen, Beziehungen*, ed. Chantal Metzger and Hartmut Kaelble (Stuttgart: Franz Steiner Verlag, 2006), 152–70.

38. *Fremont Courier*, August 11, 1870; *Cincinnati Wahrheitsfreund*, September 7, 1870; *Cincinnati Volksfreund*, August 2, 1870. For reviews of the Catholic press on the war, see *Cincinnati Volksfreund*, August 26, 1870; *Seebote Wöchentliche Ausgabe*, August 10, 1870.

39. *Cincinnati Volksfreund*, August 3, 1870.

40. Schurz provided the translation in the Senate. "Soul" was probably his rendering of "Geist." *Congressional Globe*, 1155 (February 22, 1872).

41. For a treatment emphasizing slightly later criticism of the German Empire, see Trefousse, "The German-American Immigrants and the Newly Founded Reich," in *America and the Germans: An Assessment of a Three-Hundred-Year History*, ed. Frank Trommler and Joseph McVeigh, 2 vols. (Philadelphia: University of Pennsylvania Press, 1985), 1:160–75.

42. *St. Charles Demokrat*, January 26, 1871, December 15, 1870. See also *Seebote Wöchentliche Ausgabe*, January 23, 1871. German Americans sometimes communicated these points by quoting Anglo-Americans. See *Cincinnati Volksfreund*, August 23, September 1, 1870; *Watertown Weltbürger*, September 3, 1870.

43. For positive descriptions of the military, see *New Philadelphia Deutsche Beobachter*, August 25, 1870; and *Cincinnati Volksfreund*, February 13, 1871, September 29, 1870. For some wariness, see *Wächter am Erie*, April 11, 1871; *Illinois Staatszeitung*, January 7, 1871.

44. *Mississippi Blätter* [Sunday edition of the *Westliche Post*], September 25, 1870.

45. *Cincinnati Volksfreund*, September 8, 1870. See further civil service examples later in this chapter.

46. *New York World*, October 4, 5, and November 3, 4, 1870; *New York Times*, October 4, 5, 1870; *The Nation*, October 4, 5, 1870; *Cincinnati Enquirer*, October 5, 1870; *Cincinnati Commercial*, October 6, 1870.

47. *New-York Tribune*, October 4, 1870.

48. *New-York Tribune*, October 5, 1870.

49. *New-York Tribune*, October 5, 1870. For the original statement of the policy, see U. S. Grant, Proclamation, August 22, 1870, in *Papers of Ulysses S. Grant*, 20:235–40.

50. *New-York Tribune*, October 13, 1870.

51. *Wochenblatt der New-Yorker Staats-Zeitung*, December 3, 1870.

52. *Cincinnati Volksfreund*, October 5, 1870.

53. *Seebote*, January 30 and February 6, 1871.

54. *Illinois Staatszeitung*, January 9, 1871.

55. Listing the protests, see *Wochenblatt der New-Yorker Staats-Zeitung*, January 21, 28, 1871; *Cincinnati Commercial*, January 27, 1871; *Cincinnati Volksfreund*, January 10, 26, 1871; *Illinois Staatszeitung*, January 9, 20, 1871; Wilhelm Hense-Jensen, *Wisconsin's Deutsch-Amerikaner bis zum Schluß des neunzehnten Jahrhunderts*, 2 vols. (Milwaukee: Verlag der Deutschen Gesellschaft, 1900), 1:234.

56. Schurz to Emil Preetorius, January 16, 1871, reel 89, Carl Schurz Papers (microfilm edition, 1971), Library of Congress (hereafter LOC), Washington, D.C.

57. *Westliche Post*, December 22, 1870. For a similarly cautious approach by a paper closely allied with Schurz, see St. *Charles Demokrat*, February 16, 1871.

58. *Congressional Globe*, 1048 (February 15, 1872).

59. Hamilton Fish to Schurz, January 23, 1871, reel 5, Schurz Papers, LOC, Washington. See also William Belknap to Schurz, January 24, 1871, reel 5, Schurz Papers, LOC. Francis Lieber also petitioned Fish. Lieber to Hamilton Fish, October 8 and November 17, 1870, February 14, 1871, vol. 73, 74, 76, Hamilton Fish Papers, LOC.

60. On the original *Westliche Post* notice, see *St. Louis Missouri Republican*, January 27, 1871. For a selection of fairly substantial stories, see *Cincinnati Volksfreund*, January 27, 1871; *Illinois Staats-Zeitung*, January 27, 1871; *St. Paul Minnesota Staats-Zeitung*, February 2, 1871; *Scranton Wochenblatt*, February 2, 1871; *Baltimore Deutsche Correspondent*, January 27, 1871. Nothing appeared in the *New York Times*, *New-York Tribune*, and *Chicago Tribune*, but there were a few lines on February 26, 1871 in small newspapers such as the *Boston Daily Advertiser*, *Central City (Colorado) Register*, and *Arkansas Gazette*.

61. Senate Report No. 183, 268–71. Chambrun's stake in the matter was never clear, but it appears that he expected that proving the culpability of Remington & Co. would lead to the exoneration of certain of his countrymen. Ibid., 336–411.

62. Ibid., 388, 271; *New York Times*, January 25, 1872.

63. *Congressional Globe*, 1017–18 (February 14, 1872); 1047 (February 15, 1872); 1066–67 (February 16, 1872).

64. Ibid., 1016 (February 14, 1872).

65. Ibid., App. 70, 69, 71 (February 20, 1872).

66. Ibid. 1048 (February 15, 1872), App. 72 (February 20, 1872).

67. James Harlan of Iowa, Morton, and Conkling made these points on different occasions before and after Schurz's speech on February 20. *Congressional Globe*, App. 50–51 (February 14 and 15, 1872), 1070 (February 16, 1872), App. 62–63, 65–66 (February 19, 1872), 123–27 (February 29, 1872).

68. Ibid., App. 124 (February 29, 1872). Harlan came closest to Carpenter. Ibid., 1015 (February 14, 1872).

69. Ibid., 1287 (February 29, 1872). For references to the Claims in the Senate, see Ibid., 1069–70 (February 16, 1872), App. 58 (February 19, 1872), App. 72 (February 20, 1872). See also *New York Times*, January 18, 1872; Adrian Cook, *The Alabama Claims: American Politics and Anglo-American Relations, 1865–1872* (Ithaca: Cornell University Press, 1975); Tom Bingham, "The *Alabama* Claims Arbitration," *International and Comparative Law Quarterly* 54, no. 1 (January 2005): 1–25; Jay Sexton, "The Funded Loan and the Alabama Claims," *Diplomatic History* 27, no. 4 (September 2003): 460–61.

70. Schurz, "Political Morals," November 18, 1858, in *Speeches of Carl Schurz* (Philadelphia: J. B. Lippincott, 1865), 40; Republican National Convention, *Presidential Election, 1868: Proceedings of the National Union Republican Convention, Held at Chicago, May 20 and 21, 1868* (Chicago: Evening Journal Print, 1868), 89.

71. *Congressional Globe*, 41st Cong., 2nd sess., 236–38 (December 20, 1869).

72. Slap, *Doom of Reconstruction*, 132.

73. Thomas Barclay, *The Liberal Republican Movement in Missouri, 1865–1871* (Columbia: State Historical Society of Missouri, 1926), 243–46; William E. Parrish, *Missouri under Radical Rule, 1865–1870* (Columbia: University of Missouri Press, 1965), 291–99; Efford, *German Immigrants, Race, and Citizenship*, 174–81.

74. Rutherford B. Hayes to S. Birchard, September 15, 1872, reel 172, Hayes Papers, HPC; *Wächter am Erie*, March 15, 1872; *Cincinnati Volksfreund*, April 29, May 2, 1872; *St. Charles Demokrat*, November 30, 1871; *Westliche Post*, April 17, 1872; Nagler, "Deutschamerikaner und das *Liberal Republican Movement*, 1872," 415–38; W. A. Fritsch, *Aus Amerika: Alte und Neue Heimat* (Stardgard i. Pom: Verlag von Wilhelm Prange, [c. 1905–1908]), 50.

75. Schurz to Horace Greeley, May 6, 1872, reel 7, Schurz Papers, LOC.

76. Efford, *German Immigrants, Race, and Citizenship*, 173.

77. *St. Charles Demokrat*, September 21, 1871. See also the issue of March 9, 1871.

78. *Cincinnati Volksfreund*, February 6, 1871. See also issues of August 25 and September 14, 1870 and *Watertown (Wisc.) Weltbürger*, August 6, 1870.

79. *Westliche Post*, October 20, 1870.

80. *Westliche Post*, February 7, 1872.

81. *Congressional* Globe, App. 74 (February 20, 1872).

82. Ibid., 1048 (February 15, 1872).

83. Ibid., 1287 (February 29, 1872).

84. Ibid., App. 111 (February 27, 1872).

85. Ibid., 1069 (February 16, 1872), App. 58 (February 19, 1872), App. 72 (February 20, 1872).

86. Ari Hoogenboom, *Outlawing the Spoils: A History of the Civil Service Reform Movement, 1865–1883* (Urbana: University of Illinois Press, 1961), 33–87; James J. Sheehan, *German History, 1770–1866* (Oxford: Clarendon, 1989), 425–30; Ferrel Heady, *Public Administration: A Comparative Perspective*, 2nd. ed. (New York: Marcel Dekker, 1979), 159–60; Ernest Barker, *The Development of Public Services in Western Europe, 1660–1930* (London: Oxford University Press, 1944), 21–24; Christopher Clark, *Iron Kingdom: The Rise and Downfall of Prussia, 1600–1947* (Cambridge: Belknap Press of Harvard University Press, 2006), 251, 312–44.

87. Hoogenboom, *Outlawing the Spoils*, 16–17, 29, 31; Horace White to Schurz, June 9, 1872, in *Speeches, Correspondence and Political Papers of Carl Schurz*, 2:382.

88. Hoogenboom, *Outlawing the Spoils*, 73. Schurz had not emphasized them when he introduced his bill. *Congressional Globe*, 41st Cong., 2nd sess., 236–38 (December 20, 1869).

89. *Congressional Globe*, 42nd Cong., 2nd sess., App. 107 (February 26, 1872). For earlier remarks, see 1040 (February 15, 1872).

90. Ibid., App. 120, 126 (February 29, 1872). See also charges of improper contact with the Prussian legation. Ibid., App. 64–65 (February 19, 1872).

91. Ibid., 1069 (February 16, 1872). See especially further remarks by Morton and Frelinghuysen on pages 1132 (February 20, 1872) and 1041 (February 15, 1872).

92. Ibid., 1069 (February 16, 1872), App. 58 (February 19, 1872), 1040 (February 15, 1872).

93. U. S. Grant to Congress, February 7, 1871, in *Papers of Ulysses S. Grant*, 21:163–64.

94. *The Nation*, August 11, 25 and September 29, 1870; *Cincinnati Commercial*, August 31, 1870; Gazley, *American Opinion of German Unification*, 348–58.

95. Efford, *German Immigrants, Race, and Citizenship*, 182–83, 184.

96. *Congressional Globe*, 703 (January 30, 1872). For further debate on the amendment, see 928–29 (February 9, 1872).

97. Ibid., 699 (January 30, 1872). He also mentioned "new guarantees for the rights of the colored people," a policy that he had already said he did not favor.

98. Ibid., 699, 700 (January 30, 1872). He had made the same point at an important Nashville speech calling for a complete break with the Republican Party in September 1871. Schurz, "The Need for Reform and a New Party," September 20, 1871, in *Speeches, Correspondence and Political Papers of Carl Schurz*, 2:283–84.

99. Ibid., App. 83 (February 23, 1872).

100. Ibid., 1075, 1076 (February 16, 1872).

101. Ibid., 1133 (February 20, 1872).

102. Ibid., 1110 (February 19, 1872). On Klan skepticism, see Elaine Frantz Parsons, "Klan Skepticism and Denial in Reconstruction-Era Public Discourse," *Journal of Southern History* 77, no. 1 (February 2011): 53–90.

103. Nast's cartoon was no mere sideshow; it was a part of his obsession with Schurz and the Liberal Republican bolt. Albert Bigelow Paine, *Th. Nast: His Period and His Pictures* (New York: Benjamin Blom, 1904), 230–31; Fiona Deans Halloran, *Thomas Nast: The Father of Modern Political Cartoons* (Chapel Hill: University of North Carolina Press, 2012), 145, 154–57.

104. Thomas Nast, "Mephistopheles at Work for Destruction," *Harper's Weekly*, March 9, 1872, 185.

105. For Republican examples, see *New York Times*, February 24, 1872; *Harper's Weekly*, March 9, 1872, 185; *Milwaukee Sentinel*, February 21, 1872; *Bangor Daily Whig & Courier*, February 22, 1872; *Philadelphia North American and United States Gazette*, February 22, 1872. For the opposition, see *New-York Tribune*, February 28, 1872. See also *Chicago Tribune*, February 21, 1872; *Atlanta Daily Sun*, February 22, 1872; *Brooklyn Daily Eagle*, February 27, 1872.

106. Louis Phillip Salterbach to Schurz, February 22, 1872, reel 7, Schurz Papers, LOC. See also other German-language letters on this reel from February and March.

107. *Seebote*, March 4, 1872. See also *Cincinnati Volksfreund*, February 27, 28, 1872.

108. *Illinois Staatszeitung*, March 26, 27, 28, 1872. On Raster, see H. Holst to Schurz, New York, March 13, 1872, reel 7, Schurz Papers, LOC.

109. Schurz to Friedrich Hecker, March 1, 1872, reel 3, Friedrich Hecker Papers (microfilm), State Historical Society of Missouri, Columbia; *Wächter am Erie*, March 9, 1872.

110. *Congressional Globe*, 1156 (February 21, 1872); Senate Report No. 183, 825, 11.

111. Ibid., 264–68, 334.

112. Ibid., 26, 177.

113. Ibid., 190, 472–74.

114. Ibid., xii.

115. Ibid., liv.

116. *Congressional Globe*, App. 531, 538, 533, 539 (May 31, 1872).

117. *New York Times*, June 1, 1872; *New-York Tribune*, June 1, 1872; *Chicago Tribune*, June 1, 1872; *Illinois Staats-Zeitung*, June 2, 3, 1872; *Cincinnati Volksfreund*, June 3, 1872; *Seebote*, June 2, 1872. For campaign references, see *Cincinnati Volksfreund*, October 8, 1872; *Cincinnati Volksblatt*, November 5, 1872; *Seebote*, September 23 and October 14, 1872; *Cleveland Anzeiger*, August 8, 1872; *Toledo Express*, September 4, 1872.

118. Slap, *Doom of Reconstruction*, 200–1; Summers, *Era of Good Stealings*, 153–65.

119. Foner, *Reconstruction*, 524–34, 558–63.

120. Ibid., 575–87; Trefousse, *Carl Schurz*, 239–41.

121. Rodgers, *Atlantic Crossings*, 29.

122. Sheehan, *German History*, 430–35; Leonard Krieger, *The German Idea of Freedom* (Boston: Beacon Press, 1957), 125–38. Self-described Hegelians in the United States were interested in the liberal potential of Hegel ideas, although a group of post–Civil War philosophers did defend the importance of institutions; see James A. Good, "A World-Historical Idea: The St. Louis Hegelians and the Civil War," *Journal of American Studies* 34, no. 3 (December 2000): 447–64.

123. Anja Werner, *The Transatlantic World of Higher Education: Americans at German Universities, 1776–1914* (New York: Berghahn Books, 2013), 52–61.

124. Rodgers, *Atlantic Crossings*, 84–106.

125. Richard R. Ely, "The Prussian Civil Service," *Overland Monthly* 1, no. 5 (1883): 458, 451.

5

"The Failure of the Men to Come Up"

The Reinvention of Irish-American Nationalism

Caleb Richardson

On May 24, 1870—Victoria Day in Canada—the President of the Fenian Brotherhood, John O'Neill, waited at the railway station in St. Albans, Vermont, for an invasion force. O'Neill planned to command "upwards of four thousand men": ten to twelve hundred from Massachusetts and Rhode Island were coming on the first train; six hundred more from Vermont and New York on the second, with equally full trains following them within twenty-four hours.[1] Combined with the one thousand to fifteen hundred troops assembling 75 miles away in Malone, New York, five to six thousand Fenians were to sweep across the border. They would occupy the town of Saint-Jean-sur-Richelieu and destroy the Grand Trunk Railway line at Richmond to slow the advance of Canadian troops. Then, assisted by Fenians from Detroit and points further west, and possibly even by supporters of the Métis leader Louis Riel in the recently created Province of Manitoba, O'Neill and his men would hold strategic locations, resist Canadian counter-attacks, and, somehow, parlay all of this into freedom for Ireland.[2]

O'Neill himself acknowledged the flaws in this plan. In an account published after the raid, he defended his motivation—"in striking at England through Canada we attempted no more than was done by the American Republic in the war of the Revolution"—but also admitted that "the liberation of Ireland through an invasion of Canada had not me for its author; and I very much question if its originators had not lost all faith in it [by 1870]."[3] The arrival of the first train that morning of the Queen's birthday would have given pause to the most indefatigable nationalist. Instead of over a thousand men from Massachusetts, "twenty-five or thirty" stepped onto the platform in St. Albans. "Eighty or ninety" Vermonters and New Yorkers appeared, instead of the expected six hundred.[4] Over the next twenty-four hours, the pattern repeated itself. Fifteen hundred to two thousand men were rumored to be on the way from New York and New Jersey; "not over two hundred and thirty or forty men arrived."[5] Another report of a thousand men arriving in St. Albans "from the South" produced sixty, all of whom had apparently missed their stop, ended up in New York, and had to catch a return train.[6] O'Neill's invasion was reduced to a symbolic gesture: He was left clinging to the hope that he just "might be able to cross the line with a respectable force."[7]

Although 1870 represented a particularly dire manifestation of Fenianism's weaknesses, that raid—or "attempted invasion," to use O'Neill's term—featured all of the flaws that beset the Fenians throughout the first two decades of their existence. Inadequate training, committed Canadian opposition, experienced but incoherent leadership, poor communications, and a complete absence of operations security—O'Neill's adjutant-general throughout the affair was Thomas Beach, aka "Henri le Caron," one of the most distinguished British spies of his generation—all played important roles.[8] But the main reason the Fenians failed in 1870 was the same reason that they'd failed in an earlier attempt in 1866: a simple lack of manpower, or what O'Neill later called "the failure of the men to come up."

O'Neill's disappointment is understandable, considering that he led the largest Irish-American nationalist group in history. Fenian "circles" could be found in every state; tens of thousands of people attended Fenian speeches and fundraisers. O'Neill himself had addressed the cheering crowds at many of these events. But what he and other Fenian leaders failed to appreciate was the enormous gap between the leadership's understanding of Fenianism and that of the rank-and-file. For many postbellum Irish-Americans, Fenianism had more to do with sociability than revolution. As only one of many options in the crowded postwar landscape of voluntary organizations, it offered these people the chance to express both halves of their increasingly hyphenated identity. Fenianism makes sense only when we consider the movement in the context of the rich associational life that was integral to the period's politics. The majority of those attending Fenian events supported Irish independence as an ideal, but only a small minority was willing to take up arms to fight for it. This was a "Brotherhood"; it was no army. The efflorescence of Fenianism attests to both how devoted Irish immigrants were to their homeland, but also how integrated they were into the life of their new country. As the following suggests, the character of the Fenian movement in the United States underscores how unfettered Irish-American public life was in the North, especially when compared to the experiences of Fenians in Ireland or African Americans in the South.

Founded in New York and Dublin in 1858, the Fenian Brotherhood had itself been a response to failure. A decade earlier, inspired by political activities throughout Europe and disgusted by the British Government's inadequate response to the Great Famine, the "Young Ireland" movement attempted to add Ireland's name to the list of 1848's revolutionary success stories. Unfortunately, in a precursor of what would happen twenty years later, the movement was undercut by government infiltration, popular incomprehension, clerical hostility, and a lack of military experience. After an abortive attempt at an uprising in Ireland in July 1848, its leaders fled, or were imprisoned or transported.[9]

The leaders of Young Ireland—William Smith O'Brien, James Stephens, John Mitchel, John O'Mahony, Thomas Francis Meagher, and Michael Doheny, among others—came away convinced that the only hope for Irish freedom lay in transforming their movement into an international one. Some former Young Irelanders hoped to make a deal with Russia; in New York, the Irish Republican Union, founded by veterans of the U.S.-Mexican War, encouraged a more intuitive link with Irish America. The Irish Civil and Military Republican Union and the Emmet Monument Association, both founded in the mid-1850s, were short-lived but potentially fruitful models of what a truly international Irish movement would look like. The organization that became known as the Irish Republican Brotherhood (IRB) in Ireland and the Fenian Brotherhood in the United States—named for the Fianna, the followers of the mythical hunter and warrior Fionn mac Cumhaill—was better funded, better organized, and more consciously Atlantic in its orientation than earlier groups. With the outbreak of the Civil War, the Fenians seemed poised to be that rarest of creatures: an Irish nationalist organization in the right place at the right time. When the war was over, Fenians hoped, tens of thousands of battle-hardened Irish-American troops would be ready to carry the fight onto Irish soil.[10]

But cracks within the movement quickly appeared, starting at the very top. John O'Mahony and John Mitchel found themselves on opposing sides of the Civil War. Their reasons were ideologically consistent: O'Mahony saw Abolition as another word for Liberty, while Mitchel argued that the Confederacy had just as much right to self-governance as Ireland.[11] But the conflicting loyalties that resulted just gave Irish-Americans one more reason to focus on the fight for freedom in their new home, rather than in their old one. Staunch opposition to the group by Irish and Irish-American clergy added another cause for dissension; the pronounced lack of Irish-American unity on issues such as emancipation or nationwide conscription contributed another. And divisiveness did not stop at the coastline: Back in Dublin, the Irish Republican Brotherhood president James Stephens saw Irish-Americans primarily as a source of funds and, possibly, manpower in a revolution in Ireland, while many Irish-American Fenian leaders hoped to attack the British Empire a little closer to home.

After the war ended, Fenian fortunes surged—in 1865 they raised $228,000 for their cause—but the divisions remained. O'Mahony's leadership was challenged: first by the County Cork–born Manhattan department store magnate William Roberts, and then by the veteran Union Army General Thomas William Sweeny. Roberts and Sweeny, partly inspired by the actions of pre-war filibusterers, proposed the invasion of Canada as the best way of taking advantage of the upsurge in Irish-American support. Somewhat reluctantly, and in the face of outright resistance from Stephens in Ireland, O'Mahony came to support the idea as well. Encouraged by what they interpreted as at best enthusiasm, and at worst forbearance, from Secretary of State William Seward, and convinced that a crackdown on IRB activities in Ireland made a revolution there unlikely, both American "wings" of the organization began planning for invasions of Canada in the spring of 1866.

The previously hesitant O'Mahony was the first to strike. In March and April, small groups of Fenians assembled in Maine under Bernard Doran Killian, the County Down–born publisher and veteran. Their plan was to seize Campobello Island, which would either precipitate a war between the United States and Britain, or—failing that—provide the Fenians with a launching point for future invasions of Ireland. Although hundreds of Fenians mustered at Eastport, this invasion was hardly "attempted" at all, thanks largely to a firm response by the Royal Navy. The "Eastport Fizzle" was a public relations disaster for the Fenians, and O'Mahony was impeached as Fenian leader, but plans for a Canadian invasion continued under Sweeny.

On May 31, Fenian troops under the leadership of John O'Neill made another attempt. After crossing the Niagara River, Fenians occupied the village of Fort Erie and raised the green flag of the Irish Republic above the Fort Erie courthouse. In the next few days, O'Neill's men fought successful engagements against both British regulars and Canadian volunteers at Ridgeway, in what is now Ontario. But after expected reinforcements failed to materialize, they had to retreat to Buffalo on June 2nd. While crossing the river, they were intercepted by U.S. Navy and Revenue ships, charged with violations of the 1819 Neutrality Act, and taken into U.S. custody. Their leaders were arrested, and, except for one last attempt on Quebec on June 7 and 8, the Fenian Invasion of 1866 was over.

But the Fenian Revolution continued. In 1867, Fenians finally attempted a long-postponed plan to use Irish-American Fenians to assist the IRB in an uprising in Ireland. Although several of the leaders of this Irish uprising were experienced veterans of the Union Army, they were less successful at fighting in the very different circumstances of rural Ireland, and authorities quelled the attempted revolution in early March within days. The largest successes of the attempted 1867 uprising were propaganda victories, albeit tragic ones. In September, a spectacular rescue attempt freed two IRB men from prison but took the life of an English sergeant. The resulting manhunt resulted in the execution of three young IRB volunteers who became known as the "Manchester Martyrs."[12]

O'Neill would make two more unsuccessful attempts at invading Canada in 1870 and 1871. But by the mid-1870s the torch of militant Irish-American nationalism was already passing into the hands of the smaller, more cohesive, and more effective Clan na Gael, led by the former Fenian John Devoy. In the end, Fenianism was most successful in inspiring not Irish but Canadian nationalism. In March 1867, the British Parliament recognized the creation of the Dominion of Canada, uniting Ontario, Quebec, New Brunswick and Nova Scotia. Although plans for Confederation had begun before the invasions, Fenian activities certainly reinforced the commitment of the plan's supporters. Ironically or not, one of the new Dominion's most eloquent champions was Thomas D'Arcy McGee, a former Young Irelander who had become one of the Fenians' strongest critics. A suspected Fenian sympathizer would assassinate him less than a year later.[13]

In contemporary scholarship, Irish-American Fenians play a significant role within a variety of different historiographies.[14] Scholars of nationalism, immigration, ethnicity, and political and diplomatic history have found in them a rich source of material. But many of these efforts have neglected the Fenians below officer rank.[15] In his nuanced discussion of Fenianism in his history of Irish emigration to North America, *Emigrants and Exiles*, Kerby Miller criticized this historiographical blind spot, arguing instead for the centrality of common people: "impoverished Irish-Americans were most homesick and most attracted to the nationalist dream."[16] Recent scholars of the movement have begun to correct for this. In their survey of the Fenians, Patrick Steward and Bryan McGovern present the back-room negotiations of officials, and more popular manifestations of the movement, as part of one complicated canvas.[17] Mitchell Snay puts the movement in even broader perspective, comparing the Fenian Brotherhood to the Ku Klux Klan and southern freedpeoples' Union League Clubs.[18] Snay's application of the concept of civic—rather than ethnic—nationalism to the Fenians allows him to recapture the diversity of a group that included both Republicans and Democrats, Northerners and Southerners, rich and poor. And it goes a long way toward explaining "the failure of the men to come up."

But not all the way. The great virtue of some of the recent contributions to the historiography of Fenianism outlined earlier is that these authors take the movement seriously: as a political organization and as an expression of concerns within the Irish community both at home and abroad. But this respect for the movement's ideological and political significance can also misrepresent the way that nineteenth century Americans and Irish-Americans actually experienced Fenianism. In some ways, contemporary historians of Fenianism are making the same mistake that John O'Neill made: To them, the tens of thousands of Fenians who showed up at Fenian-sponsored events were all potential fighters for Irish freedom, united by a hatred for Britain and bound by a desire to free—and in many cases return to—their homeland. According to this approach, if O'Neill and others had a hard time getting them to show up, the reason must have been clerical disapproval, economic problems, or one of Fenianism's considerable institutional weaknesses.

In fact, for thousands of Irish-Americans, Fenianism had as much to do with American citizenship, and participation in American civic and associational life more generally, as with Irish nationalism. The success of Fenian fund-raising events during Reconstruction could imply a widespread Irish-American commitment to Irish independence. Or it could imply a widespread Irish-American commitment to picnics. Which is not to suggest that involvement in civic and associational life is in any way a less serious or constructive way of achieving many of the goals that Fenianism was supposed to promote: as historians of the Irish in the American West, particularly in California, have argued, the Irish were often most influential where they were least militant.[19] In some ways, the lack of Fenian involvement in the invasions of Canada is less surprising when one remembers that Fenians were not just Irish but American. Or, to put it more expansively, they were free participants in the United States' lively, mid-nineteenth-century democratic public sphere, scorned by many for their culture and religion, but accepted by others and, ultimately, not persecuted by systematic violence.

Developing this argument requires a more generous definition of what the term "Fenian" encompasses. Snay's emphasis on the secrecy of the Fenian Brotherhood is in many ways deserved—it was exactly the organization's secrecy that played a key role in its condemnation by the Catholic Church.[20] But this focus on the secrecy of the Fenian inner circle can misrepresent the true nature of the wider movement in which sworn members were a minority. And it is important to acknowledge how unsuccessful, and, at times, how uninterested, the Fenians were in maintaining secrecy. Some of Fenianism's greatest successes came in spite of, rather than because of, the movement's secrecy. The tens of thousands of people who donated to the cause did so in large part because of the publicity that the movement received in the late 1860s. The more public the movement became, the more money it made. And the more money it made, the more it came to resemble other voluntary groups and Fenians those "associated Americans" identified by Mary Ryan, participating in "a democratic public life . . . acted out on the national stage."[21]

The tens of thousands of Irish-Americans who attended Fenian meetings, contributed to the Fenian cause, and failed to show up at that railway station in 1870 deserve to be placed at the center of the story of Irish-American Fenianism. In later years, "Fenian" would become a catchall term for any Irish nationalist or republican: It deserved that broader application even earlier. Not all Fenians were sworn members of the Brotherhood: John Mitchel, one of its most influential leaders, did not officially become a Fenian until 1865.[22] More importantly, not all of those who supported the Fenians were willing to take up arms for Irish freedom. Most Fenian supporters were passionately committed to the cause of Irish independence but did not necessarily agree on how to achieve it. These men and women deserve to be brought back into the story. David A. Wilson has written of a "Fenian subculture in Canada" that has escaped both contemporary and scholarly recognition.[23] In the United States, that Fenian subculture shed its prefix, to the point that it overwhelmed the movement's official component.

Grasping the full significance of Irish-American Fenianism, then, requires a more expansive definition of who qualified as a "Fenian" and an acknowledgement that the openness of the movement was as influential as its secrecy. Fenian leaders could never decide whether they wanted to be behind or ahead of their time. They retained their faith in filibustering and a kind of universalist nationalism long after most had given up on both, while their non-sectarian and even anti-clerical approach to politics anticipated that of twentieth-century Irish militant groups.[24] But their Fenian followers found themselves perfectly in tune with Reconstruction-era America's lively public life. Fenians were engaging in many of the same debates that other Reconstruction-era Americans were, and in many cases were adding new voices to that debate.[25] To establish a broader and more diverse vision of what Fenianism could be, then, and to restore it to its context, we should start at the same place that most postbellum Americans would have been introduced to the movement: a picnic.

To fully understand Irish-American Fenianism, one has to reconcile two facts about the movement. The first is that the Fenian Brotherhood was a violent international paramilitary organization, committed to the destruction of the British Empire, which at several times during its existence tried to foment world war to achieve its aims. The second is that, for much of the late 1860s, the Fenian Brotherhood was, in many towns and cities in the United States, a reliable source of a pleasant afternoon outing, complete with games, songs, and light refreshment. The Irish-American writer Finley Peter Dunne famously satirized the Irish-American penchant for combining revolution and recreation by having his hero, Mr. Dooley, opine that "if Ireland cud be freed be a picnic, it 'd not on'y be free to-day, but an impire, begorra."[26] In fact, picnics were crucial to the Fenian Brotherhood's balance sheet: Far from being distractions from revolution, they were essential to it. There was no better way to bring together large numbers of sympathizers, and nothing could match the picnic's capacity for fundraising. As early as 1865, Fenian Brotherhood financial officers were stressing that "every effort possible on the part of the Fenians in America should be made at once to furnish the sinews of war," and that "Pic-Nics [sic], excursions, and all that may be within the power of a circle as a means of realizing these should be taken advantage of."[27]

Picnics were the best, but not the only, means of raising money. The Fenian Brotherhood issued bonds, redeemable six months after the establishment of an Irish Republic. At the time, these bonds were probably seen by their buyers more as keepsake than investment, and by their issuers as a line of credit— O'Mahony was able to "pay" Fenian officers in bonds.[28] Nevertheless, they had staying power. When, more than half a century later, the new President of the Irish Republic, Eamon de Valera, visited the United States, he was surprised to meet Irish-Americans anxious to redeem Fenian bonds, passed down from parents and grandparents.[29]

The Fenians also hosted small-scale public events to promote their cause. In many communities, the Fenian Brotherhood organized lectures on Irish culture and history.[30] In mid-1865, the *New York Herald* referred to a "Fenian literary branch" in New Haven.[31] Also, like many other Reconstruction-era voluntary organizations, Fenians hosted balls. St. Patrick's Day was, predictably, the height of the season. The Fenians of San Francisco hosted a "Ball and Gift Distribution" on St. Patrick's Day in 1865. Ads promised a raffle and a flag presentation, and— conveniently for British or Canadian intelligence agents keeping an eye on the group—a comprehensive list of the leaders of the organization.[32] Apart from the fact that, amongst the decorations, green flags were interspersed among the Stars and Stripes, Fenian balls were indistinguishable from those organized by other groups.[33] In part, the lack of a distinctively "Irish" identity was because, as the balls became more popular, the Fenians could no longer host them in their own facilities: They had to rent space from other groups. The Wolfe Tone Circle in Macon, Georgia, celebrated its Second Grand Ball in Macon City Hall in January 1866, as their lodge had proven too small the previous year.[34] At these balls, political messages were conveyed with a light touch. Announcing an upcoming ball in Bennington, Vermont in December 1866, the local branch of the Brotherhood admitted that the ball's purpose was to raise funds for "a uniform Company of the Fenian Brotherhood of Bennington, who are expecting shortly to be called upon to take the field, for Freedom's cause," but assured their "American friends" that they were welcome to an event "lighted up in grand style," with a "band of the best musicians."[35] By the mid-1860s, in smaller cities or towns, the Fenian brotherhood was known more for its conviviality than its militancy. The Brotherhood of Jackson, Michigan, was not exaggerating when it boasted in an advertisement that "the Fenians are noted for giving Social Entertainments."[36]

In using these social events as fund-raising methods, Fenians were hardly alone, either in Irish-America, the North, or in the United States generally. During the picnic season from May to September, Odd Fellows, Turners, Masons, Sons of Temperance, fire departments, high schools, singing societies, religious organizations, and virtually every other association imaginable held fund-raising picnics across the country. During the first three days of the week of July 16, 1865, the pleasure-seeking citizen of Albany could have attended three different picnics—the Fenian picnic on Tuesday was sandwiched between the Brotherhood of St. Barnabas's outing on Monday and the Y.M.U.D.S.'s excursion on Wednesday.[37] In many small towns and cities, the local Fenian circle was often just one of many picnic-giving organizations. Partly as a result of this, before the raids of the late 1860s, Fenians were rarely considered dangerous, or even particularly political.

This proved to be a major difference between Fenians in the United States and elsewhere. While Fenians and IRB members in Ireland and throughout the British Empire often had ties to other voluntary organizations—Brian Clarke has highlighted links between the Hibernian Benevolent Society and the Fenian Brotherhood in Toronto, for instance—that relationship was of a very different character. In places where Fenian membership was proscribed, these other associations served as vital bridges to the wider Irish community. If the associations did not necessarily realize that they were being used this way, so much the better. Clarke notes that, in Toronto, "the Hibernians, wittingly or not, were a front for the Fenian Brotherhood."[38] In Canada, Australia, Britain or Ireland, Fenians associated themselves with legal groups because they had to: raising money or attracting members required the veil of legitimacy that these groups provided. In the very different context of the United States, however, Fenians had no need of a "front." At times, they would be lumped into the Irish wing of the "mottled group of ethnic brotherhoods" characteristic of the time: In the Fourth of July parade in the Irish stronghold of Lowell, Massachusetts in 1865, the Fenians followed the Lowell Irish Benevolent Society and the Young Men's Catholic Library Association.[39] But in many cases they weren't even implicitly categorized as Irish: In Norwich, Connecticut, on that same momentous Fourth, the local Fenian circle marched, presumably somewhat uneasily, between the Masons and the Temperance and Benevolent Society.[40] By 1867, the Fenians of Portland, Oregon were confident enough in their American bona fides to schedule a Fenian fundraiser on the Fourth of July.[41]

Picnics, then, became the quintessential form of Fenian fundraising. Picnics were more profitable than other methods: At a picnic in New York in 1866, a reporter noted that "The Irishmen were as liberal . . . with their fifty-cent stamps [the cost of admission] as ever they were with money for the [Fenian] bonds."[42] Picnics drew larger crowds than balls, the only limiting factor being the weather. And their open, public, highly visible nature reinforced the Fenians' argument that they were a legitimate organization. Irish-American Fenians, unlike their counterparts in the British Empire, could present themselves as just one more public association. Importantly, as time went on, this became less and less of a convenient fiction.

The only problem with this engagement with the wider culture of the Reconstruction-era United States was that Fenians also had to compete with those other associations for customers. One of the ways that they did this was through a kind of refreshment arms race. Fenian financial records indicate some of the pleasures to be found at their events. For one picnic in Buffalo, New York in July 1867, the Muldoon Brothers of 79 Main Street provided 2700 cigars.[43] The same picnic featured 402 hams.[44] But Fenian organizers also competed with other picnic organizers by downplaying the ethnic character of their events. Advertisements made a point of emphasizing that the proceedings would not be too "Irish": The advertisement for a "Mammoth Picnic" in Cincinnati in May 1865 highlighted an address on "Irish Freedom" but also made clear that "The Society having charge of the Refreshments, will take special pains in furnishing a first-class Dinner, Ice Cream, Lemonades and all other articles usual on such occasions."[45] More typical was an advertisement for a picnic in Portland, Oregon in May 1866, which did not refer to politics at all, but highlighted the "refreshments, liquors, etc." available from a "stock of the best materials to be found in the city."[46] If the food and drink were not particularly Irish, neither were the activities. Especially outside the large urban concentrations of Irish-Americans on the Eastern seaboard, Fenian picnics were often just picnics that happened to be sponsored by the Fenians: The only thing Irish about a picnic in New Orleans in 1866 was that "the fairer portion of [the dancers] were 'wearin' of the green.'"[47] Whereas picnics hosted by the Turnverein and other German-American organizations often featured German music, culture and food, Fenian picnics could be indistinguishable from non-"ethnic" events.[48]

Well into 1866, Irish-American Fenians were not widely associated with militant nationalism. If anything, Fenianism seemed to mitigate the more violent aspects of Irishness. A visitor to a picnic in Jones's Wood in New York remarked upon how "everything passed off quietly and satisfactorily, showing conclusively a self-respect and dignity that augurs well for Fenian influence on the impulsive Irish character."[49] Some argued that Fenian picnics were actually *less* dangerous than other picnics, precisely *because* they were run by militants. The editors of a New Orleans paper warned prospective attendants at a picnic that "if there should be any persons foolish enough to intend making unfriendly demonstrations, or creating a disturbance on the grounds, we advise them to remain at home, for the Fenian soldiers will certainly handle them roughly."[50] Thanks at least in part to their role as picnic organizers, the Irish-American branch of the Fenian Brotherhood developed a reputation for respectability that stunned their critics in Canada or Britain. In the midst of the invasions of Canada in the spring of 1866, The *Times-Picayune* praised a multi-day Fenian picnic in terms that would have embarrassed the most sentimental novelty songwriter: "there were green shirts and jackets ad infinitum and green cravats and green dresses, and green ribbons fluttering in the wind, as the bonnets went round in the dance upon the heads of the beautiful daughters of Erin."[51] While positive stereotypes would be tolerated, negative ones would not: When, in July 1865, the author of "Town Talk" in the *New Orleans Times* satirized the Fenians as shillelagh-waving conspirators, he felt the need to apologize a few days later, insisting that the article "was [actually] intended as a burlesque upon those persons who affect to see political danger in the Fenian brotherhood."[52]

Because much of this positive media coverage was accompanied by extensive advertising campaigns paid for by the Fenian Brotherhood, it is no wonder that editorial comment was fairly positive. But even after the raids, when newspaper editorials regularly criticized Fenians for their dangerous militancy, they continued to praise Fenian picnics for their orderly nature. While some newspapers highlighted sporadic outbreaks of violence at these events—"Donnybrook Fair" was liberally invoked—in general they treated Fenian picnics as an unexceptionable, and even admirable, part of the fabric of American life.[53] Picnics functioned not only as a means for Fenians to connect with a wider American audience, but also as a safe way for Americans to engage with Irish nationalism. For instance, after the first invasions of Canada, U.S. military personnel were wary of being publicly linked to the Fenians—who had, after all, tried to foment a war between Britain and the United States. But many soldiers and officers were also sympathetic to the Fenian cause. Picnics were a way of demonstrating that sympathy. In 1867, soldiers in the 1st and 4th Artillery Regiments participated in a Fenian picnic in Black Rock, New York, donning Fenian uniforms and parading with local Fenian soldiers. This was not only a breach of the military code; it was also deliberately provocative, as Black Rock was just outside Buffalo, the primary launching point for one of the raids a year earlier. The soldiers were court-martialed and convicted of "conduct prejudicial to good order and military discipline" and associating with "an institution reported to be in armed hostility to the Government of Great Britain and Ireland." But the President later remitted their sentences.[54] It was just a picnic, after all.

Fenian picnics followed a pattern. The event would typically open with the presentation of an Irish flag, often sewn by the local branch of the Fenian Sisterhood. One aspect of Reconstruction America echoed in Fenian picnics is the strong and visible role played by women in supporting and organizing for the cause even as its public face was male. Nearly all newspaper reports of picnics mentioned the large number of women in attendance: In many cases they formed a majority.[55] Although the Fenian Sisterhood is conspicuously absent from most official Fenian Brotherhood military records, they figured prominently in the history of Fenian picnics. On several occasions, they hosted major picnics themselves: In Jones's Wood in New York in September 1866, they entertained three thousand people with an event that featured shooting galleries, an address by the IRB leader James Stephens, and dancing into the night.[56] If anything, the surviving evidence suggests that the Fenian Sisterhood might have made better managers of these events than their male counterparts. They were certainly more committed to financial transparency: on June 10 of 1866, the Sisterhood of New York published an advertisement detailing the funds raised at a recent picnic, and proudly declared that 100 percent of the net was "forwarded to Ireland."[57]

The flag presentation or opening ceremony would be followed by speeches from prominent local members of the Brotherhood, capped by a sort of keynote address by a distinguished visitor. Most speakers were Fenians themselves: during the various splits among the leadership, different Fenian officials competed with each other for prime picnic spots. During and just after the war, Irish-American Fenian picnic speeches became a sort of genre unto themselves. With few exceptions, the speaker explained what the Fenians stood for, stressed the Brotherhood's dual loyalty to both America and Ireland, and declared their in-

tention to free Ireland from British tyranny. Depending on the inclinations of
the speaker, he would lay heavier emphasis on some of these aspects than others. John O'Mahony and James Stephens, for instance, tended to focus more on
Ireland than America, while Roberts and Sweeney often played to their audience in language that could have been lifted straight from the repertoire of any
Irish-American politician. "As [England] acted in supplying the South with ships
and other munitions of war, so the American Republic will act toward the Irish
Republic, assisting it in the same neutral manner," Roberts promised a New York
audience in July 1865—with better irony than prophecy.[58]

Before Reconstruction, Fenian picnic speakers were sometimes criticized for
blurring the line between Irish and American politics. In 1864, describing a recent picnic, the *Plain Dealer* praised this "organization among our Irish citizens,
having for its object the freedom of Ireland," and suggested that "from the numerous specimens of Irish female beauty we saw on the grounds, we have come
to the conclusion that the Irish Rose can bear transplanting to American soil."
The editor highlighted the loyalty of all present, noting that "America, the Home
of their adoption, was toasted," and singled out the Galway-born Brigadier-
General James Lawlor Kiernan, who addressed the crowd on the topic of "Ireland
and America versus England." "In this short notice," the editors gushed, "it is
impossible to do justice to the address delivered by General Kiernan. It was eloquent, argumentative and replete with telling passages which called forth again
and again the Irish 'hurrah.'"[59] But when, in Cincinnati a few days later, Kiernan
spoke again at a Fenian meeting, the same paper criticized him for commenting
directly on American politics. "[A]dressing the Fenian Brotherhood, a society
which tolerates no discussion relative to American politics, he went out of his
way to make a McClellan speech . . . the respect of gentlemen of all parties for
this General Kiernan is forever lost."[60] During the war, discussion of U.S. politics
in an "Irish" context was unacceptable, apparently.

During Reconstruction, however, the nature of Fenian picnic speeches shifted,
and speakers openly addressed current issues in American politics. The conflict
between support for a newly powerful government and a commitment to federalism, for instance—what Eric Foner has called "the moderate's dilemma"—was
often echoed in Fenian picnic speeches.[61] John O'Neill had more of a reason than
most to resent the federal government after it played a key role in quashing the
June 1866 invasion. But he made a point of distinguishing between "high officials
of the Government" and the American people. "We were defeated not by the
British government, nor by their troops, but by the government which we were
led to believe would aid us—by officials who desired to crush us," he told an

audience in Baltimore only months after his retreat, "but they do not represent the American people."[62]

The rhetoric of Fenianism also changed during Reconstruction, as an emphasis on universal liberty began to replace the more limited focus on British interference in Irish affairs.[63] This emphasis on liberty, not coincidentally, attracted the attention of Republicans seeking Irish-American votes. Partisan politics came to play an important role in Fenian picnic speeches: at times the Fenians could almost appear to be an Irish wing of the Republican Party. At a meeting in Chicago in July 1866, the Fenians adopted the following resolution:

> That it is a foul libel upon the patriotism and the intelligence of Irish Americans to assert that we are the property, the voting chattels, of any political party, and that we will satisfactorily repel that calumny, by hereafter, on all occasions, voting for that party which finds no excuse in musty laws, in vested rights, in ancient prejudices, for degrading or enslaving men, or for preventing free men, with arms in their hands, recovering that liberty and nationality of which they and their race have long been cruelly and infamously deprived.

How did the Fenians demonstrate this liberation from party politics? By planning a picnic, and inviting as guests of honor the prominent Republicans Schuyler Colfax, John A. Logan, and Horace Greeley.[64]

This was not the only case in which Fenianism undermined traditional assumptions about Irish-American political loyalties. Republican policies could align surprisingly smoothly with Fenian concerns. Whereas the contradictions inherent in Fenian ideology had threatened to overwhelm the movement during the Civil War, during Reconstruction its devotion to "liberty" meant that it fit right in. This meant not only that Fenians found a receptive audience among Republican politicians looking for votes, but that Republican politicians received a favorable response from Fenians. In Chicago in August 1866, Illinois governor Richard J. Oglesby addressed a picnic of fifteen to twenty thousand "Fenians and their friends," amidst a field in which "The Stars and Stripes and the green flags of Ireland were gaily intermingled all over the ground." Recounting his travels in Ireland, he noted that everywhere he was "kindly received, because I came from America, the land of equal rights . . . wherever I traveled in Ireland I met no man or woman, high or low, whose heart was not attached to liberty." While he was careful to distance himself from the assembled company—"I meet you not as Fenians but as American citizens," he announced, and "I am not a Fenian, nor never shall be"—he urged his listeners to "go to the polls with liberty loving patriots, and vote against Andy Johnson and Jeff Davis." He was followed by General Logan, who reminded the audience that "every friend of freedom is the friend of Irish freedom, and to lovers of universal and impartial suffrage only can Irish patriots go to find true friends."[65]

Democrats were quick to respond to what they considered a cynical attempt to buy votes. The Democratic *Weekly Patriot and Union* described Oglesby's speech as "wooing by insult," and highlighted the "derision and contempt" in his deceptively smooth remarks, asking the audience "did your Fenian leaders betray you to welcome your enemies that you might be thus entertained?"[66] Although the paper's concern was overblown—plenty of Irish-Americans remained strong Democrats—the appeal of these calls for "liberty" demonstrated how the period altered the Fenian movement. As it became more integrated into American society, Fenianism shed some of the more narrowly "Irish" characteristics of its politics.

Fenianism's new focus on "liberty" could transcend national boundaries. In a kind of return to its roots in 1848 and the Young Ireland movement, some Fenians and their supporters began connecting the struggle for Ireland not only to Reconstruction in the United States but to republican or democratic movements throughout the world. In 1869, at the start of the Ten Years' War, New York Fenians invited prominent Cubans to attend their annual picnic at Jones' Wood.[67] In a speech at a Fenian picnic in Framingham, Massachusetts in August 1866, Senator Henry Wilson declared himself to be a Fenian—in spirit if not in name—because "the cause of Fenianism is the cause of liberty everywhere the wide world over." He placed the Fenians in a long tradition stretching from the French Revolution through English Chartism to Kossuth's campaign in Hungary to Emancipation.[68] At times, these international connections could be bewildering. At a picnic on Staten Island in 1866, Antonio López de Santa Anna was the gracious guest of honor. His speech made the occasional convolutions of Fenian orators seem almost straightforward. "When Mexico was invaded by that noble enemy on whose hospitable soil I am now living, when I had arrayed against me the powerful armies of the United States under that immortal hero General Scott," he declared, "the flower of my army then were two companies composed of men from the Green Isle, with the image of their Patron Saint on their flag."[69] Although the internationalism of Irish-American Fenians was generally less concrete—and less complex—than that presented by Santa Anna, it highlighted the widening of their perspective, and that of Reconstruction-era Americans generally.

As Fenian picnickers became more engaged with American and international affairs, they became increasingly disconnected from the official Fenian

organization. Their response to the key events affecting the movement demonstrates this. In most histories of Irish nationalism, "1867"—the year that the attempted Fenian uprising in Ireland occurred and the year the Manchester Martyrs were executed—is synonymous with "Fenian" just as "1798" means "United
Irishmen" and "1848" signifies "Young Ireland." But Irish-American Fenians acknowledged 1867 only in an offhand way. Partly this is because the timing of the
key events of 1867—the attempted uprising in Ireland occurred early in the year,
and the executions in November—did not directly overlap with picnic season.
It is important to remember that, as one of the Fenians' most important fund-
raising techniques, picnics often occurred at low points in Fenian fortunes: From
a financial standpoint, it made perfect sense to schedule picnics immediately after defeats or reverses for the movement. Still, the contrast between official concerns and the wider movement could be jarring. On St. Patrick's Day 1867, in the
immediate wake of the failure of the uprising in Ireland—which was, after all, the
reason the group had been founded in the first place—the Fenians of Cincinnati
held a "Fenian Demonstration and Grand Civic and Military Ball."[70]

At times, the popularity and frequency of Fenian picnics seemed to rise in
inverse proportion to the military or political successes of the Fenians more
broadly. By the summer of 1868, Fenianism had suffered through two failed invasions of Canada, a thwarted revolution in Ireland, and the final collapse of the
original plan to import Irish-American veterans to fight on Irish soil. The Brotherhood's reputation was further sullied by political division, financial trouble and
a link to two assassination attempts: An Irish-Australian Fenian sympathizer had
shot Queen Victoria's son in the back at a picnic, and although Prince Alfred survived, the attempted murderer was hanged in April. Also that month, the former
Young Irelander Thomas D'Arcy McGee was assassinated in Ottawa.[71]

How did Irish-American Fenians mark this *annus horribilis*? With some of
the largest picnics in their history. In May, three days after a Fenian prisoner,
Michael Barrett, had been hanged in London, the Fenian Guard of Portland, Or-
egon planned its Third Annual Target and Basket Picnic Excursion to nearby
Pine Grove, featuring a full brass band.[72] In the middle of June, the Fenians of
Cincinnati gathered for a picnic at the zoo, featuring the rather un-Hibernian
Heidel's Band, and got "all the pleasure out of the occasion that was possible."[73]
While John O'Neill and Fenian Secretary of War Michael Kerwin were struggling to raise money for another invasion, Fenians in Harrisburg, Newark, Columbus, Jamestown, Cleveland and Baltimore were celebrating.[74] In Buffalo,
twenty-five thousand people gathered at the end of July.[75] In early September,
when a planned Fenian picnic in Montreal was canceled by Canadian authori-

ties, Fenians in Cleveland and Baltimore more than made up for it.[76] This pattern continued in subsequent years. In May 1870, weeks before John O'Neill would face those empty train cars in St. Albans, Bay Area Fenians had no trouble mustering twelve thousand people to a picnic in Redwood City.[77]

Picnics had always been a way of bringing the triumphs of Fenianism to larger audiences. Increasingly, this took the form of pure entertainment.[78] In perhaps the most striking conflation of patriotism and pastime, Fenian supporters in Buffalo planned a picnic to coincide with John O'Neill's trial in Buffalo in August 1866. Originally, they had hoped to hold this on Grand Island, in the Niagara River, but authorities, worried about provoking their Canadian neighbors, relocated it to the city.[79] Nevertheless, the picnic featured a parade of various civic societies "carrying the Irish and American colors," a speech by O'Neill—who stopped by after his trial ended in a nolle prosequi—and a recreation of the fight at Ridgeway, "in which the Canadians figured ludicrously."[80] As the years went on, and Fenians met with fewer and fewer military successes, these "sham battles" became more about commemoration than inspiration: In September 1867, Fenian reenactors refought the battle of Ridgeway in Jones's Wood.[81] Here again the Fenians were reflecting an American, rather than an Irish, practice: Sham battles would become a fixture of picnics during the second half of the nineteenth century. But their popularity at Fenian events highlights the increasing disconnection between Fenian supporters and Fenian leadership.

That disconnection also meant that the money raised at successful picnics did not always make it into official Fenian coffers. In the Finance Committee's Report to the Fifth National Fenian Congress in September 1866, acting Secretary of the Treasury P. W. Dunne reported with dismay that "a very small amount" of the total receipts (amounting to more than $200,000) came from the West, despite a good deal of picnic activity: "The Western Circles must have a large amount of funds on hand," he mused.[82] None of this should necessarily suggest corruption. Quite possibly, local picnic organizers often found that their lavish entertainments cost a good deal more than they had expected. Undoubtedly some profits were withheld for future picnics. On the other hand, this lack of communication between Fenian leaders and the wider membership does suggest a broader disconnection.

The expansive version of Fenianism expressed most clearly at these picnics did not imply a lack of commitment to the cause of Irish freedom, or an ignorance or apathy among the working- and middle-class Irish-Americans who attended these events. On the contrary: reporters were repeatedly struck by how well-informed and passionate the attendees at picnics were. At one giant picnic in Jones's Wood, the reporter for the *New York Herald* was impressed when the gates opened and "the men gave the seductive whiskey stands the go-by, and the women and children passed confectionary booths without so much as a glance," preferring instead to "[talk] earnestly about 'ould Ireland' and the prospects of the Brotherhood." "It was a peculiar kind of holiday for them," he concluded, approvingly.[83]

"Peculiar" but not inexplicable. By failing to understand how Irish-American Fenians could combine politics and recreation, whiskey or no whiskey, the reporter was making the same mistake that many Fenian leaders did. On one level, the disconnection between Irish Fenian leaders and their Irish-American counterparts is straightforward: the two operated in completely different legal and political environments. Attending a Fenian gathering in Buffalo or Cincinnati was a fun night out; attending one in Limerick or Birmingham or Toronto or Sydney was treason. The difference goes a long way to explaining why Fenian leaders in Ireland—and to some extent, their Irish-American counterparts, some of whom were recent immigrants—so misjudged their followers. Allying oneself with the movement within the British Empire, as opposed to within the United States, implied a completely different kind of commitment to the cause.

In some respects, British, Canadian, or Australian Fenians had more in common with the black fraternal associations and secret societies of the American South than they did with their own Irish-American "Brothers."[84] The network of "obligations and responsibilities of kinship" that had sustained African American slaves against their masters, the wide range of "'societies, leagues, combinations, meetings, with little of routine or record, but much of speech making and sage counsel'" that marked the end of the war for many freedmen, or the widespread paranoia that met black drilling companies during Reconstruction, would not have been unfamiliar to that generation of Fenian leaders that operated within the borders of the British Empire.[85] Fenians in the British Empire faced repression from an organized state seeking to secure its territory, whereas southern freedpeople confronted a more decentralized campaign of racial violence embodied in the Ku Klux Klan. But the two were similar in their difference from the situation of Irish Americans in the North and the South, who were remarkably free to engage in public demonstrations and even failed military uprisings. Irish-American Fenians in Memphis, Tennessee would dramatically underscore this difference in the riot of 1866.[86]

The problem was that, by the 1860s, the vast majority of the attendees at Irish-American Fenian picnics could not relate to the experience of Irish Fenians at all. Most had never known what it meant to be outlawed; others had likely forgotten. Fenian leaders had misjudged the extent to which Irish-Americans had been changed by their adopted home. Picnics offered Reconstruction-era Irish-Americans the opportunity to contribute to a cause they believed in, in a way that linked their commitment to Ireland to their increasing integration into America. During Reconstruction, Fenian picnics represented a kind of middle ground where the cause of Ireland morphed into a general celebration of liberty that could, at moments, even start to bring Irish Americans into the orbit of the Republican Party. Increasingly, these were people interested in building a new country rather than destroying an old one.

This at least partially explains why O'Neill and the others made such a profound miscalculation about the numbers of men who would "come up" to join their attempts at invasion. From the outside, the thousands of people cheering rhetorical assaults on Britain at massive Fenian picnics could look like an army-in-waiting. But O'Neill and the others were, to some extent, stuck in a pre-war mindset. The vast majority of these postbellum picnickers were not, as Fenian leaders hoped and Fenianism's enemies feared, Irish revolutionaries. They were Irish-Americans.

Notes

The author thanks the contributors to this volume and the participants in the History Department Colloquium at the University of New Mexico and the American Conference for Irish Studies for comments on an earlier version of this essay.

1. John O'Neill, *Official Report of Gen. John O'Neill, President of the Fenian Brotherhood; On the Attempt to Invade Canada, May 25th, 1870* (New York: John J. Foster, 1870), 15.

2. Ibid., 16–17.

3. Ibid., 4, 5.

4. Ibid., 16.

5. Ibid., 18.

6. Ibid.

7. Ibid.

8. Henry le Caron, *Twenty-Five Years in The Secret Service: The Recollections of a Spy* (London: William Heinemann, 1892), 82. Le Caron's influence in derailing the invasion is somewhat belied by O'Neill's admission that he relied on "newspapers and telegraphic reports" to track the movements of "his" men. See O'Neill, 17. On le Caron, see Peter Edwards, *Delusion: British Agent in the Fenian Ranks* (Toronto: Key Porter Books, 2008), and Joseph Clark, "The Spy Who Came in from the Coalfield: A British Spy in Illinois," *Journal of Illinois History* 10, no. 2 (Summer 2007): 90–106.

9. See Richard P. Davis, *The Young Ireland Movement* (Dublin: Gill and Macmillan, 1988); Robert Sloan, *William Smith O'Brien and the Young Ireland Rebellion of 1848* (Dublin: Four Courts Press, 2000); Christine Kinealy, *Repeal and Revolution: 1848 in*

Ireland (Manchester: Manchester University Press, 2009); Seamus Deane, "The Famine and Young Ireland" in *The Field Day Anthology of Irish Literature* 1 (1991): 115–21; John Belchem, "Nationalism, republicanism and exile: Irish emigrants and the revolutions of 1848," *Past and Present* 146, no. 1 (February 1995): 103–35.

10. See Marta Ramón, *A Provisional Dictator: James Stephens and the Fenian Movement* (Dublin: University College Dublin Press, 2007), William D'Arcy, *The Fenian Movement in the United States 1858–1886* (Washington, D.C.: Catholic University of American Press, 1947); W. S. Neidhart, *Fenianism in North America* (University Park: Pennsylvania University Press, 1975); Hereward Senior, "The Place of Fenianism in the Irish Republican Tradition," *University Review* 4, no. 3 (Winter 1967): 250–59; Richard Davis, "The IRB: 'A Natural Outcome of Young Irelandism?' " *History Ireland* 16, no. 6 (November/December 2008): 21–23.

11. As the most prominent former Confederate supporter active in the Fenians, John Mitchel is a crucial figure. See Bryan P. McGovern, *John Mitchel: Irish Nationalist, Southern Secessionist* (Knoxville: University of Tennessee Press, 2009). For the more general role of Irish Americans in the Confederacy, see David T. Gleeson, *The Green and the Gray* (Chapel Hill: University of North Carolina Press, 2013); Chapter 6 captures the world in which Southern Fenians operated. Finally, for an examination of how Mitchel's experience was by no means unique, see Paul Quigley's *Shifting Grounds: Nationalism and the American South, 1848–1865* (New York: Oxford University Press, 2011).

12. See Robert Kee, *The Green Flag: A History of Irish Nationalism* (London: Penguin, 2000), Chapters 18 and 19; Leon Ó Broin, *Fenian Fever: An Anglo-American Dilemma* (New York University Press, 1971); Joseph O'Neill, *The Manchester Martyrs* (Mercier Press, 2012).

13. David A. Wilson, "Was Patrick James Whelan a Fenian and Did He Assassinate Thomas D'Arcy McGee?" in David A. Wilson, ed., *Irish Nationalism in Canada* (Montreal: McGill-Queen's University Press, 2009).

14. Some recent cases, other than the ones discussed later, include David Sim, "Filibusters, Fenians and a Contested Neutrality: The Irish Question and U.S. Diplomacy, 1848–1871," *American Nineteenth Century History* 12, no. 3 (2011); Brian Jenkins, *Irish Nationalism and the British State: From Repeal to Revolutionary Nationalism* (McGill/Queens University Press, 2006).

15. The most important work in this tradition is Thomas Brown, *Irish-American Nationalism, 1870–1890* (Philadelphia: J. P. Lippincott, 1966). Perhaps ironically, historians of Fenianism in Canada—where the movement was much more proscribed than in the United States—have moved ahead of their U.S. counterparts in capturing the experience of common Fenians. See David A. Wilson, *Thomas D'Arcy McGee: The Extreme Moderate, 1857–1868* (McGill/Queens University Press, 2011); *Irish Nationalism in Canada* (McGill-Queens University Press, 2009). For work that places Fenians in the broader context of U.S.-Canada relations and the politics of policing in liberal states, see Brian Jenkins, *The Fenian Problem: Insurgency and Terrorism in a Liberal State, 1858–1874* (McGill-Queens University Press, 2008); *Fenians and Anglo-American Relations During Reconstruction* (Ithaca: Cornell University Press, 1970). Canadian historians also dominate the field when it comes to narrative and military histories of the Fenians:

See Peter Vronsky, *Ridgeway: The American Fenian Invasion and the 1866 Battle That Made Canada* (Toronto: Penguin Global, 2012); and Robert Dallison, *Turning Back the Fenians: New Brunswick's Last Colonial Campaign* (Fredericton, New Brunswick: Goose Lane Editions, 2006). Historians of Fenianism in Ireland and Britain have also begun to pay attention to a broader spectrum of Fenian activities in those countries, thanks to the pioneering work of R. V. Comerford. See R. V. Comerford, "Patriotism as pastime: the appeal of fenianism in the mid-1860s," *Irish Historical Studies* 22, no. 86 (September 1980): 239–50, and *The Fenians in Context: Irish Politics and Society, 1848–1882* (Dublin, 1985). For a critical review and a response by Comerford, see John Newsinger, "Fenianism Revisited: Pastime or Revolutionary Movement?" *Saothar* 17 (1992): 46–52, and R. V. Comerford, "Comprehending the Fenians," *Saothar* 17 (1992): 52–56.

16. Kerby A. Miller, *Emigrants and Exiles: Ireland and the Irish Exodus to North America* (New York: Oxford University Press, 1985), 342. Miller's view influenced many subsequent scholars, sometimes in unexpected ways: Many scholars of "whiteness," in particular, have rooted their arguments in Irish-American disaffection and alienation. See Matthew Frye Jacobson, *Whiteness of a Different Color: European Immigrants and the Alchemy of Race* (Cambridge: Harvard University Press, 1998); David Roediger, *The Wages of Whiteness* (London: Verso, 1991); Noel Ignatiev, *How the Irish Became White* (New York: Routledge, 2008). For a counter-argument, making the case that support for Irish nationalism and economic and social success could mutually reinforce each other, see Christian G. Samito, *Becoming American Under Fire: Irish Americans, African Americans, and the Politics of Citizenship During the Civil War Era* (Ithaca: Cornell University Press, 2011). And for a counter-argument to that counter-argument, demonstrating the complexity and, at times, incompatibility of Irish-American allegiances during the war, see Susannah J. Ural, *The Harp and the Eagle* (New York: NYU Press, 2006).

17. Patrick Steward and Bryan McGovern, *The Fenians: Irish Rebellion in the Atlantic World, 1858–1876* (Knoxville: University of Tennessee Press, 2013).

18. Mitchell Snay, *Fenians, Freedmen and Southern Whites* (Baton Rouge: Louisiana State University Press, 2007), 49. See also Snay's "The Imagined Republic: The Fenians, Irish American Nationalism, and the Political Culture of Reconstruction" in *Proceedings of the American Antiquarian Society* 112, no. 2 (2002): 291–313.

19. See R. A. Burchell, *The San Francisco Irish, 1848–1880* (Berkeley: University of California Press, 1980); the essays in James P. Walsh, ed., *The San Francisco Irish, 1850–1976* (San Francisco: Irish Literary and Historical Society, 1978); and Timothy J. Sarbaugh, "The Irish in the West: An Ethnic Tradition of Enterprise and Innovation, 1848–1991," *Journal of the West* 31, no. 2 (1992).

20. See Snay, Chapter 2, passim.

21. Mary P. Ryan, *Civic Wars: Democracy and Public Life in the American City During the Nineteenth Century* (Berkeley: University of California Press, 1997), 10.

22. Bryan P. McGovern, *John Mitchel: Irish Nationalist, Southern Secessionist* (Knoxville: University of Tennessee Press, 2009), 193.

23. Wilson, "Was Patrick James Whelan a Fenian?," 59.

24. See M. J. Kelly, *The Fenian Ideal and Irish Nationalism, 1882–1916* (Woodbridge: Boydell, 2006).

25. Samito, *op. cit*, is particularly insightful here.

26. Finley Peter Dunne, "The Freedom Picnic," in *Mr. Dooley in the Hearts of His Countrymen* (Boston: Small, Maynard & Company, 1898), 92.

27. "Official Monthly Circular—Financial Statement, No. 6, Headquarters, Fenian Brotherhood, May 10–June 10, 1865," Fenian Brotherhood Records, Catholic University of America, http://dspace.wrlc.org/view/ImgViewer?url=http://dspace.wrlc.org/doc/manifest/2041/4885.

28. Steward and McGovern, 79–80.

29. Dave Hannigan, *De Valera in America: The Rebel President and the Making of Irish Independence* (New York: Palgrave Macmillan, 2010).

30. "Fenian Brotherhood," *Newark Daily Advertiser*, May 27, 1865.

31. "The Fenians," *New York Herald*, July 24, 1865.

32. "Ball and Gift Distribution of the Fenian Brotherhood," *Daily Evening Bulletin*, March 14, 1865.

33. "Grand Ball of the Fenian Sisterhood at Buffalo," *Daily Age*, November 23, 1865.

34. "Pleasure in Anticipation," *Macon Daily Telegraph*, January 16, 1866.

35. "Grand Ball of the Fenian Brotherhood," *Bennington Banner*, December 20, 1866.

36. "Fenian Ball," *Jackson Daily Citizen*, September 5, 1866.

37. "First Annual Pic-nic of the Fenian Brotherhood," *Albany Argus*, July 13, 1865.

38. Brian P. Clarke, *Piety and Nationalism: Lay Voluntary Associations and the Creation of an Irish-Catholic Community in Toronto, 1850–1895* (Montreal: McGill-Queens University Press, 1993), 170.

39. Daly, 59. "Celebration of the Fourth of July, 1865, in Lowell," *Lowell Daily Citizen and News*, July 1, 1865.

40. "The Nation's Holiday," *Connecticut Courant*, July 8, 1865.

41. "Fourth of July Excursion: The Fenian Guard," *Morning Oregonian*, June 17, 1867.

42. "The Irish Republic," *New York Herald*, May 16, 1866.

43. "Receipt from Muldoon Brothers to Fenian Picnic," July 18, 1867, Fenian Brotherhood Collection, American Catholic Historical Society, http://digital.library.villanova.edu/Item/vudl:249327.

44. Receipt from Miles Jones & Sons, July 1867," Fenian Brotherhood Collection, American Catholic Historical Society, http://digital.library.villanova.edu/Item/vudl:249439.

45. "Mammoth Picnic of the Fenian Brotherhood," *Cincinnati Daily Enquirer*, May 23, 1865.

46. "The Fenian Picnic!" *Morning Oregonian*, May 1, 1866.

47. "The Fenian Picnic," *New Orleans Times*, May 15, 1865.

48. See Brookins's chapter in this volume.

49. "The Fenians in New York," *The Daily Age*, July 27, 1865.

50. "Success of the Fenian Picnic," *New Orleans Times*, May 14, 1866.

51. "The Fenian Picnic," *The Daily Picayune*, May 15, 1866.

52. "Town Talk's Article on the Fenians," *New Orleans Times*, July 26, 1865.

53. "The Donnybrook Fair in Chicago," *Boston Herald*, August 17, 1867.

54. "General News," *Buffalo Express*, August 1, 1867; *New-York Tribune*, October 12, 1867.

55. "Great Fenian Pic-Nic," *Albany Evening Journal*, August 21, 1866.

56. "The Fenians," *New York Herald*, September 25, 1866.

57. "Report of Trustees of the Fair of the Fenian Sisterhood," *New York Herald*, June 10, 1866.

58. "The Fenians in New York," *The Daily Age*, July 26, 1865.

59. "Picnic and Excursion in Aid of the Cause of Irish Liberty," *Plain Dealer*, September 20, 1864.

60. "Brigadier General Kiernan," *Plain Dealer*, September 28, 1864.

61. Eric Foner, *Reconstruction: America's Unfinished Revolution, 1863–1877* (New York: HarperCollins, 2014), 242.

62. "Gathering of the Fenians," *The Sun*, September 13, 1866.

63. See Snay, "Imagined Republic," and his *Fenians, Freedmen and Southern Whites*, 43–47.

64. "New Political Platform—Coalition Between the Fenians and the Republicans," *Commercial Advertiser*, July 14, 1866.

65. "The Fenians," *Cincinnati Daily Gazette*, August 16, 1866.

66. "Wooing by Insult," *Weekly Patriot and Union*, September 6, 1866.

67. "From New York," *Cincinnati Daily Gazette*, August 24, 1869.

68. "Grand Fenian Picnic at Framingham," *Boston Daily Journal*, August 27, 1866.

69. "The Fenians' Picnic on Staten Island," *New York Herald*, October 9, 1866.

70. "St. Patrick's Day," *Cincinnati Daily Enquirer*, February 17, 1867.

71. Steward and McGovern, 192, and see also David A. Wilson, "Was Patrick J. Whelan a Fenian?"

72. "The Fenian Guard," *Morning Oregonian*, May 23, 1868, 2. In the end, the picnic had to be postponed, but not out of respect for Barrett—Portland was having an unusually wet "picnic season."

73. "Fenian Picnic—Civil and Military," *Cincinnati Daily Enquirer*, September 6, 1868.

74. "Brevities," *New York Herald*, June 14, 1868; "From Columbus," *Cincinnati Daily Gazette*, June 17, 1868, p.3; "County News," *Jamestown Journal*, June 26, 1868; "Fenian Brotherood," *Plain Dealer*, June 30, 1868; "Amusements," *The Sun*, July 27, 1868.

75. "The Fenians," *New York Herald*, July 28, 1868.

76. "Personal and Other Scraps," *Plain Dealer*, September 9, 1868; "For Ireland," *The Sun*, September 10, 1868.

77. "The Fenian Picnic," *Daily Evening Bulletin*, May 9, 1870.

78. "The Third Annual Grand Picnic of the Roberts Circle Fenian Brotherhood," *Newark Daily Advertiser*, August 1, 1866.

79. "The Fenian 'Picnic,' " *Evening Post* (New York), August 21, 1866.

80. "The Fenians," *New-York Tribune*, August 22, 1866; "Great Fenian Pic-Nic," *Albany Evening Journal*, August 22, 1866.

81. "Fenian Picnic and Sham Battle," *New York Tribune* September 13 1867; "News Items," *Providence Evening Press*, July 27, 1868.

82. "Abstract of Report of Finance Committee on Receipts and Expenditures from December 8th, 1865 to August 31st, 1866," Fenian Brotherhood Collection, American Catholic Historical Society, http://digital.library.villanova.edu/Item/vudl:248000.

83. "The Irish Republic," *New York Herald*, May 16, 1866.

84. Foner, 95, 120.

85. Steven Hahn, *A Nation Under Our Feet: Black Political Struggles in the Rural South from Slavery to the Great Migration* (Cambridge: Belknap Press of Harvard University Press, 2003), 20, 138, 172–76.

86. Steven V. Ash, *A Massacre in Memphis: The Race Riot That Shook the Nation One Year After the Civil War* (New York: Hill and Wang, 2013), 57–59, 168.

6

Incorporating German Texas

*Immigrant Nation-Building
in the Southwest*

Julia Brookins

In April 1873, U.S. Secretary of War William Belknap stopped in San Antonio, Texas, on his inspection tour of the army's military posts on the Texas frontier. The former mayor of the city, German immigrant, engineer, and architect Wilhelm Thielepape, joined with other local German and Republican leaders in welcoming Belknap and his entourage. They had arranged a torchlight parade to the city's main outdoor recreational area, San Pedro Springs, which was run by Swiss landscape architect John Duerler. Unfortunately, gusty winds kept blowing out the torches. Following the parade, the assembled company repaired to the Menger Hotel next to the Alamo, where German immigrant and proprietor Mary Menger, recently widowed, had prepared one of her famously elegant menus for the visiting dignitary.[1]

Texas attracted significant numbers of German immigrants from before it became a U.S. state in 1845 until 1900. People from the German-speaking states formed ethnic communities that were distinctive in Texan culture and politics well into the twentieth century. Throughout the period, Germans and German Americans in Texas engaged with diverse groups of Anglos, Tejanos, and others through economic and political activity, but their geographic clustering, ethnic organizations, and use of German language, including an active German-language press, reinforced their differences from the Anglo-American cultural mainstream. During Reconstruction, German Texans and others attached new meanings to these ethnic differences. Most German Texans had supported the Union, few volunteered for Confederate military service, and some resisted the Confederate draft, in certain cases fleeing to Mexico. By contrast, Anglo-Texans had overwhelmingly supported secession, exposing themselves in immigrants' eyes as obstacles to political stability and economic progress.

Reconstruction provided members of the German-Texan minority with unprecedented opportunities to make claims to full membership and participate in the government while they retained their cultural difference. German Texans, on the whole, supported both the Republican Reconstruction policies for expanded black rights and a new Southern political order and the ongoing project of westward expansion under federal (Union) authority. Several factors shaped the roles that German Texans played in the period following the U.S. Civil War, including: a close community relationship with the U.S. army; a robust associational life in the midst of frontier social conditions; ideas about government administration formed in response to European experiences; and education levels, including training in technical subjects. These factors help explain how German Texans provided important but temporary social and political support for Republican policies, as well as long-term ideological backing and some trained personnel in service of Union authority in the Southwest.

German immigrants in Texas did not settle indifferently on land claimed by the United States. They and their descendants did not just seek formal U.S. citizenship, but went further to support nation-building. Individuals advocated and took responsibility for assisting the U.S. economic and political consolidation in the West. They not only accepted American political and legal institutions, formal naturalization, and participation in local self-government; they also endorsed the rhetoric and reality of the nation's growth in the world as a vital mission for humanity, one in which they and other immigrants could and should participate.

In the U.S. West, the Reconstruction agenda gave urgency and a new political form to processes of federal consolidation that had been reshaping the region for many years. Recent historiography of the post-war period in the United States has described the ways that conquering and incorporating western lands had already exposed some of the same divisive questions that the North-South conflict brought to the fore. Whereas earlier histories tended to emphasize Reconstruction in the East and discussed western incorporation as a separate, and somewhat subordinate, development, a number of historians have recently found ways to analyze these two processes as interconnected. Elliott West, for example, has reframed the long-term centralization of national authority into a "Greater Reconstruction," which encompassed the Civil War and the conquest of the far west, lasting from the annexation of Texas in 1845 to the Nez Perce War and the end of Reconstruction in 1877.[2] Heather Cox Richardson has emphasized the extent to which a new ideology centered on the middle class arose to address the politics of Reconstruction and of western consolidation.[3] The realities of territorial expansion alongside foreign immigration in the West ensured that questions about how big and diverse a republic could be, how to make federalism dynamic as new states came into being, and how to define citizenship were long important to the region.[4] This was especially true in the borderlands of Texas, where complex and highly mobile communities evolved under a succession of governments. The case of the German ethnic community in Texas allows us to see how one set of transnational actors tried to answer these questions from within a state that was deeply involved in both major developments of the period.

Texas had seen repeated upheavals that accompanied changes in sovereignty between 1800 and 1865. It went from a frontier region of New Spain to part of newly independent Mexico in 1821, only to break away into a separate republic in 1836 before successfully joining the United States in 1845. In 1861 Texas seceded to join the Confederacy. These changes were symptomatic of the Texan region's shifting position in the conflicts that accompanied U.S. territorial conquests. They also point to wrenching social and demographic transitions that would eventually allow Washington to consolidate its control over those vast lands. By 1836, Anglo-American migrants from the South and the North were numerically dominant in Texas. Throughout the nineteenth century, they interacted with Indians, Tejanos (native Hispanic Texans), African Americans, and Mexicans, as well as European immigrants.[5]

Texas was the lynchpin of the United States' continental empire in the mid-nineteenth century, connecting plantation slavery and Northeastern capital to the Hispanic and indigenous peoples of the arid, mineral-rich Southwest. Consolidating U.S. authority there was difficult. In a unique arrangement, the U.S. government allowed the Texas state government to retain ownership of all public lands, meaning the state also kept significant leverage in managing American Indian populations.[6] The state of Texas during the nineteenth century constituted a nation within the nation and an empire within an empire.[7] Anglo-American Texans pressed their boundary claims against neighbors on all sides, both domestic (Louisiana, New Mexico) and foreign (Mexico).[8] Impractical to govern as a unit, it stretched 800 miles from Galveston to El Paso and dwarfed available means for transport, communication, and defense. There were (and still are) many distinct regions within Texas's borders, each with a different human ecology.[9]

Postbellum political opportunities for German migrants and their continuing distinction from Anglo-Americans have received relatively little attention in a Texas Reconstruction historiography which, understandably, focuses on the conflict among the state's larger groups. Recent scholarship on Reconstruction Texas draws out the period's deep changes, political realignments, and widespread violence. There have been a number of significant studies since 2000 that build a strong but incomplete picture of post-war society. Much of the recent historiography is constructed around a model of groups in violent conflict with each other: Republicans and former Confederates, former slave-owners and freedmen, Anglos and Mexicans. Historians use terms such as pandemonium, turmoil, mayhem, and, of course violence to evoke the troubled post-war years.[10] Most do not consider European immigrants as important and distinctive players, despite the actual growth of immigration from Germany after the war and the continuing prominence of Germans in Texas's economic, political, and cultural life. None offers a conceptual framework for understanding the ongoing divisions between Anglos and Germans or how Reconstruction affected those distinctions.[11]

German-speaking immigrants to Texas in the nineteenth century were part of a complex multi-ethnic and multi-racial society. Sizeable numbers of people from the German states began to move to Texas around 1844, when a group of princes—called the Society for the Protection of German Immigrants, or Adelsverein—recruited emigrants from the crowded villages of the German states to found colonies on a large land grant in western Texas. The organizers were motivated by philanthropy and expected profits from land appreciation. Due in part to poor logistics and planning, as well as a lack of accurate information about the grant in which they had invested, they quickly went into debt. Many of their immigrants died of exposure and disease on the shores of the Gulf of Mexico.[12] Notwithstanding these failures, by 1850 Texas counted over 8,000 German-born individuals among its population.[13]

Despite the Adelsverein's rapid collapse, the initial colonies prompted chain migrations. The first waves of settlers became farmers concentrated, first, in a line east and north from Austin to Houston and the port city of Galveston in the zone of plantation agriculture, and second, in frontier agricultural settlements in the Hill Country north and west of San Antonio, distant from slave agriculture and closer to American Indian and Hispanic populations.[14] By 1850, German-born individuals formed over 30 percent of the non-native (i.e., not Tejano), free population in nine counties. While most of these immigrants had agricultural backgrounds, many also possessed valuable artisanal or craft skills and were accustomed to the more concentrated farming settlements common in Germany. As a result, Germans were disproportionately resident in cities, especially San Antonio, Galveston, Houston, and later Austin. German immigration produced the city of New Braunfels, the town of Fredericksburg, and many smaller settlements. Germans constituted just over 5 percent of the state's white population in 1850 (which included Tejanos and Mexicans), but 25 percent of its urban population. Urbanism magnified Germans' exposure to other groups in the state and their visibility to outsiders.[15]

The interdependence of the communities of German settlers in the Hill Country and the U.S. Army shaped German-speaking migrants' experiences and opinions of the Union and the U.S. Civil War. Between the end of the U.S.-Mexican War in 1848 and the closing of the Hill Country forts by the 1880s, federal forces tried to protect the settlers of the area militarily from Indian (mainly Comanche and Kiowa) raiding, from attacks by bandits, and from any threats from across the Mexican border. The security threats could be real and deadly, especially for those who lived on isolated farms. Many Germans dreaded secession, as it meant the withdrawal of nearby troops.[16]

Except during the Civil War, the Union Army continued to occupy an important role in day-to-day life in German communities, particularly those near the frontier.[17] The give-and-take in the German-Army relationship had two main aspects: the Army offered security and economic opportunities in fulfilling its frontier functions, and the German community offered individual public servants as well as civic and social networks through its extensive and well established organizations, including hotels and schools.

Along with security, the Army provided business to many in the area of Fredericksburg and San Antonio. The U.S. Army spent around 6 percent of its national budget in Texas in the 1850s, and in the 1870s, spending $27.9 million from 1869 to 1879. This included contracting for food and supplies, the purchase of horses and other stock, construction, rents, civilian employment, and contracting for the transportation of goods to the forts. The number of civilian employees in the Department of Texas fluctuated widely, from just twenty-six in 1849 to 488 in 1851 and 230 in 1878; wages usually included daily rations and were higher than similar, private employment.[18] Many of the settlers who drove ox-teams for the army were Germans.[19] Some of the blacksmiths, teamsters, clerks, and other workers were hired locally, while others might have been recruited from distant cities. Workers and soldiers all spent at least part of their pay in the towns nearest the posts. The money the army spent on shipping raw materials for construction and provisions developed the freighting industry and made San Antonio the major commercial hub for the Texas frontier.[20] Army officers and their families tended to stay at German hotels in San Antonio and Fredericksburg on their way to frontier posts.[21]

Antebellum German immigrants were known as a pro-Union element within the South. Like Tejanos and Mexicans, German Texans tended to vote for

Democratic candidates, especially after a crisis of political nativism in 1855.[22] But support for the Democrats did not mean German immigrants were proslavery. Most Germans who settled in Texas between 1845 and 1861 tended to be indifferent or hostile to slavery.[23] Several leaders of the ethnic communities that formed in this period were liberal revolutionaries who had been exiled from Germany for their involvement in the 1848 revolutions. As the national press correctly reported, slave-holding rates among German Texans were extremely low, even in households that could have afforded the outlay.[24]

Several scholars have analyzed the forces at play in the secession choices made by Germans and other unionist-leaning populations within Texas.[25] While geographer Terry Jordan and historian Walter Buenger have argued that the focus on Germans as strong anti-slavery unionists distorted the record,[26] more recently Walter Kamphoefner's work with precinct-level voting results on the secession question has pinpointed Unionist support more narrowly, and this has revealed that most of the pro-union votes throughout central Texas could be attributed to each county's German residents (along with Mexican and Tejano residents in Bexar County). With the exception of Comal County, even counties where secession narrowly won, like Bexar, were polarized at the precinct level. Anglo precincts recorded very high levels of support for secession, but there was little, if any, among the German voters.[27] Among the reasons for unionism among Texas Germans was a reluctance to give up the frontier protection of the U.S. Army, low slave-holding rates, and perhaps a more strongly felt duty to the United States as naturalized citizens.

During the Civil War, immigrant settlements across Texas experienced unwelcome attention from Confederate authorities. When few German men volunteered for military service, conscription and martial law were instituted in both the western Hill Country areas and in the eastern German belt. German men, as well as some women and children, headed to Mexico or to larger towns like San Antonio for safety in numbers, as the Hill Country settlements became the scene of a number of lynchings, often by Texas state troops (as opposed to Confederate troops). A widely publicized battle in the summer of 1862 killed several dozen young German Unionists who were fleeing to Mexico. When a few of the Germans survived to report that nine wounded prisoners were shot by one of the officers of the Texas State troops, this incident came to be known as the Nueces Massacre. The Nueces Massacre served as a rallying cry against the Confederacy and helped to radicalize some of the German community during the war. The incident solidified bitterness against the Confederacy in certain localities well into the twentieth century.[28] There were important costs for real and perceived

German Unionism, but there would be correspondingly important rewards for German Texans during Reconstruction. The Union victory marked significant changes for German immigrants. Their access to power increased with slave emancipation and with new immigrants buying lands in the plantation region of East Texas, as well as the imposition of temporary political disabilities on many Anglo-Texan Confederates.

At the end of the U.S. Civil War, the Union Army's priorities in Texas were to reassert federal control over the settled areas of the state, set up a loyal government, oversee the end of slavery, and secure the Indian and Mexican frontiers against criminal and military attacks. The military again became critical to the state's economy, helping its recovery. Spending resumed, but the army was now, awkwardly, both an occupying and a protective force. In the midst of this complex situation, a rapid demobilization constrained Union commanders who sought meaningful social change. The number of troops available within Texas went from 39,000 in 1865 to just 8,500 in 1866 and 4,733 the following year. As one historian of the Texas Reconstruction Army concluded, "in reality there was little Federal presence beyond the fringes of Texas." In order to meet their objectives, Army officers needed the help of local individuals. Members of the Army looked to German Texans as reliable allies in regaining control of the state and in reestablishing governance in the chaotic post-war environment.[29]

German Texans, including some who had departed for Europe or Mexico and who returned after the war, now faced altered circumstances. Emboldened by Union victory and the promise of an occupying Northern army, they recognized their unusual opportunity to play a prominent role in mainstream postbellum political life. One historian has called Reconstruction "the chance of a lifetime" for many Germans in Texas. This opportunity coincided with and reinforced the broader national pivot: from debates on expanding slavery to a wholesale effort to incorporate and exploit western lands.[30]

Some prominent German-speaking Unionists tried to rework mainstream, Anglo-Confederate society in Texas into a more open and orderly polity of broader political participation and economic opportunity. Relieved at the cessation of hostilities, these optimistic and confident Germans accepted military appointments to government offices during the federal occupation, ran for elected office, served in the state constitutional conventions (1866, 1868–69, and 1875), and used their Republican newspapers to influence opinion on the questions of Reconstruction. Reconstruction also marked an ongoing shift for some German Texans away from state-level loyalties and toward national citizenship. German Texans asked themselves whether they could best embody their loyalty by staying in Texas, leaving for the North, or, most radically, by dividing Texas into multiple states.

The careers of four German immigrant men who were skilled and respected enough to achieve public prominence demonstrate how Texas's German communities transitioned from exile and persecution into new opportunities for political engagement and office-holding after 1865. Gen. J. J. Reynolds, the occupation military commander, appointed Wilhelm Thielepape mayor of San Antonio; Edward Degener was elected a U.S. Representative; and Jacob Kuechler oversaw the biggest business in the state as Commissioner of the General Land Office. August Siemering also took advantage of the new meanings attached to German-ness in the post-war Texan public sphere and launched three new newspapers to serve English- and German-speaking publics. He even wrote a novel about the German-Texan war experience that won a national German-American book prize.[31]

The trajectories of these four local elites reveal different views on the changing meaning of German ethnicity in post-war Texas. They show the unique and temporary nature of political opportunity in the Reconstruction period, as well as the permanent end of the German Texans' pre-war marginality. While mainstream Anglo-Texan society accommodated itself at least partially to the persistent cultural differences of Germans in their midst, the first generation of German Texan leaders conceded the defeat of their ambitions to establish a truly new, liberal society at the United States' southwestern frontier. Degener, Kuechler, Thielepape, and Siemering emerged from the war ready to fight for their own kind of Union. By the mid-1870s, though, each had made a separate peace with his adopted state and nation.

It took the U.S. Army two years to move its headquarters inland from its wartime beachhead in Galveston to the political capital in Austin and then to its previous headquarters in San Antonio.[32] The Union Army also needed to rebuild the supply networks and system of posts, stables, armories, and warehouses that had been abandoned to Confederates. While physical damage to Texas had been mild in comparison to that in other Confederate states, it was nonetheless a *tabula rasa* for frontier army operations.[33]

German Texans welcomed renewed contact with the Union Army and showed the troops warm hospitality.[34] One local German Texan even became engaged to a Union officer.[35] German hotelier William Menger provided a temporary home for officers in his San Antonio hotel and supplied provisions for the army's horses and mules.[36] Menger mobilized considerable resources to hold onto the city's advantageous position as a center of the army network in the Southwest. The Army's move back to San Antonio was not a foregone conclusion, nor was its decision to stay there. The Army initially merely rented four buildings in San Antonio, including the Alamo.[37] In 1867, residents received the news that the Army ordered the headquarters to move to another city because of inadequate facilities. San Antonio locals, including Germans, were eager to keep the Army in the city for its economic impact and because Unionists benefited from the added security and direct ties to Washington, D.C., provided by face-to-face relationships with officers. In response to the army's threatened departure, William Menger commissioned a local German contractor to build a warehouse for the Army between his hotel and the San Antonio River at a cost of over twenty thousand dollars.[38]

The Menger Hotel on Alamo Plaza had been a symbol of local civilian-military interdependence almost since its founding in 1859. German immigrants William A. and Mary Menger combined and elaborated upon the basic functions of Mary's previous boardinghouse business, and William's famous beer, which he brewed onsite with another German immigrant. One of the best-known hotels in the Southwest, renowned for its comfort and luxury, the Menger Hotel was popular with army personnel as well as civilians. Officers and their families were frequent guests; merchants seeking contracts to supply the frontier forts with hay, beef, corn, or other goods came to town to negotiate and network. The Mengers did serve Confederate customers throughout the war, but afterwards their hotel became a center of German Unionist and Republican events.[39]

German immigrants in San Antonio founded numerous voluntary associations that appealed mostly to other Germans.[40] But they also made a fabric of institutional structures that connected them to non-German groups within the city and across Texas by providing the spaces, beer, food, planning, and sometimes the agenda where many people met and interacted with each other.[41] Like some of the Fenian picnics Caleb Richardson describes in his essay in this volume, the appeal of German ethnic groups extended beyond the migrants and their families, and served a more inclusive function for the towns and cities where they held their events. The vibrancy of German social organization and the construction of physical public spaces for socializing and cultural enrichment shaped inter-ethnic contact. This phenomenon was especially consequential in the German community's relationship with the U.S. Army. San Antonio's Germans expanded on the tradition of the Hispanic plazas and created a remarkable infrastructure of civic life that in turn formed the foundation for post-war celebrations of everything from Independence Day, the Humboldt Centennial, and Juneteenth (the celebration of emancipation in Texas).[42]

To celebrate U.S. Independence Day in 1867, for example, Germans' and freedmen's organizations marched together in a large procession through the city, with the members of General Mason's Union Army command leading the way. Employees of the Army's Quartermaster's Depot followed, mounted and carrying small flags. Municipal officers and officers of Bexar County were next, followed by the two fire companies in the city, the Turners, mutual aid society members, the Laborers Association (Arbeiterverein)—all of which were German-run and composed mainly of Germans—and more than seven hundred members of the Union League, most of whom were freedpeople, as well as "some of our most prominent citizens and Union men." A column of carriages brought up the rear of this display, which the San Antonio *Express*, a Republican paper, estimated at over two thousand people. These Union-friendly residents marched through the city and returned to their starting place in front of the Menger Hotel, where the organizers had put up a speaker's stand. A lawyer named Anderson read the *Declaration of Independence*. James P. Newcomb, a white, Anglo Unionist, who had immigrated to Texas from Nova Scotia at the age of two, then read the *Emancipation Proclamation* after explaining some of its context. The *Express* boasted that it was the first time the *Proclamation* had been read publicly in Texas. A German judge and an elderly Hungarian liberal exile gave the final speeches in praise of liberty, and the crowds dispersed to enjoy various picnics around the city. In the evening the firemen held a ball for hundreds at the Turners' Hall, and the Casino Club hosted another large gathering at their facilities, where they also welcomed several military guests.[43] Together, German associations and army personnel led another large July Fourth celebration in 1868, in spite of bad weather.[44]

The tight connection between the Army and German Texan associational life was also evident in San Antonio's Casino Club and German-English School. The Casino Club (1855), a voluntary, membership association founded by Germans, served as a meeting place for Germans, the U.S. Army, and Anglo Texans. For most of this period, the Club had a policy from its inception of welcoming army officers—and only officers—from the nearby posts as guests of the club without membership.[45] The cordial relationship between the German members and Union Army guests resumed after 1865.[46] Several members of the Casino Club were also on the board of the German-English School, which left its mark on the city's leadership for a generation. In 1869, the army participated in a large, day-long public celebration and school fundraiser in honor of the 100th anniversary of the birth of Prussian scientist and explorer Alexander von Humboldt. The Humboldt Centenary program was apparently a great success, and nearly 60 years later, the city press recalled the army's participation with pride.[47]

German support for the Republican Party and its Reconstruction agenda in San Antonio was strong until internal disputes, higher taxes, and the ouster of several German officials provoked ethnic voters to become more independent after 1872. Carl Schurz's Liberal Republican movement at the national level and its critiques of the Grant administration, discussed by Alison Clark Efford's chapter in this volume, would have undermined German Texans' enthusiasm for the San Antonio Republican coalition as well. The closeness between the Army and the German elites was not always matched by warm feelings or mutual respect from the local head of the Republican Party, James Newcomb. Newcomb and his associates, including M. G. Anderson and the sharp-penned columnist Alex Sweet, referred to Germans with derision. They called German leaders "the Casino Clique," or "Bismarck" and "Kaiser," while one-time U.S. Representative Edward Degener became "old aunty" in their private correspondence. Sweet could read German and translated relevant articles for Newcomb. Newcomb and other white Republicans needed German votes but lamented that there were not more "Americans" "to represent American Republican principles."[48] Even after much of the Republican political agenda for Reconstruction had collapsed locally, the German ties to the army, now focused on western incorporation, held strong, as on the night when San Antonio hosted Secretary of War Belknap.[49]

From 1867 to 1869, a set of proposals to divide Texas into two or more states underscored German Texans sense of political influence in Republican circles, but also their naïveté. So, too, did these proposals demonstrate the complex interplay of local, state, national, and international trends during German Texans' greatest political influence. Some of the extreme former Confederates endorsed these plans, too, but they lacked support in Washington and would ultimately become lost amidst many more pressing Reconstruction issues. Plans to divide Texas were not new. They had, in fact, been proposed numerous times in the 1840s and 1850s, and were even provided for in the bill annexing Texas into the Union in 1845.[50] The enormous state was possible to administer only because so few people lived west of the Hill Country, except along the Rio Grande, where communities were tied to the towns of New Mexico.[51] The advocates for division, had they succeeded, would have drawn themselves out of their old state, dominated by Confederates, and into a new one, untainted by rebellion, with San Antonio as the capital. The post-war Unionist plan, championed by several leading Germans, allowed Unionists to envision a fresh model for frontier development under their own control, instead of the messy, unpredictable process that had evolved to that point.

The push for division indicated that Germans after the Civil War believed their aspirations and political goals diverged from those of southern Anglos. While there had been some general discussion of creating a free state out of West Texas before the war, a renewed discussion took place in German newspapers late in 1866, after slavery was off the table as an issue and the shape of Reconstruction was in question. Ferdinand Flake's *Galveston Union* and August Siemering's *Freie Presse für Texas* had a lively exchange on the plan in their pages. Siemering's paper advocated the measure against fellow German Ferdinand Flake's *Galveston Union* paper, which represented merchant interests of East Texas. Both papers were looking west to see their economic future and used analogies of unionism and unity to justify their opposite conclusions. The main features of this argument within the German Texas Unionist press was a disagreement over whether East Texan interests were thwarting the economic development of the western portions of the state, including San Antonio. The San Antonio interests argued that the East was thwarting their ambitious efforts to build railroads. They also blamed the conservative, formerly slaveholding cultural and political forces of East Texas for discouraging foreign immigration to the state.[52]

In rebuttal, the *Union* argued that the railroad concerns would build railroads when and where they thought profitable, and that this did not reflect any conspiracy or ill-will from the capitalists in Galveston or elsewhere. And, the *Union* wrote, the issue of fostering more immigration was not a regional one within the state, but a general political one. As the *Union* responded to the two main pro-division concerns, immigration and railroads, it based its opposition on three practical points. First, agitation on the subject of division would add more confusion to an already confused post-war situation. Second, the interests of the East and West were not actually incompatible. Third, division was being pushed in part by office-seeking politicians eager to create a new state government in order to multiply state bureaucracies. Flake's paper added that, ideologically, the most important reason to oppose division was that it flew in the face of the lesson of the Civil War and the spirit of the times. Even in Europe, it explained, "small-state-ness" was a thing of the past, while the principle of secession would lead states to be "dissolved into their atoms" and turn the rule of the majority into a senseless concept. "Consolidation and concentration of powers is the keyword of our time," the paper added.[53]

Notably, this discussion of the implications of national unity and state division was taking place as Bismarck was consolidating the German states through his own state-building process of Prussian dominance.[54] In light of Alison Efford's work on how the German Empire affected German-American notions of citizenship and state power, we might observe in these opposing views from the *Galveston Union* and the *Freie Presse für Texas* an emphasis on the size and imperial success of a state versus an emphasis on its democratic processes. As Efford has found, the unification of a German nation (which did not include Austria or Switzerland) under Bismarck made the late 1860s a major turning point in German-American notions of citizenship and nationality.[55]

In 1867, after Texas came under military authority, Edward Degener corresponded with the Union Army commander about putting the division question on the ballot for the new, congressionally mandated constitutional convention. He believed that the monopolistic money influence of Galveston could not be outvoted in the state as it then existed, and that East Texas representatives in Congress did not fairly advocate for the interests of the western portion of "our hitherto neglected state." In the long term, Degener wanted to levy a tonnage tax against ships entering Matagorda Bay to go toward the building of a western railroad. Before this could happen, officials had to charter companies to develop Matagorda Bay into "what nature has adapted it to be, the best port on the Mexican Gulf," i.e. better than Galveston's notoriously shallow harbor. Because it was too much to expect Galvestonians to support this project, "We have no choice but divide our State in such a shape, as to make our own legislature a Unit, and have two Senators in Washington, who will fairly stand by our interests." Degener went on to explain that the measure would not interfere with Reconstruction politics. Degener implied that, while the Reconstruction moment provided the occasion for this discussion, the real difference between East and West Texas went deeper than Civil War politics. On its surface, the disagreement was correlated with Civil War loyalties, but underneath it was about different visions for the future of the Southwest. He argued that the East Texas interests would be able to send men to the constitutional convention who had not been active in the Confederacy but were nonetheless unacceptably conservative. He also explained to Reynolds that pro-division representatives would be more successful if they went into the constitutional convention with an electoral mandate.[56]

The commander General Reynolds demurred, however, telling Degener that the ballot had to be a simple question—yes or no to the new constitutional convention. There could be nothing to distract voters from that issue, he insisted. If the convention failed to carry statewide, any results from Western Texas could be considered by Congress in Washington to advance a particular regional agenda later.[57]

A subsequent 1868 proposal was to call the new, western state Lincoln, which, as the Republican *San Antonio Express* reported, "would be able to put the seal of condemnation upon the rebellion." During the summer of 1868, the *Express* considered that Lincoln should include the land west of the Colorado River to the Rio

Grande and south of the Thirty-Second Parallel, or the Brazos River. This would amputate that part of Texas which the paper's German Republican leaders found most objectionable. In the eastern part of Texas, the *Express* explained, where former masters were unable to escape bitterness against "those who have been instrumental in depriving them of their slaves," there was no appreciation for the values of general progress and economic development: "Republicanism with them means robbery; free labor means destruction; free schools means poverty"; and as far as they were concerned, justice would only be served by reinstituting servitude. According to the *Express* "there was no middle ground" for the former slaveholders, who were "determined to rule or ruin."[58] The second post-war constitutional convention of 1868–69 eventually collapsed without much agreement, but the delegates debated the question of division, with some German delegates like Edward Degener supporting the idea.[59] There was even a state constitution drafted and printed.[60] Nothing came of the idea, but if successful, it would have put the German and Mexican communities in a much stronger demographic position relative to Anglo-Americans, and it would have reserved to the new state most of the sparsely settled and undeveloped land. The new state also would have encompassed the areas fortified by federal troops in the Indian Wars, securing for the new state the lucrative contracts for labor and provisioning that supported Texas's economy throughout the period from statehood to 1900.

These partition schemes were representative of the fleeting nature of German-Texan political power. Reconstruction in Texas, particularly the period of federal military occupation (May 1865 through March 1870), offered a few prominent German Texans unprecedented paths to political power. Simultaneously, German San Antonians were instrumental in reopening access to local networks for Union authorities by including them in German cultural life. Outside of the most heavily German counties, however, the chances for many German leaders to influence Texan society through political power narrowed after 1870, especially as former Confederates resumed widespread political participation. San Antonio's Reconstruction Mayor Thielepape and other prominent Germans departed in the years after 1865, especially after Reconstruction. These exits confirmed the shrinking space for immigrants' political activism in an Anglo-dominated state. Slavery ended with the Thirteenth Amendment, making obsolete one of the central arguments that Anglos and some Germans had used to underscore German distinctiveness up to that point.[61] Culturally, German institutions such as the Casino Club and the Menger Hotel continued to be centers of networking for important local leaders and visitors to San Antonio for decades, while the German-English School literally trained the next generation of elites from Anglo-American, Tejano, and German families in Central Texas.

The waning of German-Texan political influence coincided with a decline in their commitment to racial equality. Germans' more liberal racial attitudes during the 1850s and 1860s had emanated from substantive, conceptual differences with most Anglo Texans on the roles that minority cultures and group affiliations could play in a polity based on individual rights. The tests of the Civil War distilled these conceptual differences, and Reconstruction gave a small but vocal minority of middle-class German Texans a platform to express themselves and act on social policies. Yet white supremacist violence against black rights, generational transition, Republican factionalism, and even the unification of Germany took their toll on German Texans' racial liberalism. These forces narrowed the channels of racial liberalism's popularity and eroded its political relevance as southern white supremacy hardened into segregation and disfranchisement in the 1880s and 1890s. The vestiges of German-Texan difference remained visible into the twentieth century as scattered anomalies, but their lasting influence was modest and localized.[62]

Yet even as German-Texan political leadership faded from statewide prominence, the immigrants' active support of U.S. nation-building continued. German political ideals and cultural efforts stood out more than other aspects of ethnic distinctiveness in the heated period between the 1840s and the 1860s. Politics always existed alongside other features of the community, however, such as high levels of economic activity, technical expertise, devotion to education, and social organization. Over the course of the Reconstruction era and then after it, these other traits became the most notable features of German Texans, which in turn created a particular niche for Germans in the state. Germans' work in technical and scientific occupations and increasing economic activity suggests the breadth of immigrant settlers' contributions to U.S. nation-building in the Southwest.

By the 1870s, it was German entrepreneurs who were highly visible in their community. Visitors to Central Texas confirmed a shift away from German prominence in politics towards business. Journalist Edward King noted in his report on Texas for *Scribner's Monthly* in 1874:

The Germans have settled several thriving places west of San Antonio, the most noted of which is Fredericksburg. German and Jewish names are certainly over the doors of more than half the business houses in San Antonio;

and German or Hebrew talent conducts many vast establishments which have trade with the surrounding country, or with Mexico.[63]

German traders and merchants had long built and maintained ties to mainstream American financial and commodities networks, in part drawing on their connections to credit, goods, and information from Europe.

Immigration to Texas from the German states and other areas of Europe resumed after 1865, and even increased. The number of German-born residents was close to 20,000 in 1860, nearly 24,000 in 1870, and more than 48,000 in 1890. The total number of German Texans and natives with at least one German parent was 41,000 by 1870 and 157,272 in 1900. While the early immigrants were predominantly farmers, they were less uniformly so than Anglo-Americans in the state, and the later German immigrants tended to pursue other occupations. Artisans, craftsmen, surveyors, lithographers, engineers, doctors, and other professions important to the consolidation of administrative control in the region figure prominently in many German-Texan biographies. These skills brought from European universities quietly became instrumental in the winning of the American West.[64]

German-speakers' presence in engineering, cartography, surveying, and related scientific fields, in Texas and elsewhere, was a feature of their migration before and long after the Civil War. The mass emigration from German states resulted in a transnational dispersal of accumulated technical knowledge and methods, and an extension of scientific networks in some cases. Trained technical or scientific workers like Maria von Blücher's surveyor husband, Felix, mapmakers such as the von Rosenberg brothers, all from Prussia, and engineers such as Gustav Schleicher, a Hessian, were not in the majority, but they did skilled work that was instrumental to increasing administrative control of the region. They received their education in German schools and universities as well as during military service, which was compulsory in Prussia.

This qualified them for the demanding work in the American West, with their world-views and personal ambitions also leading them into certain types of positions, typically working for the government, mining outfits, or railroad companies. Here they found occupations—naturalist, geologist, surveyor, engineer, cartographer, draftsman, even artist—for measuring, mapping, and reorganizing western land and its resource potential. In these positions, immigrants joined Anglo-American colleagues in advancing the cause of nation-building by connecting the chaotic and often violent events of settlement to the rhetorical and bureaucratic systems that linked American communities to each other and to the nation's financial and political centers in New York and Washington. Although German immigrants were a minority, their work was of particular significance. The successful extension of bureaucratic control was one of the key enabling factors in the broad transition in the West from a political economy centered on trade to one based on land acquisition.[65]

The U.S. conquest of western North America was a joint public-private project, one that allowed many Germans to provide service to Texas from knowledge gained abroad. During the mid- to late nineteenth century, many German-speaking migrants and settlers contributed their own day-to-day work and even entire careers in service of centralizing control of the West in the hands of the U.S. government and its citizens. Some Germans were in a position to do intellectual and technical work that helped remap the spaces of the American West and Southwest into places that were known and duly recorded portions of the U.S. continental empire, and they embraced this possibility. Perhaps their early exposure to the more bureaucratic apparatus of governance in Central Europe inclined some of them to "see like a state" in ways that were less familiar to Anglo-Americans and less established within the traditions of U.S. statecraft in the decades before 1840. Technically minded German-speaking immigrants contributed to this American bureaucratization even as most of them sought greater freedom from the state surveillance and domination of political and economic life in Central Europe. Possibly they believed that the cause of individual liberty was best served by bringing the republican forms of U.S. government to bear on ever larger swaths of the earth.[66] Their Unionist credentials endeared them to the new federal regime that came with Confederate defeat.

Trained immigrants from the German and Austrian states sought out opportunities to survey, map, and engineer the Southwestern borderlands during their uneven transition to firm U.S. control between 1845 and 1890. Wilhelm Thielepape and his older brother Georg contributed their surveying skills to support themselves and their families as soon as they arrived in Texas. Other German Americans brought unique skills to Texas. Expertise in engineering and chemistry helped build the Confederate defenses at Galveston, for example. German engineers and architects contributed to infrastructure in developing cities, frontier forts, and railroads. A group of German-born miners and engineers formed the Sonora Mining and Exploring Co. A Habsburg native, Anthony Lucas, discovered oil at Spindletop in 1901. Several German settlers used their proficiency in surveying and cartography for the government. Jacob De Cordova's famous 1849 map of Texas was used by the General Land Office, where several German draftsmen worked. Ethnic political leaders contributed their knowledge in other government agencies, and even through establishing the German-language school in San Antonio.[67]

The domestic political context of German technical contributions in the Southwest put them on the side of an expanding bureaucratic state, regardless of their attitudes toward Reconstruction issues. Surveyor Jacob Kuechler—a Republican—and then engineer Johann Groos—a conservative—were each elected commissioner of the General Land Office. Former Confederate supporter Gustav Schleicher was also an engineer, surveyor, entrepreneur, socialite and disillusioned communist who contributed to work on railroads, bridges, mills, restaurants and government. These immigrants engaged in scientific work ranging from collecting climate data from tree rings to recording tidal information along the coast.[68]

In small and large ways, German immigrants in Texas aided Reconstruction and influenced the course of political and social reorganization between 1865 and 1872 while also participating in an ongoing project of national consolidation. The pivot to centralized power and military might as true expressions of national worthiness was less dramatic than in the eastern United States because those more competitive, military dimensions of nationalism were never far from the surface of daily life in the Southwest from the 1830s through the 1870s. Frontier settlement exposed immigrants to a different aspect of the U.S. state than could be seen on the streets of other cities with large German populations, such as New York or Baltimore, before the Civil War. The nation-building project was not a rhetorical exercise or merely a question of population growth and industrial expansion, but also of physical conquest of territory and an accommodation with non-American peoples.

German Texans embraced U.S. nation-building in Texas and the Southwest before, during, and after Reconstruction. Their active commitments to the longer-term processes of U.S. territorial expansion and consolidation influenced their community's position in postwar society and their understanding of the political stakes of the Reconstruction agenda. This alternative emphasis helps to account for German Texans' enthusiasm for a new order in post-Confederate Texas and for their relative quiescence as public attention reverted from questions of fairness and justice for freedmen to the conquest of the West.

One of the most insightful perspectives on the roles that German Texans played in the post-war United States comes from an unexpected source. "The Ballad of Gregorio Cortez" is a famous *corrido*, or border ballad, that circulated among Mexican and Hispanic migrants as they traveled in Northern Mexico and the U.S. Southwest in the early twentieth century. In this tale of social banditry, German immigrants' enthusiasm for settling western lands for the Union appeared as a grotesque counter-example to the Mexican hero's anti-establishment principles. As the story went, the bandit Gregorio Cortez was sentenced to prison in the United States for 99 years. He was offered release if he accepted the marriage proposal of President Lincoln's beautiful (fictional) daughter. Visiting Cortez in prison, Lincoln's daughter tries to persuade him with a vision of future wealth and freedom:

> "I have many rich farms," President Lincoln's daughter said. "They are all my own. Marry me and we will farm together."
>
> Gregorio Cortez thought about that. He could see himself already like a German, sitting on the gallery, full of ham and beer, and belching and breaking wind while a half-dozen blond cockroaches played in the yard. And he was tempted. But then he said to himself, "I can't marry a Gringo girl. We would not make a matching pair."
>
> So he decided that President Lincoln's daughter was not the woman for him, and he told her, "I thank you very much, but I cannot marry you at all."[69]

When the Mexican outlaw imagines what it would be like to "go straight" and assimilate to the United States, why does a German farmer come to mind? In the world of the ballad, Germans played the ultimate Americans: complacent, prosperous, and unquestioning. They chose to accept U.S. nationalism and their private lives stood as an endorsement of U.S. territorial conquest.

Unlike conquered Mexican-Americans, who were marginalized and discriminated against following Texan statehood, German immigrants found their way of belonging in the nineteenth-century United States. Cultural maintenance— "ham and beer" was shorthand for German cultural distinctiveness—remained an important distinguishing characteristic of German Texans through the mid-twentieth century. But this did not preclude greater roles for Germans in both Reconstruction and post-war economic development, indicated here by their association with Lincoln's legacy. Their close ties to the Union Army in Central Texas as well as their high levels of education and commercial activity had shown them a path to full American citizenship through nation-building. Their status as foreign migrants to the Southwest did not undercut their commitment to U.S. territorial conquests or to the consolidation of national, federal authority in the Southwest.

The German immigrants in Texas, despite early similarities with Tejanos—
including opposition to nativism—were participants in the structural changes
that negatively impacted indigenous Tejanos and Mexican immigrants in subsequent years. Reconstruction marked a turning point for German Texans, as their
politics melded into the mainstream. Unionism was manifest in Reconstruction
office-holding, continued Republican voting patterns in some areas, and popular
memory of the war. The meaning of this German connection to federal unionism
was never unitary or simple, particularly during the confusion of Reconstruction. But its meaning to the federal project of territorial incorporation was crys-
tallized in "The Ballad of Gregorio Cortez." While rejecting cultural assimilation,
German immigrants nevertheless became U.S. nationalists *par excellence*.

Notes

The author would like to thank the contributors to this volume for their detailed
feedback on multiple earlier drafts.

1. *Freie Presse für Texas*, April 12, 1873; Vinton Lee James, *Frontier and Pioneer, Recollections of the Early Days in San Antonio and West Texas* (San Antonio, Tex.: Press Artes
Graficas, 1938), 122–23. Sam Woolford, "Menger Was Oasis," *San Antonio Light*, February 22, 1959.

2. Elliott West, *The Last Indian War: The Nez Perce Story* (New York: Oxford University Press, 2009).

3. Heather Cox Richardson, *West from Appomattox: The Reconstruction of America
after the Civil War* (New Haven: Yale University Press, 2007).

4. Immigrants were more heavily represented in western than eastern states. In 1890,
a larger proportion of the population was foreign-born in the West (17.3 percent) than
in the United States as a whole (14.7 percent), a situation which would continue into
the twentieth century. Some western states had very high proportions of foreign-born
residents: California had a large total population, but was still thirty percent foreign-
born in 1890; in the same year immigrants made up twenty-five percent of residents in
Washington and Colorado; smaller western states such as Montana and Nevada were
thirty percent foreign-born. Elliott R. Barkan, *From All Points: America's Immigrant
West, 1870s–1952* (Bloomington: Indiana University Press, 2007), 463, 464.

5. "Census and Census Records," *Handbook of Texas Online*, (http://www.tshaonline
.org/handbook/online/articles/ulc01).

6. W. E. S. Dickerson, "Indian Reservations," *Handbook of Texas Online* http://www
.tshaonline.org/handbook/online/articles/bpi01.

7. See D. W. Meinig, *Imperial Texas: An Interpretive Essay in Cultural Geography*
(Austin: University of Texas Press, 1969).

8. Handbook of Texas Online, s.v. "Boundaries," https://www.tshaonline.org/
handbook/online/articles/mgb02.

9. Treatments of regional specificity in Texas are numerous and include David
Arreola, *Tejano South Texas: A Mexican American Cultural Province* (Austin: University

of Texas Press, 2002); Sean Kelley, *Los Brazos De Dios: A Plantation Society in the Texas Borderlands, 1821–1865* (Baton Rouge: Louisiana State University Press, 2010); William D. Carrigan, *The Making of a Lynching Culture: Violence and Vigilantism in Central Texas, 1836–1916* (Urbana: University of Illinois Press, 2004); for the early twentieth century, an elegant and concise overview is in Neil Foley, *The White Scourge: Mexicans, Blacks, and Poor Whites in Texas Cotton Culture* (Berkeley: University of California Press, 1997).

10. See, for example, Kenneth Howell, ed., *Still the Arena of the Civil War: Violence and Turmoil in Reconstruction Texas, 1865–1874* (Denton: University of North Texas Press, 2012).

11. Sean Kelley analyzes German-Anglo differences in familial and household relations along the lower Brazos River region in *Los Brazos del Dios* but does not focus on the post-war period. For the period of 1872–1884, Patrick G. Williams considers frontier, borderlands, and post-slavery issues in his analysis of white Democrats in *Beyond Redemption: Texas Democrats after Reconstruction* (College Station: Texas A&M University Press, 2007). David Johnson's painstaking narrative of a feud between a group of Germans and Anglos in the Hill Country, *The Mason County "Hoo Doo" War, 1874–1902* (Denton: University of North Texas Press, 2006), is another exception but lacks grounding in the historiographies of violence or Reconstruction. On the latter, see also Carrigan, *Making of a Lynching Culture*; Carl Moneyhon, *Texas after the Civil War: the Struggle of Reconstruction* (College Station: Texas A&M University Press, 2004); James Smallwood, Barry A. Crouch, and Larry Peacock, *Murder and Mayhem: the War of Reconstruction in Texas* (College Station: Texas A&M Press, 2003). On African Americans, see Barry A. Crouch, *The Dance of Freedom: Texas African Americans During Reconstruction* (Austin: University of Texas Press, 2007); Donald G. Nieman, "African-American Communities, Politics, and Justice: Washington County, Texas, 1865–1890," in Christopher Waldrep and Donald G. Nieman, eds., *Local Matters: Race, Crime, and Justice in the Nineteenth-Century South* (Athens, Ga.: University of Georgia Press, 2001), 201–24. The leaders of the radical and conservative camps have both received full-length biographical monographs: Kenneth Wayne Howell, *Texas Confederate, Reconstruction Democrat: James Webb Throckmorton* (College Station: Texas A&M University Press, 2008); and Carl H. Moneyhon, *Edmund J. Davis: Civil War General, Republican Leader, Reconstruction Governor* (Fort Worth: Texas Christian University Press, 2010).

12. There are many histories of the Adelsverein and early migrations. See Gilbert Giddings Benjamin, *The Germans in Texas: A Study in Immigration* (Philadelphia: University of Pennsylvania, 1909); Rudolph Biesele, *The History of the German Settlements in Texas, 1831–1861* (Austin: Von Boeckmann-Jones, 1930); Hubert G. H. Wilhelm, *Organized German Settlement and Its Effects on the Frontier of South-Central Texas* (New York: Arno Press, 1980); Chester William Geue and Ethel Hander Geue, *A New Land Beckoned: German Immigration to Texas, 1844–1847* (Waco: Texian Press, 1972); and for a German perspective, see Stefan von Senger und Etterlin, *Neu-Deutschland in Nordamerika: Massenauswanderung, nationale Gruppenansiedlungen und liberale Kolonialbewegung, 1815–1860* (Baden-Baden, Germany: Nomos, 1991), esp. 214–322, 355–68. See also Theodore Gish and Richard Spule, eds., *Eagle in the New World: German Immigration to Texas and America* (College Station: Texas A&M University Press, 1986); Beate Rese, *Texas: Ziel Deutscher Einwanderung im 19. Jahrhundert* (Pfaffenweiler, Germany: Centaurus, 1996).

13. 1850 U.S. Census figures from tables in Dagmar Ausperg-Hackert, *Deutsche Aus-wanderung nach Texas im 19. Jahrhundert* (Ph.D. dissertation, Ruhr-Universität Bochum, 1984), 56.

14. An earlier German colony around the town of Industry, in the east, was founded by Friedrich Ernst in the 1830s. Glen E. Lich, *The German Texans* (San Antonio: University of Texas Institute of Texan Cultures, 1981), 38.

15. Lich, *German Texans*, 38; Terry Jordan, "Population Origins in Texas, 1850," *Geographical Review* 59, no. 1 (January 1969): 83–103, esp. 85, 97–100; Terry Jordan, *German Seed in Texas Soil Immigrant Farmers in Nineteenth-Century Texas* (Austin: University of Texas Press, 1966), 48–53; Terry Jordan, "Germans and Blacks in Texas," in Randall M. Miller, ed., *States of Progress: Germans and Blacks in America over 300 Years, Lectures from the Tricentennial of the Germantown Protest Against Slavery* (Philadelphia: The German Society of Pennsylvania, 1989), 90.

16. On Texans' decision-making on whether to support Secession and the Confederacy, see Walter Buenger, *Secession and the Union in Texas* (Austin: University of Texas Press, 1984), and James Marten, *Texas Divided: Loyalty and Dissent in the Lone Star State, 1856–1874* (Lexington: University Press of Kentucky, 1990). On the Comanches, see Pekka Hämäläinen, *The Comanche Empire* (New Haven: Yale University Press, 2008).

17. See, for example, Esther Mueller, "Hulda Walter—In Her Life and Poetry," typescript, Walter (Hulda) Papers, Briscoe Center for American History, University of Texas Austin (hereafter CAH).

18. Thomas T. Smith, *The U.S. Army and the Texas Frontier Economy, 1845–1900* (College Station: Texas A&M University Press, 1999), 8-9, 11, 131–33.

19. Rena Mazyck Andrews, "German Pioneers in Texas: Civil War Period" (M.A. thesis, University of Chicago, 1929), 22, 21.

20. Smith, *The U.S. Army*, 10.

21. Char Miller and David R. Johnson, "The Rise of Urban Texas," in Char Miller and Heywood T. Saunders, *Urban Texas: Politics and Development* (College Station: Texas A&M University Press, 1990), 1–31, esp. 13. Menger Family Papers, University of the Incarnate Word Library, San Antonio; Subject Files, "Germans—Menger, William A.," and "Germans—Menger Hotel," Institute of Texan Cultures Library, San Antonio (hereafter ITC).

22. Buenger, *Secession and the Union*, esp. 80–105; Frantz; Mike Kingston, "Democrats in the 19th Century," in Mike Kingston et al., eds., *The Texas Almanac's Political History of Texas* (Austin: Eakin Press, 1992), 37–46.

23. Walter D. Kamphoefner, "German Texans: In the Mainstream or Backwaters of Lone Star Society?," *Yearbook of German-American Studies* 38 (2003), 119–38, esp. 120–21. See also Cornelia Küffner, "Texas-Germans' Attitudes toward Slavery: Biedermeier Sentiments and Class-consciousness in Austin, Colorado, and Fayette Counties" (M.A. thesis, University of Houston, 1994); Melvin Johnson, "A New Perspective for the Antebellum and Civil War Texas German Community" (M.A. thesis, Stephen F. Austin State University, 1993); and Lauren Ann Kattner, "Ethnicity Plus: Historical Roots of Slavery for the Germans of Louisiana and East Texas, 1719–1830" (Ph.D. dissertation, University of Texas at Austin, 1997); and Sean Kelley, *El Brazos de Dios*. On German Unionism,

Walter Buenger stresses its limits in "Secession and the Texas German Community: Editor Lindheimer vs. Editor Flake," *Southwestern Historical Quarterly* (*SWHQ*) 82, no. 4 (April 1979), 379–402. See also Buenger, *Secession and the Union*. Anne J. Bailey lays out the necessity of Confederate army intervention in "Defiant Unionists: Militant Germans in Confederate Texas," in John C. Inscoe and Robert C. Kenzer, eds., *Enemies of the Country: New Perspectives on Unionists in the Civil War South* (Athens: University of Georgia Press, 2001), 208–28. James Marten investigates attitudes toward and participation in the Confederacy in *Texas Divided*. The most prominent German-Texan abolitionist is the subject of Justine Davis Randers-Pehrson, *Adolf Douai: The Turbulent Life of a German Forty-Eighter in the Homeland and in the United States* (New York: Peter Lang, 2000). On Indians and Germans, see Karl A. Hoerig, "The Relationship between German Immigrants and the Native Peoples in Western Texas," *SWHQ* 97, no. 3 (January 1994): 422–51.

24. Walter Kamphoefner delves into the data on German slave-holding rates in "New Perspectives on Texas Germans and the Confederacy," *SWHQ* 102, no. 4 (April 1999): 441–55, esp. 442. On the press, see for example, "The German Immigration," *New York Daily Times*, January 6, 1855, 4, and "The German Loyalists," *New York Times*, March 16, 1862, 4; "Texas," *Debow's Review, Agricultural, Commercial, Industrial Progress and Resources* 23, no. 2 (August 1857): 113–32.

25. See Buenger, *Secession and the Union*; Martern, *Texas Divided*; Bailey, "Defiant Unionists"; Kamphoefner, "New Perspectives."

26. Buenger, *Secession and the Union*, 83–84; Jordan, *German Seed*.

27. Kamphoefner, "New Perspectives," esp. 448. The only major exception to this pattern was in Comal County, where the influential German newspaper editor (and botanist) in New Braunfels, Ferdinand Lindheimer, supported secession and persuaded many of his readers to follow suit. As an old-timer in Texas, Lindheimer had lived through many flag changes; he counseled others to adapt to the Confederate transition, as well. Lindheimer was subject to sustained intimidation for his southern sympathies, however.

28. See Kamphoefner, New Perspectives, 451–55. On the Nueces incident, see Stanley S. McGowen, "Battle or Massacre?: The Incident on the Nueces, August 10, 1862," *SWHQ* 104, no. 1 (July 2000), 64–86.

29. William L. Richter, *The Army in Texas during Reconstruction, 1865–1870* (College Station: Texas A&M University Press, 1987), 27. Figures from Thomas T. Smith, *The Old Army in Texas*, 104–6; Smith, *The U.S. Army and the Texas Frontier Economy*, 39–40. See also Robert Shook, "Toward a List of Reconstruction Loyalists," *SWHQ* 76, no. 3 (January 1973): 315–20.

30. Andreas Reichstein, *German Pioneers on the American Frontier: The Wagners in Texas and Illinois* (Denton: Univ. of North Texas Press, 2001), 144. The Germans' change of fortune, of course, was much less dramatic than the shift for millions of black freedpeople across the country.

31. Theodore Albrecht, "San Antonio's Singing Mayor: Wilhelm Carl August Thielepape, 1814–1904," ts. (Cleveland, Ohio: n.p., 1976); and Albrecht, "Thielepape, Wilhelm Carl August," *Handbook of Texas Online* http://www.tshaonline.org/handbook/online/

articles/fth41; ITC subject files: Germans, Thielepape. On Thielepape's mayoral administration, resignation, and departure to Chicago, see *San Antonio Express*, December 19, 1867; July 16, August 20, 1869; March 28, August 29, 1871; and January 11, 1874; *San Antonio Herald*, January 23, 1869; January 4, January 5, January 6, January 10, January 11, March 6, March 12, 1872; William Corner, *San Antonio de Bejar: A Guide and History* (San Antonio: Bainbridge & Corner, 1890), 9, 45, 50–54. On Edward Degener's life and career, see Anne W. Hooker, "Degener, Edward," *Handbook of Texas Online*, http://www.tshaonline.org/handbook/online/articles/fde28. On his prosecution for sedition during the Civil War and bitterness toward the Confederacy, see Alwyn Barr, ed., "Records of the Confederate Military Commission," *SWHQ* 73, no. 2 (October 1969): 246–68 and August Siemering, *The Germans in Texas During the Civil War: Taken from the Records of Judge August Siemering, 1876*, Helen Dietert, trans. (privately printed, 2000), 31. On his term in Congress, see Edward Degener, *Open Letter of Edward Degener, Member of the Forty-First Congress, to His Constituents* (Washington, D.C.: Congressional Globe Office, 1871). On Kuechler, see the Kuechler (Jacob) Papers, 1840–1907, CAH, and Adolf Paul Weber, *Deutsche Pioniere: zur Geschichte des Deutschtums in Texas* (San Antonio: self-published, 1894), 44–51. On Siemering's war experience, see Siemering, *The Germans in Texas During the Civil War*. On his publishing venture, see A. Siemering letter to C. H. Guenther, June 19, 1865, Guenther Papers folder, Oscar Haas Papers, 1844–1955, CAH. Karl J. R. Arndt and May E. Olson, *German Language Press of the Americas*, Vol. 1 (Munich: Verlag Dokumentation Publishers, 1976), 629–30. Frances Donecker, "San Antonio Express-News," *Handbook of Texas Online*, http://www.tshaonline.org/handbook/online/articles/ees03. August Siemering, *Ein Verfehltes Leben* (San Antonio: Freie Presse für Texas, 1870. See also his obituary, "A Texas Journalist," in *Texas Siftings* (Austin, Texas) October 6, 1883; Ella Gold, "Siemering, August," *Handbook of Texas Online*, http://www.tshaonline.org/handbook/online/articles/fsi06; and Richard L. Puglisi, "Bexar County Chief Justice August Siemering, 1830–1883," *Journal of the Life and Culture of San Antonio* online, http://www.uiw.edu/sanantonio/sapublications.html.

32. On the early occupation along the Texas Gulf Coast, see Charles Spurlin, "The World Turned Upside Down?: The Military Occupation of Victoria and Calhoun Counties, 1865–1867," in Howell, ed., *Still the Arena of the Civil War*, 113–31.

33. See maps of the army supply system in 1860–61 and 1870 in Smith, *U.S. Army and the Texas Frontier Economy*, 20–21.

34. Kamphoefner notes the regret with which some Yankees left New Braunfels, "Mainstream or Backwaters," 132.

35. See Maria von Blücher, *Maria von Blücher's Corpus Christi: Letters from the South Texas Frontier, 1849–1879*, ed. Bruce S. Cheeseman (College Station: Texas A&M University Press, 2002), 162–63

36. Clippings and Joseph A. Menger, "William A. Menger: Hotel Founder," unpublished typescript, in Subject Files, "Germans—Menger, William A.," ITC. Smith, *The U.S. Army*, 41–42.

37. *San Antonio Express*, May 18, 1869; J. E. Conrad, "Phases of the History of the San Antonio Quartermaster Depot" (n.p., 1944), San Antonio Historical Society Papers, San Antonio Public Library (hereafter SAPL).

38. *San Antonio Express*, May 18, 1869. Newspaper clipping in Subject Files, "Germans—Menger, William A.," ITC. The contractor was John Kampmann, who had also built Menger's hotel and the Casino Club and Theater; "Menger, William A." typescript, in Subject Files, "Germans—Menger, William A.," ITC.

39. Menger Family Papers; Subject Files, "Germans—Menger, William A.," and "Germans—Menger Hotel," ITC. Eleanor Stuck, "Menger Hotel," *Handbook of Texas Online* (http://www.tshaonline.org/handbook/online/articles/dgm02). On the closure during the war, see Inez Strickland Dalton, "The Menger Hotel: San Antonio's Civic and Social Center, 1859–1877," *West Texas Historical Association Year Book* 32 (October 1956), 90. See also Julia Brookins, "William Achatius Menger," in *Immigrant Entrepreneurship: German-American Business Biographies, 1720 to the Present*, vol. 2, edited by William J. Hausman. German Historical Institute, http://www.immigrantentrepreneurship.org/entry.php?rec=29.

40. Daniels, *Coming To America*, 146–47. On the German *Verienswesen* in the United States, see Heike Bungert, "Feste und das ethnische Gedächtnis: Die Festkultur der Deutsch-Amerikaner im Spannungsfeld zwischen deutscher und amerikanischer Identität, 1848–1914" (Habilitation, Köln, 2004).

41. Keeth, "Sankt Antonius: Germans in the Alamo City of the 1850's." *SWHQ* 76, no. 2 (October 1972): 183–202; Mary Lou LeCompte, "The Texas Turnvereins," paper given at the Texas State Historical Association meeting, Fort Worth, March 1, 1985, in German Association: Turnverein, Vertical Files, ITC, 4–7, quotation on 5; LeCompte, "German-American Turnvereins in Frontier Texas, 1851–1880," *Journal of the West* 26, no. 1 (January 1987): 18–25; LeCompte, "Turnverein Movement," *Handbook of Texas Online*, http://www.tshaonline.org/handbook/online/articles/vnt02/; Christa Luise Carvajal, "German Theaters in Central Texas: 1850–1915" (Ph.D. dissertation, University of Texas at Austin, 1977); "He Writes From Germany," *San Antonio Daily Express*, May 15, 1895; Albert F. "Rick" Grimm. Swiss-run San Pedro Springs was also the site of freedmen's picnics. *San Pedro Springs: A Scrapbook* s.n., 2001, Institute of Texan Cultures; notice of a freedmen's picnic is in *San Antonio Express*, May 9, 1871.

42. On parades, see Judith Berg-Sobré, *San Antonio on Parade: Six Historic Festivals* (College Station: Texas A&M University Press, 2003).

43. *San Antonio Express*, July 6, 1867.

44. *San Antonio Express*, July 4 and July 7, 1868.

45. Siemering, 11. Revenue lists and Inventory/Monthly dues in San Antonio and Casino Club Records, University of Texas at San Antonio Special Collections (hereafter UTSA). *Handbook of Texas Online*, s.v. "Casino Club," https://tshaonline.org/handbook/online/articles/vnc01; Casino Club letterpress copybook, 1875–82, Daughters of the Republic of Texas Library (hereafter DRT).

46. "Fremdenliste," San Antonio and Casino Club Collection, UTSA.

47. *San Antonio Express*, September 24, 1869; *San Antonio Express*, March 4, 1928.

48. See, for example, M. G. Anderson to Newcomb, July 19, 1871, and Stanley Welch to Newcomb, July 12, 1871, ts. transcription in J. P. Newcomb Letters, SAPL.

49. *Freie Presse für Texas*, April 12, 1873.

50. See "Western Texas a Free State," *San Antonio Herald*, March 8, 1856.

51. See Weston Joseph McConnell, *Social Cleavages in Texas: A Study of the Proposed Division of the State* (Ph.D. dissertation, Columbia University, 1925), which has the flaws common to works in the Dunning School but also extensive detail on division schemes.

52. *Freie Presse für Texas*, October 27, November 17, and December 15, 1866; *Galveston Union*, November 3 and 24, 1866.

53. *Galveston Union*, "Theilung des Staates," November 24, 1866.

54. Ibid.

55. Alison Efford, *German Immigrants, Race, and Citizenship in the Civil War Era* (Cambridge University Press, 2013).

56. E. Degener to General Reynolds, October 24, 1867, Microfilm M1193, "Registers of Letters Received and Letters Received of the Department of Texas, the District of Texas, and the 5th Military District, 1865–70," RG 393, National Archives and Records Agency, Washington, D.C. (hereafter NARA DC).

57. November 14, 1867, M1165, "Letters Sent by the Department of Texas, the District of Texas, and the 5th Military District, 1856–58 and 1865–70," RG 393, NARA DC.

58. Editorial, *San Antonio Express*, July 2, 1868.

59. Texas, Constitutional Convention, 1868–1869, *Journal of the Reconstruction Convention Which Met at Austin, Texas*, 2 volumes (Austin: Tracy, Siemering, 1870), esp. v. 1, 148, 323, 326. Jacob Kuechler supported a modest division plan but cautioned against surrendering land to the federal government because, as a surveyor, he was reluctant to give up lands before their value, including their mineral potential, was fully understood. Ibid., 171–72.

60. *Constitution of the State of West Texas* [Austin? 1869?]. *San Antonio Express* (San Antonio, Texas), July 4, 1868.

61. See Julia Brookins, "Immigrant Settlers and Frontier Citizens: German Texas in the American Empire, 1835–1890" (Ph.D. dissertation, University of Chicago, 2013).

62. See Kamphoefner, "New Perspectives" and "Mainstreams or Backwaters?" On regional cultures of violence, see Carrigan, Moneyhon, "Texas after the Civil War."

63. Edward King, "The Great South: Glimpses of Texas, I," *Scribner's Monthly* 7, no. 3, January 1874, 302–31, quotation 320.

64. These figures do not include German-speaking Austrians, Swiss, or Alsatians, even though such distinctions were not always important in Texan society. Terry Jordan, *German Seed*, 51, 55, 57. A rare treatments of post-war immigration is Jordan's, "The German Settlement of Texas after 1865," *Southwestern Historical Quarterly* 73, no. 2 (October 1969), 193–212.

65. On this broad transition and its consequences for racial mixing, see Anne F. Hyde, *Empires, Nations, and Families: A History of the North American West, 1800–1860* (Lincoln: University of Nebraska Press, 2011), esp. 306. On the Southwest as an object of Eastern scientific study, see George E. Webb, *Science in the American Southwest: A Topical History* (Tucson: University of Arizona Press, 2002).

66. On seeing like a state, see James C. Scott, *Seeing Like a State: How Certain Schemes to Improve the Human Condition Have Failed* (New Haven: Yale University Press, 1998). On the partnership between the U.S. military and commercial interests in the exploration of Texas, see William Goetzman, *Army Exploration in the American West, 1803–1863* (New Haven: Yale University Press, 1959), 225–39.

67. On the defenses at Galveston, see W. T. Block, "The Ghostly-Silent Guns of Galveston: A Chronicle of Colonel J. G. Kellersberger, The Confederate Chief Engineer of East Texas," *East Texas Historical Journal* 33, no. 2 (1995), 23–34. On the Von Rosenberg family's work at the General Land Office, see Nan Thompson Ledbetter, "Three Generations of Texas Topographers," *SWHQ* 64, no. 3 (January 1961), 384–47. Adelsverein immigrant Charles A. Pressler led surveying parties for De Cordova and checked his map for accuracy before publication. "Pressler, Karl Wilhelm," *Handbook of Texas Online*, http://www.tshaonline.org/handbook/online/articles/fpr07. Friedrich Schenck was another German immigrant engineer at the GLO; see H. T. Schenck, Edward Hertzberg, trans., "Notes and Documents: A Letter from Friedrich Schenck in Texas to His Mother in Germany, 1847," *SWHQ* 92, no. 1 (July 1988), 144–64, esp. 164. Robert Wooster, "Lucas, Anthony Francis," *Handbook of Texas Online*, http://www.tshaonline.org/handbook/online/articles/flu04. Texas Revolution veteran Hermann Ehrenberg, mining engineer Carl Schuchard, and geologist Frederick Brunckow worked together on the Sonora Mining and Exploring Co. Ernst F. Schuchard Papers, 1832–1973, DRT; Natalie Ornish, *Ehrenberg: Goliad Survivor—Old West Explorer* (Dallas: Texas Heritage Press, 1997), 46–51; Ben W. Huseman, *Wild River, Timeless Canyons: Balduin Möllhausen's Watercolors of the Colorado* (Fort Worth, Tex.: Amon Carter Museum, 1995), 76n; Kathleen Doherty, "Schuchard, Carl," *Handbook of Texas Online*, http://www.tshaonline.org/handbook/online/articles/fsc77. Pressler and Wilhelm von Rosenberg helped to found Austin's German Free School. Lich, *German Texans*, 139; "The German School," *Southern Intelligencer* (Austin, Tex.), February 9, 1859.

68. Hubert Plummer Heinen, "Schleicher, Gustav," *Handbook of Texas Online* http://www.tshaonline.org/handbook/online/articles/fsc09, June 7, 2016. Samuel Wood Geiser, *Men of Science in Texas, 1820–1880* (Dallas, Southern Methodist University Press, 1958), esp. 270–84. See also Geiser, *Naturalists of the Frontier* (Dallas: Southern Methodist University Press, 1948).

69. Américo Parades, *"With His Pistol in His Hand": A Border Ballad and Its Hero* (Austin: University of Texas Press, 1958), 52–53.

7   Reconstruction, from Transatlantic Polyseme to Historiographical Quandary

David Prior

For over two decades, the drive to explain how developments in the United States related to those abroad has enriched historical scholarship. Yet the transnational turn, as it is often known, has had comparatively little influence on the study of Reconstruction. This lack of engagement is, in part, a recent manifestation of Reconstruction scholarship's longstanding tendency to treat transnational connections as of marginal interest to the field. It is not that Reconstruction scholars are provincial; the field has several brilliant comparative studies. But as narrative histories of Reconstruction make clear, the field has long limited its attention to the world beyond to a handful of topics.[1] Diplomacy features briefly in many Reconstruction narratives, sometimes tucked into separate chapters.[2] Likewise, African-American colonization, planters' attempts to import European and "coolie" labor, and Confederate emigration to Latin American and elsewhere occasionally garner passing mention.[3] The rise of industrial capitalism and changing class relations in Western Europe have at times featured as an important part of Reconstruction's backdrop.[4]

Transnational connections have long remained marginal to the study of Reconstruction due in good measure to the elaboration of two loosely formed rival approaches—one national, one southern—to the writing of Reconstruction's narrative. These approaches have formed a dialectical relationship with each other that, over time, has tended to draw scholarly attention inward. This is not to say that individual scholars have focused on either just the nation or just the South. Most specialists would concur that Reconstruction concerned northern-made federal policies toward the defeated Confederacy and the slave South. Moreover, scholars have long been concerned with how the interplay of northern policies and southern actions transformed national citizenship and identity. What defines these two approaches is not their exclusive focus on the nation or the South but how they balance these in Reconstruction's narrative and how they relate them to Reconstruction's meaning. Here, there has long been substantial and persistent disagreement, and this disagreement has worked to limit interest in transnational connections.

But where have these two approaches come from and why have they been so resilient? Ironically, the answer involves the transatlantic history of the word *reconstruction*.[5] Before the Civil War, this term circulated in Europe and the United States as a name for two historical processes. First, it referred to the resurrection of individual polities—states, nations, and empires—and reflected in part the romantic fascination with the idea that modern peoples had premodern forerunners. Second, *reconstruction* referred to the transformation of the very fabric of society, especially as advocated by socialists and other radical reformers.[6] These understandings of *reconstruction* with a small-r (a name for general historical processes) explain why Civil War–era Americans took *Reconstruction* with a big-R (a proper noun referring to something specific to America) to mean two things.[7] From very early on, *Reconstruction* could refer to the reunification of the United States, the transformation of southern society, and no doubt sometimes both at once.

We will need more research to fully examine how small-r *reconstruction* morphed into big-R *Reconstruction* and how subsequent scholars further adapted these terms. But we can show here that the connections between the two sets of meanings mattered. Small-r *reconstruction* bequeathed to Civil War–era Americans and subsequent scholars a persistent ambiguity concerning what the name *Reconstruction* referred to. As one leading scholar has recently noted, "I confess to feeling more than a little confusion about what Reconstruction really is."[8] Over time this ambiguity has evolved into imprecision, and two other scholars have recently suggested abandoning the term, as it applies to the postbellum years, altogether.[9] We should not do that, however, without first understanding that the key to the field's lack of clarity about its own subject derives in part from the early history of its name.

Reconstruction's original ambiguity explains why the national and southern approaches to Reconstruction's narrative have been so persistent and so difficult to harmonize. That original ambiguity, or more precisely our failure to date to grasp it, also explains why these two approaches remain inchoate. A lack of research about what *Reconstruction* meant during the Civil War era has left these approaches free to develop over time in response to broader scholarly trends. This has lent Reconstruction scholarship even greater complexity as scholars in the field reinvent the term and reconsider how to balance the South and the nation in their narratives.[10] As a result, the history of the word *Reconstruction* has shaped the evolution of Reconstruction's narrative, but in amorphous ways.

This essay urges scholars to rethink Reconstruction by considering the term's origins and how Civil War–era Americans used it. Its main argument is that the ambiguous meanings of *Reconstruction* and its small-*r* antecedent laid the foundation for the development of two loosely formed approaches to narrating Reconstruction. It traces the co-evolution of these two approaches from the birth of professional scholarship on the United States up to recent narratives. In doing so, it draws upon the transatlantic history of the word *reconstruction* to develop new perspective on Reconstruction historiography, demonstrating that some interesting continuities mark a body of scholarship otherwise best known for its moments of rupture.

Working toward a transatlantic history of the transformation of the word *reconstruction* into the name *Reconstruction*, the following section aims to demonstrate the existence of and congruity between their two sets of meanings. Civil War–era Americans use of *reconstruction* reflected their engagement with Western European sources that relied on the term to refer to two things: the resurrection of polities and the transformation of society.[11] Both meanings of small-*r* *reconstruction* elicited commentary from people in the United States, often in response to European events.

The European revolutions of 1848 were particularly important in engaging Americans in conversations about reconstruction as resurrection. *Living Age*, which specialized in republishing European news and commentary, ran from the *British Quarterly Review* one article that referred to "the failure of the attempt made at Frankfort towards a reconstruction of Germany" and the threat that "a reconstruction of Poland" would pose to Russia.[12] In this sense, the term "reconstruction" often accompanied the word "nationality," which typically referred to peoples who lacked states.[13] *The American Whig Review*, for example, paraphrased a manifesto by France's Alphonse de Lamartine, the moderate republican minister of foreign affairs during the Second Republic, as stating that France could come to the aid of oppressed nationalities if these were on the verge of reconstruction.[14] The *Daily Crescent* of New Orleans also addressed Lamartine's speech, discussing its ramifications in Ireland and concluding that "the 'reconstruction of oppressed nationalities in Europe and elsewhere' has begun in earnest."[15] Three months later, a financial report in the *Democratic Review* stated that the German customs union "has gone far towards promoting the nationality which is now laying the foundation for a reconstruction of the German Empire."[16]

Europeans often discussed the potential reconstruction of Poland, which Austria, Prussia, and Russia had partitioned in the eighteenth century. Americans followed these discussions, especially during the Crimean War (1853–1856) as British and French sources considered aiding the reconstruction of Poland as an anti-Russian measure. *Living Age* ran at least five articles from Britain that used the term "reconstruction" to refer to the resurrection of Poland.[17] *Harper's Monthly Magazine* mentioned a British politician's belief that the "reconstruction of Poland" was the best way to carry forward the conflict with Russia.[18] When exiled Hungarian nationalist Lajos "Louis" Kossuth argued in Sheffield (June 5, 1854) and Nottingham (June 12, 1854) that England must help reconstruct Poland in order to defeat Russia, newspapers in Athens, Tennessee; Edgefield, South Carolina; Richmond, Virginia; and Brookeville, Indiana took notice.[19] Months later, *The Western Democrat* of Charlotte, North Carolina, reprinted a *Philadelphia Bulletin* editorial, "The Reconstruction of Poland," which criticized Kossuth's argument as well as his premise that there were Poles left to make a nation from.[20] Although a skeptic, the editor, like others, followed European debates and used *reconstruction* to refer to Poland's resurrection. Later in the Crimean War, at least five newspapers reported that a British M.P. had moved an address to the Queen praying that peace negotiations would include exertions for Poland's reconstruction.[21] Earlier, *The Ashland Union* of Ohio expressed interest when the *New York Tribune* reported that Duke Persigny, a French Bonapartist, urged the reconstruction of Poland as a barrier against Russian expansion.[22]

Small-*r* reconstruction's meaning as resurrection circulated up to the start of the Civil War. In 1857, the *North American Review* surveyed the Italian patriot Antonio Gallenga's *History of Piedmont*, noting that his chapter "Reconstruction of Piedmont" was one of many that highlighted the region's tumultuous political history.[23] The *Atlantic Monthly* invoked the term twice in an 1859 article on the Italian War between Austria and France. The first reference was to Napoleon III's alleged plans to bring about "the reconstruction of the First Empire," and the second was to the popularity of "the idea of the reconstruction of Poland" among some French statesmen and literati.[24]

American discussions of *reconstruction*'s second meaning, as social transformation, were also tied to events and publications in Europe, especially France. In 1848, one American magazine article explained that France's ongoing revolution "is equally social and political; indeed, with regard to its internal affairs, the reconstruction of society appears to have been the end."[25] Three years later, *Living Age* republished an article from the *United Service Magazine* of Britain that mentioned that French troops belonged to clubs devoted "not merely to the subversion of government, but the entire reconstruction of civil society in France."[26]

But the term's associations with radicalism were hardly limited to France. *Harper's Monthly* invoked the concept in an article about the utopian daydreaming of a group of British poets. As *Harper's* noted, the action that set their schemes in motion was a discussion between a young man and a bookstore owner about "the problem—ever old, yet always new—of the reorganization and reconstruction of society."[27] Responding to the revolutions of 1848, the *Philadelphia Ledger*, in an editorial reprinted by the *Indiana State Sentinel*, contemplated the looming reconstruction of European society. It warned that Europe's debt-ridden monarchies could soon default, bringing about a crisis that would proceed from violence to anarchy to more violence and finally to an unwanted "reconstruction of society."[28]

Small-*r* *reconstruction*'s meaning as social transformation also came up frequently in purely domestic conversations about reform movements within the United States. One popular newspaper editorial, which appeared in at least five newspapers in 1857, suggested that radical social reformers put the cart before the horse. Only once the people abandoned their superficial pretenses and returned to simpler ways, it argued, could they begin "to talk about the reconstruction of society upon a new basis, and not much before."[29] In 1850, *The Princeton Magazine* ran a song entitled "The Reconstruction of Society," which presented the idea as dear to those who would not work or study or listen to their own consciences. *The Star of the North*, of Bloomsburg, Pennsylvania, reprinted the song and described it as "a dash at Political and Industrial Socialism."[30] Tangentially, scholars have yet to fully explain how, after the Civil War, the term "social equality" came to refer to unregulated racial contact and economic leveling. It may be that the term "social equality" was useful to critics of Republican policies toward the South because it resonated with *reconstruction*'s preexisting association with socialism. Some publications in the United States were even more pointed in their critiques of radical ambitions to reconstruct society. In 1850, an article in the *New Englander and Yale Review* argued that recognition of human depravity, and not plans to reconstruct society, should guide social reform. The author repeatedly warned against social radicalism, variously criticizing the idea of "the reconstruction of society as the only remedy for social evils"; describing radical Associationism as marked by a goal of "disorganizing society as now established and reconstructing it upon the basis of Communism"; and concluding that "Much then as certain social reforms are needed, there is no need of a radical reconstruction of society in order to secure them."[31] One author for *The American Whig Review* argued that the New England mind was so convinced that society was but "an aggregation of individuals" that it could not fathom that society "does not readily admit of revolution and reconstruction." Hence the region was full of monomaniacal reformers who "seem impatient to tear down the universe and reconstruct it after a pattern of their own."[32]

The term "reconstruction" gradually came to refer to processes specific to the United States starting with the run-up to the Civil War, although understanding exactly how will require more extensive research. James Henry Hammond used *reconstruction* generically when he warned northerners that if the white wage-labor slaves, who drove their society, came to comprehend the true power of the ballot box, "Your society would be reconstructed, your government reconstructed, your property divided."[33] Perhaps more telling of future usage was a statement by a moderate Republican in March of 1860 that immediate abolition was implausible for it would require "[n]othing short of the reconstruction of society" in the South.[34]

The transition may have been much quicker and more striking with reconstruction as resurrection. During the secession crisis, even a radical paper like *The Liberator* took the term to refer to a potential reunification of North and South, as did the ideologically diverse sources *The Liberator* reprinted and excerpted.[35] Abraham Lincoln, Andrew Johnson, and the *Report of the Joint Committee on Reconstruction* all used *Reconstruction* to refer to the process whereby federal authority would return to the South, the southern states would return to the Union, and the country would be reunited. Often, Lincoln, Johnson, and the *Report* used *Reconstruction* interchangeably with "restore" and "restoration," which sometimes also referred to the extension of rights to former Confederates.[36] At least one source declared Reconstruction complete when Georgia returned to full statehood in 1870.[37]

By 1867, if not before, political partisans started linking Republican legislation with older ideas about the reconstruction of society, the latter already having longstanding and mostly negative connotations. At least four papers reprinted from the *New York Herald* an editorial that condemned the Republican Party for reconstruction laws that would bring "social ruin" to the South to "secure power to a coterie of politicians." The *Herald* commented that, if the Democratic Party's track record was poor, at least it could boast that if it "had ever desired to reconstruct society it was in the interests of the white man."[38] Writing in the shadow of Republican legislation, the *Charleston Daily News* editorialized about:

the social philosopher who proposes to knock into chaos the moral and religious systems under which the civilized world has prospered, and to reconstruct society after a new plan which, whenever it has been tried on a small scale, has failed utterly and scandalously.[39]

A few years later, the same paper described the presence in the South of "the respectable white . . . the determined opponent of the Radicalism which sought to reconstruct society after an idea, and made the craziest experiments upon the self-respect of the people and the public prosperity."[40] Ironically, white supremacists eager to equate the expansion of African-American rights with radicalism and socialism may have played an important role in shifting the popular understanding of big-*R Reconstruction* toward social transformation.

This may explain why Republicans sometimes attempted to disavow an interest in social transformation. In 1867, the *Dallas Herald* reprinted from the Republican *Galveston Bulletin* an article that offered some intraparty criticism of the local National Republican Association. The association, claiming to speak for the loyal people of Galveston, had declared its support of Congress's efforts to "'reconstruct society at the South.'" The *Bulletin* responded by acknowledging that there were "those who desire to reconstruct society" but then arguing that Congress was focused on a political reconstruction, not a social one, and that not all loyalists were radicals.[41] Yet such negative connotations were not ubiquitous. The *Burlington Weekly Free Press* used the term favorably when criticizing southern whites for driving away northern immigrants. When the war ended, the paper noted, many expected that northern immigration would "reconstruct society and change the face of things in every respect," but southern whites proved unwelcoming and remained "as little reconstructed as ever."[42]

Such a brief survey does not, obviously, provide a complete history of how small-*r reconstruction* became big-*R Reconstruction*. Much more remains to be said, for example, about African-American uses of the term, how nationalists and socialists abroad referenced big-*R Reconstruction*, what it meant to accuse someone of being "unreconstructed," and how the idea of a Reconstruction Period first emerged. Likewise there is much room to better explain how *Reconstruction* often meant both reunification and southern transformation at once. In the United States, the two were so closely intertwined as historical processes that it would only be natural to want to speak of them in the same breath. This section's aim has been much more limited: demonstrating that people in the United States used *Reconstruction* in two ways that reflected the earlier meanings of its small-*r* antecedent.

This essay continues by developing a historiographical argument focused on how scholars have attempted to narrate Reconstruction. It would go too far to argue that *reconstruction*'s dual meanings morphed directly into two clearly distinguished rival methods or schools of thought. But the polysemous nature of the word *reconstruction* did shape the early meanings of *Reconstruction* as a name for something specific to the history of the United States. That original ambiguity has laid the foundation for the ongoing elaboration of two loosely formed approaches to narrating Reconstruction, one of which calls attention to the South and the other to the nation. These two approaches have tended to evolve across the decades, in part because it has been uncommon in the field for scholars to demand attention to what *Reconstruction* meant at the time. Understanding the evolution of these two approaches therefore also requires a focus on broader scholarly trends. The next five sections examine historiographical moments in which both that original ambiguity and those trends were at play.

In 1936, Fletcher Green opened his obituary for Walter Fleming, then a leading Reconstruction scholar, by explaining that historians had advanced "widely divergent views" of the period. "Some of them," he explained, "have taken the position that the history of reconstruction should concern itself largely with conditions in the seceded states, and they have made the South the core of their study." "[O]thers," he continued, "have chosen to approach the problem from the opposite pole, and have devoted attention to the victorious North rather than the vanquished South."[43] While Green's diction suggests rival sectional approaches, there are but a handful of Reconstruction studies that focus exclusively on the North, most of them published well after Green's obituary.[44] What "the victorious North" must have referred to, then, was not simply the states above the Confederacy, but some combination of the cause of the Union and northerners' control of federal policy and influence on the nation more generally. If this is what Green meant, then he grasped something important. Competing claims about the centrality of the South and the nation to Reconstruction have defined the field from the birth of professional history, if not earlier.

By 1936, Reconstruction's narrative was already in its second of five moments, each defined by the influence of broader scholarly trends. The first moment came from the 1880s to the 1910s as two trends shaped historical writing on the United States. First, historians focused on writing detailed narratives concerning broad swathes of history. Second, historians took polities, especially nations, to be unproblematic and even natural narrative subjects. Together, these trends inspired national narratives concerned with specific periods of the United States' history or, for the more ambitious, all of it.[45] Narratives by three historians, William A. Dunning, James Schouler, and Peter Joseph Hamilton, exemplify how this emphasis on the nation shaped Reconstruction's narrative.

Dunning, Schouler, and Hamilton each drew upon the notion that there was a Reconstruction Period—a concept that was circulating by the 1880s if not sooner—and applied it to the nation as a whole.[46] Dunning's *Reconstruction*, for example, noted that "[f]rom the point of view of social and political science in general, the South bulks largest in the history of reconstruction," but asserted that "we must regard the period as a step in the progress of the American nation." Hamilton's 1905 study, *The Reconstruction Period*, was even more emphatic. Hamilton took exception to how "Reconstruction has been often thought of as exclusively a Southern matter," and argued that while certain features of Reconstruction were unique to the South, it "affected the North also," and was ultimately "a Federal and not a sectional matter." Explaining that constitutional lawyers might view Reconstruction as "a process establishing freedom, citizenship and suffrage for the negro," Hamilton averred that "while it was this, it was far more." Hamilton conceded that "in a peculiar sense it [Reconstruction] did especially relate to the South," but stressed shortly thereafter that "Reconstruction was of the whole Union and in it we study a period in the history of the United States as one country."[47] Schouler was less emphatic in making Reconstruction national but then again did little to define the term at all. Publishing his *History of the Reconstruction Period* in 1913, he may have taken a national definition for granted, especially since this work was volume seven in his series "History of the United States under the Constitution." Tellingly, Schouler closed the preface to his Reconstruction volume by identifying himself as "a historian of our country."[48]

There were clear differences in perspective, structure, and interpretation among these works. Schouler, a former Union soldier and amateur historian who had served as president of the American Historical Association (1897), addressed himself and his audience as loyal northern whites, whereas Dunning, who was professionally trained in scientific history in Germany, did not frequently invoke his own or his audience's identity.[49] Hamilton's editor described him as presenting a southern perspective, yet Hamilton, whose father was a northern immigrant to the South, styled himself an Anglo-Saxon American.[50] Dunning and Schouler aspired to geographical breadth in their works, discussing the transcontinental railroad, the West, political corruption, foreign affairs, the panic of 1873, and the centennial celebrations.[51] Dunning out-researched Schouler, who relied on James Ford Rhodes's *History of the United States* and his experiences in Washington, D.C.[52] All three were racist, Hamilton most elaborately so.[53] He believed that "History is the story of race development," started his volume with a concise global history of race relations, began his coverage of the South with a chapter entitled "A Study of Race Tendencies," and focused much of his volume on the South.[54]

The authors also differed in why they thought Reconstruction was national. Dunning argued that if events in the South were most dramatic, developments most evident in the North and West "transformed the nation from what it was in 1865 to what it was in 1877."[55] Though Dunning did little to elaborate this claim, he did return at times to "the progress of the American nation," decrying corruption and African-American empowerment but lauding economic development.[56] Whereas Dunning underscored the political and economic transformation of the United States, Schouler was more concerned with patriotic reconciliation between white northerners and southerners, especially with how radical Reconstruction interfered with this process. Indeed, in Schouler's view, only after Reconstruction did the United States become "less of a confederacy and more of a unified nation," with even the national centennial's "promise of national harmony and reconciliation" marred by the 1876 election.[57] Hamilton called attention to the strengthening of the federal government vis-à-vis the states, a development that he welcomed even if racial egalitarians were the primary boosters of this nationalization. He believed that Reconstruction had preserved the virtues of state sovereignty while nonetheless turning the United States into a consolidated Union.[58] Hamilton concluded his volume by claiming that "the Federal Union had been reconstructed," that "the people were a Nation," and that "the period of Reconstruction was at an end."[59]

Reviews further highlight that scholars at this moment were working through what a national narrative of Reconstruction should look like. Schouler's narrative garnered little notice, but Dunning's elicited interesting comments.[60] L. S. Rowe stated that "No one can hope to secure a true perspective of the development of the American nation" without it.[61] More critical was E. Benjamin Andrews, who thought Dunning was fair toward white southerners but neglected their efforts to suppress the "threatening barbarism" of black enfranchisement. Andrews also found that Dunning's narrative failed to weave the South and the nation together into a unitary story.[62] Hamilton's 1905 volume provoked mixed responses for stressing that Reconstruction was national while concentrating on the South.

Walter Fleming considered it among the best general treatments of Reconstruction and useful for "understanding the Southern point of view."[63] Dunning reviewed it and was particularly critical, arguing with some exaggeration that Hamilton focused almost exclusively on the South.[64] David Y. Thomas lauded Hamilton for recognizing that the North underwent changes during Reconstruction, but faulted him for having "made no attempt to write a history of the United States for this period" and for neglecting extra-southern events. Thomas emphasized, as in fact Hamilton had, that "Reconstruction was a national, not a purely sectional matter" and that "the nation itself was being transformed."[65]

These were by no means the only turn-of-the-century Reconstruction narratives. John Burgess, in particular, warrants attention for his *Reconstruction and the Constitution* (1902), which zeroed-in on federal policy-making with little detail on the southern states and contemporaneous national developments except a chapter on foreign affairs.[66] But Dunning's, Schouler's, and Hamilton's narratives stand out for presenting Reconstruction as national. In their view, nations were not intellectual abstractions or convenient shorthand terms for lumping disparate regions together. Instead, nations were akin to living things, developing through stages, of which Reconstruction was one. Hamilton said this most directly: "The history of a country is somewhat like that of an individual."[67] Reconstruction could be judged for what it had done to the nation.

The turn-of-the-century emphasis on Reconstruction as national was the product of two factors. First, many historians at this time believed that history belonged to nations rather than the opposite and that the main task of the historian was to narrate. Second, the history of the term *Reconstruction* and its small-*r* antecedent made it easy to conceive of Reconstruction as inherently national. Dunning, Schouler, and Hamilton said little about big-*R Reconstruction*'s history as a concept, with Hamilton alone devoting a brief paragraph to it.[68] But, as they likely knew from their research, *Reconstruction* had long referred to a national process, namely of reunification. Given the emphasis at the time on writing national narratives, it is therefore hardly surprising that they decided to treat Reconstruction as a period in the history of the United States. Doing so required only a modest amount of intellectual slippage and allowed them to frame their topic in ways amenable to the fashion of the day.

Interestingly, at moments Dunning and Hamilton may have also thought of Reconstruction along the lines of its small-*r* antecedent's other meaning, social transformation. Hamilton noted but never developed an argument that Reconstruction in the South entailed the reorganization of society.[69] Dunning's narrative evoked the concept by calling attention to underlying economic and political changes in the North and West. But neither scholar interrogated the term *Reconstruction* much or explained how they came to understand it, leaving us guessing how exactly its history shaped their work.

The second moment in the transformation of Reconstruction's narrative, the moment during which Fletcher Green wrote, came from the 1900s to the 1950s, when monographic works and historiographical essays proliferated. With some important exceptions, most narratives still focused on nations. Most studies, however, narrowed their focus to a specific group, institution, event, region, idea, or scholarly dispute.[70] As focuses sharpened, differences in interpretation proliferated. With Reconstruction scholarship, these developments facilitated three trends. First, emerging scholars, many working under Dunning, produced studies of individual institutions, localities, and especially states in the South. By the 1930s, these studies had rendered an impressive volume of detailed but often racist scholarship.[71] Second, scholars such as Charles and Mary Beard, Howard K. Beale, James Allen, and W. E. B. Du Bois pioneered analyses of Reconstruction that foregrounded economic interests and class conflict. Though diverse, this last group of historians shared an interest in extra-southern developments, especially the rise of industrial capitalism.[72] Third, scholars such as John R. Lynch, Alrutheus A. Taylor, Du Bois, and John Hope Franklin challenged longstanding notions that people of African descent were racially inferior and unworthy of political equality.[73]

Two synthetic works with different racial politics capture how these trends reshaped Reconstruction's narrative: W. E. B. Du Bois's *Black Reconstruction* (1935) and the popular historian Robert Selph Henry's *The Story of Reconstruction* (1938). As is well known among scholars today, in *Black Reconstruction*, Du Bois rewrote Reconstruction's narrative with African Americans as equal and active human beings essential to one of the world's pivotal democratic moments.[74] Henry is now forgotten, but at the time he was an accomplished Tennessee-born amateur historian who later served as president of the Southern Historical Association (1957).[75] Henry dissented modestly from rigidly racial interpretations of the period, arguing that African Americans worked harder and learned faster than detractors predicted.[76] Henry also cited Du Bois's and John Lynch's works favorably.[77] But Henry, who had also authored an admiring biography of Nathan Bedford Forrest, was no racial egalitarian.[78] Henry's *Story* downplayed the relentlessness of white supremacist violence and blamed the South's racial conflict on the Republican Party.[79]

Du Bois's and Henry's works drew on the new southern-centric monographs, filtering them through their distinctive perspectives. The two volumes had different messages, but both made Reconstruction's narrative more detailed and more focused on the South.[80] Federal policy-making still garnered attention, as did Reconstruction's national implications, with Du Bois stressing the betrayal of democracy and Henry, like Hamilton, the reordering of American federalism.[81] Neither attempted to cover the postbellum North or West in their own right, although some of Du Bois's chapters, especially "Looking Forward" and "The Counter-Revolution of Property," examined economics and class in the North and West to understand the fate of the South.[82] Instead, the experiences and perspectives of southerners came more to the fore, with both scholars attending to race relations from the ground up, Du Bois in more detail.[83] Henry also included chapters on daily life that dwelled on southern whites.[84] Both works evoked big-R *Reconstruction*'s meaning as the transformation of the South, even though neither addressed the term's history. In particular, both focused on the rise of interracial politics, with Henry seeing it as a great disruption in daily life while for Du Bois it embodied democracy. That said, both works, especially Henry's, expanded their coverage of the South beyond the revolutionary moments of emancipation and enfranchisement. In this sense, big-R *Reconstruction*'s second meaning laid the foundation for the writing of wider-ranging southern-centric narratives, a trend which would arguably culminate in E. Merton Coulter's prejudiced but eclectic *The South during Reconstruction*.[85]

While detailing southern developments, Du Bois's narrative also evinced an international consciousness. In particular, Du Bois situated Reconstruction within a history of capitalism and linked the interplay of race and labor in the South to the rise of racial imperialism in the late nineteenth and twentieth centuries.[86] In his view, "The unending tragedy of Reconstruction is the utter inability of the American mind to grasp its real significance, its national and worldwide implications."[87] Du Bois, moreover, sought to condemn American racism before the enlightened opinion of modern civilization.[88] Finally, the volume had a comparative sensibility that anticipated future works.[89] *Black Reconstruction*'s perspective did not entail a comprehensive treatment of the Reconstruction Period nor of international connections and contexts. Diplomacy, immigration, emigration, international trade, American opinion of foreign events, and foreign opinions of Reconstruction were treated lightly if at all.[90] Nonetheless, by proposing that the collapse of Reconstruction was tied to the global ascent of racial imperialism, Du Bois's volume was ahead of its and our own day.[91]

Henry, in contrast, neglected international connections and contexts as well as national developments aside from federal policy towards the South. For this, reviewers skewered him. Their criticisms reflected both an ongoing interest in

Reconstruction's national and international economic context and the idea that Reconstruction was a period in the nation's history.[92] Perhaps focusing more on Dunning's students than on Dunning's own work, T. Harry Williams argued that Henry, like other Dunning followers, neglected national policy, adding that "Reconstruction in the South overshadows events in Washington."[93] R. H. Woody, echoing the idea that there was a Reconstruction Period, noted that Henry's work "is not the history of the nation," adding that "one finds no discussion of important national questions—the tariff, foreign policies, and economic development," as well as the panic of 1873, political scandals under Grant, and the Tweed Ring.[94] W. G. Seabrook commented that Henry's book "does not deal adequately with the broader aspect of the history of the United States and ignores world movements," including the rise of capitalism and industrialization.[95] Henry Shanks chided the volume for discussing "only those things about the North which help to explain the national program of reconstruction," meaning federal policy toward the South. The Story, Shanks added, failed to attend to how the radicals' economic issues and policies—including railroads, tariffs, banking, and currency—ultimately divided the South and the West.[96] William Hesseltine argued that "Only recently have new historians begun to see that Reconstruction was national in its implications," and that Henry had failed to engage with this work. Hesseltine explained that Henry's volume was so preoccupied with southern events that it "ignores the problems of national politics and economics, and avoids anything more than casual attention to the conflicts and personalities of Washington."[97] James Patton was kinder, acknowledging the volume failed on these fronts but stressing that Henry was a storyteller, not a research historian.[98]

If Henry lacked Du Bois's breadth and perspective, and if Henry was a "storyteller," his volume still had its own innovations with the structure of Reconstruction's narrative. In particular, Henry used the term Reconstruction to refer to two things. First, he used it, conventionally, to refer to period from the end of the Civil War to the withdrawal of federal troops from the South (1865–77). Second, he narrowed the term to refer to the radical period from the Military Reconstruction Act (March 2, 1867) to the readmission of Georgia in July of 1870. This period transformed southern society and the Union, creating "new states, in new relations to a new sort of national government."[99] In Henry's scheme, "Restoration," defined by the more moderate policies of Lincoln and Johnson, preceded Reconstruction and "Redemption," the six years during which southern whites took power through what Henry considered unfortunate but necessary means, followed it.[100] Henry's application of these terms was not perfectly consistent, but the gist of his argument was that Reconstruction was an attempt to transform the nation and the South and not return it to its prewar shape. Henry never demonstrated that his Restoration-Reconstruction-Redemption distinction was historically consonant, but his approach did echo small-*r* and big-*R Reconstruction*'s associations with radical change.

Du Bois's and Henry's narratives were not the only ones from this scholarly moment, nor do they convey all its complexity.[101] But they do underscore how drives to chronicle southern experiences and developments and to situate Reconstruction amid the rise of industrial capitalism pulled its narrative in two directions. The first trend found fruition in Du Bois's and Henry's narratives: the South became the bulky center of Reconstruction's narrative and southern lives and experiences became even more integral to its human drama. The second trend had more limited influence, finding expression but not exhaustive elaboration in Du Bois's work.

Much like turn-of-the-century scholarship, works from the 1900s to the 1950s did not interrogate the origins and meanings of *Reconstruction* as a proper noun. They did, however, add complexity to the emerging distinction between national and southern narrative approaches. As *Black Reconstruction* demonstrates, one did not need to rely upon turn-of-the-century claims about Reconstruction as a national time period to draw attention to industrial capitalism as Reconstruction's national (and international) context. Also, if Henry's and Du Bois's volumes evoked Reconstruction's meaning as the transformation of southern society, neither was narrowly confined to this topic. Much as turn-of-the-century scholars broadened earlier meanings of *Reconstruction* as national reunification to create narratives of it as a national time period, Henry, in particular, built a southern-centric narrative that ranged beyond the radical reordering of southern society alone. Finally, both of these southern-centric narratives made claims about the nation. This reminds us that the tension in the writing of Reconstruction's narrative is not about whether to address the nation or the South, but how to incorporate them both, how to balance attention to them, and how to relate them to claims about the nature of Reconstruction and its deeper meaning.

The third moment in the transformation of Reconstruction's narrative came in the 1960s as non- and anti-racist scholarship triumphed in the writing of U.S. history. In Reconstruction scholarship, as elsewhere, historians dismantled broadly accepted beliefs about race.[102] Yet, as revolutionary as this moment was, it also had its continuities. As revisionists overhauled Reconstruction scholarship, they also shared with earlier scholars choices about how to balance the South and the nation in Reconstruction's narrative. With the form and structure of Reconstruction's narrative, claims and approaches from earlier works found not denunciation but reinvention. More so than previously, it became clear that the field had two established poles—one national, one southern—and that scholars lacked a consensus about what exactly Reconstruction was.

Of the three major revisionist narratives from this period—John Hope Franklin's *Reconstruction: After the Civil War* (1961); Kenneth Stampp's *The Era of Reconstruction, 1865–1877* (1965); and Rembert Patrick's *The Reconstruction of the Nation* (1966)—Franklin's and Patrick's best illuminate how divided scholars remained. Stampp's landmark volume was similar in structure to John Burgess's 1905 *Reconstruction and the Constitution*, focusing on federal policy-making with but one chapter on the South and little on contemporaneous national developments.[103] Stampp's narrative also refrained from arguing about the centrality of southern experiences or national developments to Reconstruction. As such, reviewers offered little commentary on its balancing of the South and the nation. Only David Donald, the foremost revisionist proponent of a national approach, commented that Stampp's work paid little attention to "political and economic changes in the North and West."[104] Franklin and Patrick, in contrast, produced concise narratives that sought to cover the South and the nation in a more comprehensive manner, although to different degrees.

As his title suggests, Patrick's volume was closest in format to the national narratives of the turn of the century, especially Dunning's and Schouler's. Like them, Patrick devoted generous space to three topics: the making of federal policy toward the South; conditions in the South; and contemporaneous national developments. In his preface, Patrick admitted that this approach "precludes the unity attainable in a specialized study."[105] Patrick included chapters on "The Grant Regime" and "Foreign Affairs," but it was his wide-ranging forty-page chapter on "The People" that he felt needed justification. Patrick conceded, "The South provides an almost irresistible central theme for the Reconstruction era." But, much like Dunning, he believed that the country as a whole went through a broader transformation during these years, or as Patrick put it, "the economic and social changes deserve summation, for they played a signal part in America's rebirth." The conquest of the West, immigration, religion, and education all got attention—much as similar constellations of topics had in Dunning's and Schouler's narratives—because they "altered the course of the nation" and therefore were "part of the Reconstruction era." Mostly revisionist in tone, Patrick's work nonetheless reiterated the turn-of-the-century notion that there was a Reconstruction period in the nation's history.[106] His reference to the nation's rebirth even appeared to echo one of small-*r* *reconstruction*'s original meanings.

Franklin's *Reconstruction* also addressed federal policy-making and broader national events but devoted more space to the struggle for interracial democracy in the South. Franklin compressed most of his commentary on national developments into a twenty-page chapter on "Social and Economic Reconstruction." Here, he discussed contemporaneous developments as diverse as industrialization, reform currents, and literature. Compared to Patrick's work, Franklin's treatment of federal policy-making was also compressed. The struggle between Johnson and congressional Republicans garnered a few chapters while the Grant presidency received passing attention and the Liberal Republicans warranted but a line and no index entry.[107] The South, in contrast, was the topic of substantial portions of seven of his twelve chapters.[108] Yet Franklin was also concerned with Reconstruction's national context, arguing that corruption in the South, often used to condemn black political participation, was part of a national trend.[109] Franklin also framed Reconstruction as the period during which the United States became "a mature, modern nation," and lamented that during this time "the Union had not made the achievements of the war a foundation for the healthy advancement of the political, social, and economic life of the United States."[110] If Franklin's discussion of contemporaneous developments was concise, he nonetheless noted how struggles over and in the South shaped the nation, even writing of the latter's growth and health. A polar opposite of Peter Joseph Hamilton when it came to racial politics, Franklin nonetheless shared with him, as did Patrick and others, a set of metaphors comparing nations to people.

Reviews made it particularly evident that scholars disagreed with each other about what Reconstruction was and how to tell its story. With Patrick's work, J. Ryan Beiser noted that it showed the reader "that Reconstruction was nationwide" but focused mostly on the South.[111] Much as some thought that Hamilton treated the North too briefly in his avowedly national narrative, David Donald commented that Patrick included chapters on extra-southern developments "rather begrudgingly."[112] Patrick Riddleberger argued that Patrick's analysis in his chapter, "The People," "might more profitably have been integrated into the story of political Reconstruction."[113] Likewise, William Brock alleged that Patrick's "general analysis" was "less satisfactory" than his handling of the South, in part because he used "the familiar but stale technique of segregating economic and social information into a single, isolated chapter."[114] Neither Riddleberger nor Brock expressed concern with Patrick's separate chapters on Grant and foreign affairs, suggesting that they took these to be natural if distinct parts of Reconstruction's narrative. LaWanda Cox argued that Patrick's chapter "The People" ranged too far and did too little to advance his central arguments about the

South. Likewise, she claimed that Patrick's book would have been more valuable if he had "reduced his treatment of the Grant regime and foreign affairs to those aspects directly relevant to Reconstruction." Such a criticism took as its starting point a definition of Reconstruction alien to Patrick's claim that there was a "Reconstruction era" that involved the entire nation.[115]

Reviews of Franklin's work were similarly divided.[116] Benjamin Quarles lauded Franklin's chapter on the North for demonstrating that the South, including its corruption, was not exceptional. He added that the Franklin's concluding sentence demonstrated, unwittingly, that "Reconstruction was a national phenomenon."[117] Edgar Toppin agreed, judging Franklin's book the most thorough and judicious short study of the "Reconstruction era," noting that it was especially successful in "fitting Southern developments into proper perspective with national issues."[118] Eric McKitrick, however, argued that Franklin's narrative failed to sufficiently analyze the experience of and connections between national and southern developments, which he partially attributed to the volume's brevity. McKitrick's dissatisfaction reflected in part Franklin's limited attention to the "national experience under Grant and 'Grantism,'" which McKitrick, in disagreement with Cox, identified as one of the three key components of Reconstruction.[119] Avery Craven argued that Franklin's emphasis, "one sincerely regrets to find, is always on how the Negro fared in this or that situation," and that "scholars sitting in Northern libraries" needed to spend more time reading manuscript letters written by southerners.[120] Craven's argument was particularly odd since he could have easily imagined the difficulties facing an African American scholar working in segregated southern archives and since the vast majority of African Americans lived in the southern states.[121] But most pertinent here is Craven's argument that Reconstruction scholars needed to focus on the experiences and voices of southerners, a claim that in its own way had the potential to transcended racial politics.

Responses to Franklin's and Patrick's volumes measure well how divided the field remained, with some lauding their works for grasping Reconstruction's national dimensions, while others thought they fell short on this mark, and still others believed that they were too northern and national. The revisionist moment made manifest tensions that had been developing within Reconstruction scholarship from at least the birth of professional history. The field now had a wealth of monographic literature and at least three loosely defined narrative models to borrow from: the wide-ranging national narratives developed by Dunning and Schouler, the southern-centric works by Du Bois and Henry, and the federal model pioneered by Burgess. It also had a number of claims, many only partially developed, about Reconstruction as a time period in the history of the nation, state centralization and the transformation of American federalism, the importance of national and international economic contexts, and the centrality of southern experiences to the meaning of Reconstruction. It is little wonder that Patrick and Franklin did not please all their reviewers, or that their works attempted to cover the South and the nation in different ways.

At the same time that Patrick's and Franklin's volumes built on earlier works, their own attempts to explain Reconstruction were perhaps now more fully autonomous from the word's original meanings than previous studies had been. It had been easy, arguably, for Dunning, Schouler, and Hamilton to present Reconstruction as national because doing so required only a modification of the earlier meaning of Reconstruction as reunion. Likewise, Reconstruction's other meaning as the transformation of southern society likely facilitated Henry's and Du Bois's decision to make the southern states the bulky center of Reconstruction's narrative. By the 1960s, scholars had so many claims about and models for Reconstruction's narrative that they did not, strictly speaking, need to rely directly on the original ambiguity in the term to provide them with interpretive leeway.

The fourth moment in the transformation of Reconstruction's narrative came in the 1980s with renewed debate about the need for and merits of narrative syntheses. The 1950s through the 1970s saw monographic scholarship grow dramatically alongside university faculties.[122] How to make sense of the welter of scholarship was, by 1980, an even more pressing question than it had been in 1930 or 1960.[123] By the 1980s, scholars such as Eric Monkonnen, Thomas Bender, and Bernard Bailyn were questioning whether and how the profession should channel the flood of research into narrative syntheses.[124] The most ambitious attempt at a new Reconstruction narrative came from Eric Foner, whose essay "Reconstruction Revisited" and magnum opus *Reconstruction: America's Unfinished Revolution, 1863–1877* directly addressed the need for synthesis.[125]

Shaping Foner's approach was his career-long drive to reintegrate the vibrant fields of social and political history and his dedication to foregrounding the experiences, voices, and actions of African Americans. Foner anchored his *Reconstruction* around four themes: the "centrality of the black experience" and black mobilization in making Reconstruction and defining its meaning; the transformation of southern society, especially through the rise of new labor relations, and the meaning of this for the black experience and Reconstruction politics; the related transformation in racial attitudes and relations in the South, particularly as class relations changed and opportunities for interracial political alliance developed; and the rise of a more powerful, activists central state committed to national citizenship and racial equality before the law and the reaction to this development.[126] Perhaps more so than any other narrative except Du Bois's, Foner's work channeled the radical social meanings of small-*r reconstruction*.[127]

Foner's narrative was in some senses national, but not along the same lines as Dunning's, Schouler's, or Patrick's. Indeed, the vast majority of Foner's narrative attended to African-American experiences, politics, and institution-building in the South. Only one of *Reconstruction*'s twelve chapters, chapter ten, "The Reconstruction of the North," focused on the North, and even here without losing sight of the South. Addressing industrialization and rising class conflict, it linked these trends to changing northern attitudes toward southern freedpeople. Similarly indicative of Foner's southern emphasis was his eighth chapter, "Reconstruction: Political and Economic," which borrowed the title of Dunning's national narrative but addressed the South. Throughout his narrative, the South remained, as he put it in his preface, "the heart of the Reconstruction drama."[128]

What made Foner's narrative national was its concern with the relationship between African Americans and the federal polity. In particular, his narrative managed a dual emphasis on "the black experience" and its meaning for the United States by foregrounding the cause of racial equality and integration.[129] If the black experience compelled attention to the South, the quest of southern freedpeople for equality made their efforts, and their ultimate exclusion, crucial to the history of United States as a nation. Built on a generation of scholarship that drew much of its energy from the Civil Rights Movement, Foner's narrative saw in African Americans' postbellum struggles the antecedents and precedents for the subsequent transformation of the United States in the twentieth century. Reconstruction was "America's Unfinished Revolution" because of and not despite the centrality of African Americans to it.

Scholars rightfully lauded Foner's *Reconstruction*, but they were also quick to argue that it was far from comprehensive in its treatment of the South and the nation. To be sure, Foner's narrative was then and still is an inspiring and daunting accomplishment. Yet, precisely because of this, its critics' concerns about its comprehensiveness are noteworthy.[130] In racial equality and integration Foner had a theme that allowed his narrative to weave the South and the nation into a common story. But in the process Foner paid only modest attention to tangentially related northern and southern developments. Michael Perman averred that Foner's emphasis on African Americans led him to neglect "the rest of southern society and how it was affected by Reconstruction," which ultimately impoverished his analysis at points.[131] C. Vann Woodward thought that Foner could have better addressed the plight of non–slave-owning southern whites, who, as he pointed out, constituted three-fourths of southern whites and a majority in several states.[132] David Donald stated that the work was "not truly a history of the South during Reconstruction, for its focus is almost exclusively on the Southern blacks—not on the Southern whites who made up 60 percent" of the former Confederate states. Donald also argued that Foner's focus on the black experience led him to slight northern developments, including electoral issues shaping southern reconstruction and developments integral to the broader history of the postbellum United States. Donald claimed that William Dunning offered a stronger treatment of the tariff, monetary policy, agrarian dissent in the West, the conquest of the plains Indians, and diplomacy. In his words, "Foner's *Reconstruction*, then, is not truly a comprehensive history of the United States during the Reconstruction decade," adding, "nor is it a history of the South during Reconstruction."[133]

Donald and two co-authors later elaborated on his critique in the third edition (2001) of what had originally been James G. Randall's *The Civil War and Reconstruction* (1937). Donald, along with Jean Harvey Baker and Michael Holt, conceded that Foner's southern approach now dominated scholarship. Still, the authors briefly expressed reservations in what was essentially a very impressive textbook. As they explained, "over three-fifths of Americans lived in the North, where much of importance occurred between 1865 and 1877 that ostensibly had nothing to do with race relations in the South," adding that the "experiences of the majority require assessment." They also noted that understanding developments in the South required sustained attention to the politically dominant North. But a few pages later, the authors emphasized that many in the North were far more concerned with their own livelihoods than with the struggles between southern freedpeople and ex-Confederates.[134]

If terse, Donald, Holt, and Baker's comments underscore a problem at the heart of Reconstruction's narrative. If distinctive southern experiences, such as those of the freedpeople, define the essence of Reconstruction, how can Reconstruction serve as a paradigm for understanding a period in the history of the entire United States? Foner's narrative offered one solution by underscoring how the cause of racial equality was integral to the experiences of southern freedpeople and to the legal, cultural, and political evolution of the United States. Yet, this approach—part of what Steven Hahn has labeled the "liberal integrationist framework"—did not allow for a more comprehensive treatment of the North and the West, and in fact neglected some aspects of southern history.[135] In this sense, Foner, not unlike Du Bois, arguably wrote less of Reconstruction as a period in the history of the nation than as a specific set of developments involving the nation but centered on the South.[136] In doing so, Foner's volume ended up speaking to the idea of Reconstruction as the social transformation of the South.

The fifth moment in the evolution of Reconstruction's narrative runs from the end of the last century up to the present. Since at least the 1990s, historians have interrogated the geographical paradigms that frame their fields of studies. Atlantic and world history, for example, moved more to the center of the profession while national, imperial, and regional histories drew criticism. It took about a decade for Reconstruction scholarship to engage with this trend, and when it did that engagement was productive but paradoxical. International connections and contexts featured in a number of monographs but otherwise remained about as marginal to Reconstruction's narrative as they had always been. Meanwhile, the field developed an innovative thread of research on the western United States. With Reconstruction's narrative, this western focus formed a part of a renewed interest in Reconstruction as national history, right as national history was elsewhere falling out of favor. The two narratives that have done the most to reimagine Reconstruction as national, both with attention to the West, are Heather Richardson's *West from Appomattox: The Reconstruction of America after the Civil War* (2007) and Mark Summers's *The Ordeal of the Reunion: A New History of Reconstruction* (2014).[137]

West from Appomattox offers a Reconstruction narrative of unprecedented scope, going far beyond the brief, compartmentalized coverage of the West common to many national narratives. Richardson argued that the conquest of the American West was integral to the emergence of a new, dominant middle-class understanding of America. Working with the longer chronology (1865–1901) that Richardson pioneered in her *The Death of Reconstruction* (2001), Richardson argued that although the federal government was pivotal to the conquest of the West, an emerging middle class associated the region with rugged individualism.[138] This western imagery limited popular sympathy for groups like former slaves who suffered from systematic inequalities and who stood to benefit from an expansive government agenda. The predominantly white members of the middle-class in the North, South, and West, came to imagine themselves as good, self-starting Americans and other groups—and some corporations—as conniving special interests.[139] For Richardson, this dynamic defined Reconstruction not as the reentry of the southern states into the Union but as "the literal reconstruction of the North, South, and West into a nation in the aftermath of the Civil War."[140] This thesis gave her volume a coherence missing in earlier national narratives of Reconstruction, such as Dunning's and Patrick's, but came at the cost of comparatively limited coverage of developments in and federal policy concerning the South.[141] Indeed, at least three reviewers deemed her book to be a narrative of the Gilded Age.[142]

In its basic outline, Summers's book is an orthodox history of Reconstruction as a period in the history of the nation. Like earlier national narratives, *The Ordeal* runs from 1865 to 1877 and focuses on the South and federal policies toward it while also covering foreign affairs, finance, the conquest of the West, and nationwide corruption and reform efforts.[143] But in addition to offering a superb synthesis on these topics, Summers's work offers two innovations. First, it emphasizes that the term *Reconstruction* referred to the process of rebuilding the nation, and in particular to having the southern states return permanently and consensually to a nation that, except for the abolition of slavery, would be recognizable to antebellum Americans.[144] Second, Summers argued that, viewed in this light, Reconstruction seems much more successful, if tragically so, than if scholars take the fate of interracial democracy in the South and the nation as Reconstruction's central story.[145] *The Ordeal* offers a valuable corrective to a generation of works that all too often lost sight of how many Americans used the term or what sort of postbellum settlement they desired. It correctly identifies the goal—reunion—that had both intense and broad support among the group that held the reins of federal power, northern white men. Yet, *The Ordeal* does not detail how Civil War–era Americans used the term *Reconstruction*, or its small-*r* antecedent, and only gets us part of the way to recapturing its history and meaning. While *The Ordeal* reminds us that big-*R* Reconstruction often referred to the moderate end of national reunification, it neglects how Civil War–era Americans, including northerners, associated the term with radicalism and used it to describe the transformation of the South.

As with previous moments, the two narratives explored here were not the only ones of note.[146] But *West from Appomattox* and *The Ordeal* stand out for returning the field to arguments first made over 100 years ago. Both presented Reconstruction as inherently national and both ranged across the nation. Yet both also testify to the complexity of Reconstruction's narrative because, in one sense, they are diametrically opposed to each other. Richardson's conceptualization of Reconstruction allowed for a narrative both sweeping and coherent, but used the term in ways that would have been unrecognizable to most Civil War–era Americans. Summers's narrative, in contrast, called attention to the term's Civil War–era meaning as reunification, and in doing so made its own innovations within the national approach. As their works demonstrate, after over a century of Reconstruction narratives, the field remains as divided as ever, with two loosely formed approaches that contain within them plenty of diversity, as was true when Dunning, Schouler, and Hamilton wrote their national narratives. As in past historiographical moments, the two approaches continue to evolve in line with broader scholarly trends and with only partial attention to the history of the term.

Over the last one hundred years scholars have crafted Reconstruction narratives. As distinctive as these have been from each other, they share a common quandary of how to balance the South and the nation. In part, this problem stems from the political history of the postbellum United States. Because of the federal structure of the American government, politics in the South and the North were tightly interwoven. Yet, if this were the only issue, the challenge of narrating Reconstruction would be straightforward; scholars would simply enumerate the myriad ways that politics in the North and South shaped each other.

The deeper problem is that scholars do not agree, at least not completely, about what the term *Reconstruction* refers to, and, because of this, their narratives draw out different meanings and messages for their readers. There is a limited consensus in that all would agree that federal policies toward the South are integral to what Reconstruction was, and this may be why Burgess and Stampp developed the federal narrative. But few would accept an exclusive concern with those policies as making for an adequate narrative of Reconstruction. Some want greater attention to the South, no doubt with an eye on its radical transformation. Others want greater attention to the nation, no doubt with a concern with its survival and rebirth.

The origin of these perspectives lies with the antebellum, transatlantic history of the word *reconstruction*. Small-*r reconstruction* commonly referred to two distinct things, the resurrection of polities and the transformation of society. *Reconstruction* as a name for something specific to the United States evolved from this term and quickly incorporated both of its meanings. But, because the field has yet to produce a detailed history of its own name, scholars have remained largely uninterested in, perhaps even unaware of, big-*R Reconstruction*'s small-*r* antecedent. This has left scholars remarkably free to add new meanings onto the name *Reconstruction*. Over time, historians have formulated and reformulated its meanings in line with broader trends shaping the profession as a whole. The result has been two loosely formed interpretive approaches, one of which holds that Reconstruction was inherently national, the other that it was quintessentially southern.

It is an irony of Reconstruction scholarship that the transatlantic history behind its name helps explain the rise of two loosely formed approaches that have in turn marginalized transnational connections in the telling of Reconstruction's story. In the coming decades, scholars will no doubt rewrite Reconstruction's narrative again. This essay would suggest that those scholars should focus less on whether Reconstruction was southern or national and more on how Civil War–era Americans transformed a polysemous word into a multivalent name. The appeal of the name *Reconstruction* at the time may have stemmed from its imprecision, as people in the United States struggled to comprehend unprecedented events in a complex and changing environment. At a minimum, the name's history reminds us that transnational connections did not merely form part of Reconstruction's backdrop. Rather, they were woven into its very fabric, so tightly so that they could disappear from plain sight.

Notes

The author thanks Durwood Ball, Joshua Burgess, Alison Efford, Andre Fleche, Tiffany Florvil, Evan Rothera, John David Smith, Mitchell Snay, Mark W. Summers, and Michael Woods for detailed comments on earlier drafts.

1. There are also a small but growing number of monographic studies that explore Reconstruction's global context. See the introduction to this volume; Mark M. Smith, "The Past as a Foreign Country: Reconstruction, Inside and Out," in Thomas J. Brown, *Reconstructions: New Perspectives on the Postbellum United States* (New York: Oxford University Press, 2006), 117–40; and Jay Sexton, "Toward a Synthesis of Foreign Relations in the Civil War Era, 1848–1877," *American Nineteenth Century History* 5, no. 3 (Fall 2004): 50–73.

2. The widest ranging chapter in this vein is Mark W. Summers, *The Ordeal of the Reunion: A New History of Reconstruction* (Chapel Hill: University of North Carolina Press, 2014), Chapter 9, "Passage to India?" See also John W. Burgess, *Reconstruction and the Constitution* (New York: Charles Scribner's Sons, 1905), Chapter 14, "International Relations of the United States between 1867 and 1877"; William A. Dunning, *Reconstruction: Political and Economic, 1865-1877* (New York: Harper & Brothers, 1907), Chapter 10, "A Critical Period in Foreign Relations (1865–1873); James Schouler, *History of the Reconstruction Period, 1865–1877*, vol. VII of his *History of the United States under the Constitution* (New York: Dodd, Mead & Company, 1913), 161–68; and Rembert W. Patrick, *The Reconstruction of the Nation* (New York: Oxford University Press, 1967), Chapter 9, "Foreign Affairs." There are several monographs on diplomacy during these years, although these only occasionally address themselves to Reconstruction scholars and in many cases are dated. See Richard Zuczek, "Foreign Affairs and Andrew Johnson" and Stephen McCullough, "Avoiding Wars: The Foreign Policy of Ulysses S. Grant and Hamilton Fish," in Edward O. Frantz, ed., *A Companion to the Reconstruction Presidents, 1865–1881* (Malden, Mass.: Wiley Blackwell, 2014), 85–120 and 311–27.

3. See, for example, W. E. B. Du Bois, *Black Reconstruction in America, 1860–1880* (New York: Free Press, 1992), 693; Robert Selph Henry, *The Story of Reconstruction*

(Gloucester, Mass.: Peter Smith, 1963 [1938]), 176–77; John Hope Franklin, *Reconstruction: After the Civil War* (Chicago: University of Chicago Press, 1961), 45, 140; Kenneth M. Stampp, *The Era of Reconstruction, 1865–1877* (New York: Vintage Books, 1965), 47–48; Patrick, *The Reconstruction of the Nation*, 37–38, 207–8, 245; Eric Foner, *Reconstruction: America's Unfinished Revolution, 1863–1877* (New York: Harper & Row, 1988), 26, 28–89, 419, 598–600. On Chinese "coolie" labor and Reconstruction, see also Moon-Ho Jung, *Coolies and Cane: Race, Labor, and Sugar in the Age of Emancipation* (Baltimore: Johns Hopkins University Press, 2006).

4. See especially the following discussions of the Paris Commune in Reconstruction narratives: Foner, *Reconstruction*, 490, 491, 530; Heather Cox Richardson, *The Death of Reconstruction: Race, Labor, and Politics in the Post–Civil War North, 1865–1901* (Cambridge, Mass.: Harvard University Press, 2001), 85–87, 89, 92, 93, 96–97, 98, 103, 185; and *West from Appomattox: The Reconstruction of America after the Civil War* (New Haven: Yale University Press, 2007), 100. See also Philip M. Katz, *From Appomattox to Montmartre: Americans and the Paris Commune* (Cambridge, Mass.: Harvard University Press, 1998).

5. Throughout the text, I use italics to indicate when I am addressing the history and meaning of the word "reconstruction" and the related proper noun "Reconstruction." Unless otherwise noted in the text, these words appear in Roman typeface when I am addressing the historical processes associated with these terms rather than their etymology and meaning.

6. In Europe, "reconstruct" could also refer to the forming of governing coalitions and cabinets, the revising of constitutions, and the making of diplomatic alliances; *The Times* (London), "The State of the Continent," January 10, 1849, 6; ibid., "The State of Europe," February 14, 1851, 6; and ibid. "The State of the Continent," February 1, 1854, 6–7.

7. The distinction between small-*r reconstruction* and big-*R Reconstruction* does not perfectly mirror how Civil War–era Americans wrote these terms. For example, Civil War–era Americans often used the word "reconstruct" as a verb and "reconstructed" as an adjective, which of course would not require capitalization. Even when they did use *Reconstruction* to refer to processes specific to the United States, they sometimes left it in lowercase.

8. See Steven Hahn's comment in Eric Foner, et al., "Eric Foner's 'Reconstruction' at Twenty-Five," *Journal of the Gilded Age and Progressive Era* 14, no. 1 (January 2015): 13–27, quotation 23; see also Eric Foner's comments in ibid., 25–26.

9. Gregory P. Downs and Kate Masur, "Introduction: Echoes of War: Rethinking Post–Civil War Governance and Politics," in their *The World the Civil War Made* (Chapel Hill: University of North Carolina Press, 2015), 1–21, especially 3–6.

10. Leading historiographical essays overlook the tensions between southern and national approaches to Reconstruction's narrative; see Howard K. Beale, "On Rewriting Reconstruction History," 45, no. 4 (July 1940): 807–27; Bernard A. Weisberger, "The Dark and Bloody Ground of Reconstruction Historiography," *Journal of Southern History* 25, no. 4 (November 1959): 427–47; Vernon L. Wharton, "Reconstruction," in Arthur S. Link and Rembert W. Patrick, *Writing Southern History: Essays in Honor of Fletcher M. Green* (Baton Rouge: Louisiana State University Press, 1965), 295–315; John Hope Franklin,

"Mirror for Americans: A Century of Reconstruction History," *American Historical Review* 85, no. 1 (February 1980): 1–14; and Eric Foner, "Reconstruction Revisited," *Reviews in American History* 10, no. 4 (December 1982): 82–100. Weisberger offers a brief paragraph critiquing "sectional" approach to Reconstruction, wherein an economically and socially uniform North attempted to shape a similarly uniform South, as simplistic and dated. Here, however, his point was to address the ways in which discussions of the North and the South often glossed over differences within these regions, not to assess how scholars should balance the two; see Weisberger, "The Dark and Bloody Ground," 443–44. Beale suggested that southern scholars too often approached Reconstruction as southern history and neglected its national context; see Beale, "On Rewriting Reconstruction History," 811–12. O. Vernon Burton, David Herr, and Matthew Cheney, "Defining Reconstruction," in Lacy Ford, ed., *A Companion to the Civil War and Reconstruction* (Malden, Mass.: Blackwell, 2005), 299–322 reviews scholarly disagreements about when Reconstruction began and ended; see page 302 for a helpful comment on the oscillating emphases on political and social factors in Reconstruction historiography. Heather Cox Richardson has asserted that Reconstruction was fundamentally national in its nature, and has synthesized studies of postbellum attitudes toward the state and political economy to elaborate this point; see Heather Cox Richardson, "Reconstruction and the Nation," in Ford, ed., *A Companion to the Civil War and Reconstruction*, 447–67; "North and West of Reconstruction: Studies in Political Economy," in Thomas J. Brown, ed., *Reconstructions: New Perspectives on the Postbellum United States* (New York: Oxford University Press, 2006): 66–90; and *West from Appomattox: The Reconstruction of America after the Civil War* (New Haven: Yale University Press, 2007).

11. On this distinction, consider also Andrew Zimmerman's comments on the Civil War and the evolution of the term "revolution" in Andrew Zimmerman, "From the Second American Revolution to the First International and Back Again: Marxism, the Popular Front, and the American Civil War," in Gregory P. Downs and Kate Masur, eds., *The World the Civil War Made* (Chapel Hill: University of North Carolina Press, 2015), 304–35, especially 304.

12. "Prussia and Austria—Monarchies *v.* Nationalities," *The Living Age* 31, no. 397 (December 27, 1851): 583–99; quotations 594 and 596.

13. Aira Kemiläinen, *Nationalism: Problems Concerning the Word, the Concept and Classification* (Jyväskylä: Kustanajat Publishers, 1964), 47–48.

14. "Foreign Miscellany," *The American Whig Review* 7 (May 1848): 537–41. A copy of Lamartine's manifesto is available at "The Revolution in France," *The Times* (London), March 7, 1848. On Lamartine's diplomacy, see William Fortescue, *Alphonse de Lamartine: A Political Biography* (New York: St. Martin's Press, 1983), 197–230.

15. "Trouble Ahead—France, Germany, Italy, Poland, Ireland," *The Daily Crescent*, April 7, 1848, 2. The *Crescent's* quotation appears to be a miss-transcription of a passage in J. B. Dillon, "Address of the Council of the Irish Confederation to the People of Ireland," which was in turn quoting Lamartine's circular. Dillon's address is available in full in the *Crescent's* article.

16. "Financial and Commercial Review," *The United States Democratic Review* 23 (July 1848): 77–84; quotation 81.

17. "M. Kossuth on the War," *The Living Age*, February 3, 1855, 319–20, especially 319; "The Continent in 1854," ibid., April 21, 1855, 131–57, especially 152; "The Reconstruction of Poland," ibid., April 28, 1855, 195–201; "War Policy of Great Britain," ibid., January 5, 1856, 38–44, especially 38, 39, and 41–42; "Poland," ibid., May 10, 1856, 380–81, especially 380.

18. "Monthly Record of Current Events," *Harper's Monthly Magazine*, June 1855, 112–16, quotation 115.

19. "Kossuth on Russia," *The Athens Post*, July 7, 1854; "Kossuth on the State of Europe," *Edgefield Advertiser*, July 6, 1854; "Another Speech of Kossuth," *The Daily Dispatch*, June 28, 1854; and "Kossuth in the Field—Of Debate," *The Indiana American*, July 7, 1854. Reprints of Kossuth's speeches are available in "M. Kossuth at Sheffield," *The Times* (London), June 7, 1854; "M. Kossuth at Nottingham," *The Times* (London), June 13, 1854; and Lajos Kossuth, *Authentic Report of Kossuth's Speeches on the War in the East, and the Alliance with Austria, at Sheffield, June 5, and at Nottingham, June 12, 1854* (London: Trübner and Co., 1854).

20. "The Reconstruction of Poland," *The Western Democrat*, November 24, 1854.

21. "Four Days Later from Europe," *Evening Star*, April 13, 1855; "Later from Europe," *The Spirit of Democracy*, April 18, 1855; "By Telegraph," *The Ashland Union*, April 18, 1855; "Arrival of the Washington," *Plymouth Banner*, April 19, 1855; and "The Latest Foreign News," *Burlington Free News*, April 20, 1855.

22. "Reestablishment of the Kingdom of Poland," *The Ashland Union*, November 8, 1854; on Persigny's politics, see Roger Williams, *Gaslight and Shadow: The World of Napoleon III, 1851–1870* (New York: Macmillan, 1957), 1–39.

23. "Sardinia," *The North American Review*, October 1857, 330–68; quotation 332. The reference is to "Reconstruction of Piedmont (1559–1580)," Chapter 1 in Antonio Gallenga, *History of Piedmont*, volume 3 (London: Chapman and Hall, 1855), 1–59, which focuses on Emanuel Philibert, the first post–occupation ruler of Piedmont. On Gallenga and his *History*, see Toni Cerutti, *Antonio Gallenga: An Italian Writer in Victorian England* (New York: Oxford University Press, 1974), especially 127–31.

24. "The Italian War," *Atlantic Monthly*, August 1859, 244–56; quotations 246 and 253.

25. "French Revolution: M. Louis Blanc," *The American Whig Review*, July 1848, 90–100, quotation 97.

26. "Military Crisis in Europe," *Living Age*, March 15, 1851, 518–28, quotation 527.

27. "Mr. Cottle and His Friends," *Harper's Monthly Magazine*, December 1853, 68–76, quotation 76.

28. "Cause and Effect," *Indiana State Sentinel*, September 27, 1849.

29. "The Passion for Display," *The Weekly Portage Sentinel*, September 3, 1857; "The Passion for Display," *Preble County Democrat*, September 10, 1857 and October 1, 1857; "The Passion for Display," *Raftsman's Journal*, September 9, 1857; "The Passion for Display," *Bedford Inquirer and Chronicle*, July 31, 1857; "The Passion for Display," *Green-Mountain Freeman*, August 6, 1857.

30. *The Star of the North*, September 5, 1850.

31. "Social Reforms," *New Englander and Yale Review*, August 1850, 452–70; quotations 456, 465, and 470; on depravity, 468.

32. "Whipple's Essays and Reviews," *American Whig* Review, February 14, 1849, 148–72; quotations 156 and 157.

33. "The Southern Side of the Great Question," *New-York Tribune*, March 11, 1858.

34. "What Shall We Do with the Negro?" *New-York Tribune*, March 13, 1860.

35. For example: "Fatuity of Mr. Seward," *Liberator*, March 15, 1861, 42; ibid., "Why Is the North United?" June 14, 1861, 94; ibid., "A Word from the Green Mountains," July 5, 1861, 107; ibid., "Dying Testimony of Senator Douglas," ibid., August 30, 1861, 1; "No Reconstruction," ibid., April 12, 1861, 1; "To the Point," ibid., March 22, 1861, 46; ibid., May 3, 1861, 71.

36. Abraham Lincoln, *Proclamation of Amnesty and Reconstruction*, in Roy P. Blaser, ed., *The Collected Works of Abraham Lincoln* (New Brunswick, N.J.: Rutgers University Press, 1953), vol. 7, 53–56; Lincoln's message on his pocket-veto of the Wade-Davis Bill, ibid., 433; "The Last Public Address," ibid., 400–1; Andrew Johnson, *Amnesty Proclamation*, in Paul Bergeron, ed., *The Papers of Andrew Johnson* (Knoxville: University of Tennessee Press, 1989), vol. 8, 128–31, especially 128–29; Andrew Johnson, *Proclamation Establishing Government for North Carolina*, ibid., 136–38, especially 137; and see *Report of the Joint Committee on Reconstruction at the First Session Thirty-Ninth Congress* (Washington: Government Printing Office, 1866), viii–xiv, xvi, xviii, xx, xxi.

37. See "Perils of the Republican Party," *Evening Telegraph*, December 5, 1870; "Thanksgiving," *The Conservative*, November 25, 1870; and "Reconstruction," *The St. Cloud Journal*, December 8, 1870.

38. "The New York Herald Gives Up for Seymour and Blair," *Lincoln County Herald*, September 3, 1868; "The Presidential Campaign," August 27, 1868; "Heraldiana," *Nashville Union and Dispatch*, August 18, 1868; "The Presidential Campaign," *Democratic Enquirer*, September 3, 1868.

39. *The Charleston Daily News*, August 23, 1867.

40. "The Situation at the South," *The Charleston Daily News*, October 8, 1869.

41. "The New Party," *Dallas Herald*, May 11, 1867.

42. "Don't Want Them," *Burlington Weekly Free Press*, August 28, 1868.

43. Fletcher M. Green, "Walter Lynwood Fleming: Historian of Reconstruction," *Journal of Southern History* 2, no. 4 (November 1936): 497–521; quotation 497. On Fleming, see Michael W. Fitzgerald, "The Steel Frame of Walter Lynwood Fleming," in John David Smith and J. Vincent Lowery, eds., *The Dunning School: Historians, Race, and the Meaning of Reconstruction* (Lexington: University Press of Kentucky, 2013), 157–77, especially 171–72.

44. Green's use of the term "North" here may have derived from William Dunning's work, which made a claim to being national in scope because of its focus on the North; see William Archibald Dunning, *Reconstruction: Political and Economic, 1865–1877* (New York and London: Harper & Brothers, 1907), xv. Works focusing on the North include Felice A. Bonadio, *North of Reconstruction: Ohio Politics, 1865–1870* (New York: New York University Press, 1970); James C. Mohr, ed., *Radical Republicans in the North: State Politics during Reconstruction* (Baltimore: Johns Hopkins University Press, 1976); and David Quigley, *Second Founding: New York City, Reconstruction, and the Making of American Democracy* (New York: Hill and Wang, 2004).

45. For analyses of the rise of national narratives as a leading genre of historical writing at this time, see Richard Hofstadter, *The Progressive Historians: Turner, Beard, Parrington* (New York: Alfred A. Knopf, 1968), especially 23–30; Peter Novick, *That Noble Dream: The 'Objectivity Question' and the American Historical Profession* (New York: Cambridge University Press, 1988), 68–80; and Christopher L. Hill, *National History and the World of Nations: Capital, State, and the Rhetoric of History in Japan, France, and the United States* (Durham and London: Duke University Press, 2008), Chapter 1, "National History and the Shape of the Nineteenth-Century World."

46. On Reconstruction as a period, see John Conness, "Some of the Men and Measures of the War and Reconstruction Period": An Address (Boston: Nathan Sawyer & Son, 1882); Frederic Allison Tupper, *Moonshine: A Story of the Reconstruction Period* (Boston: Cupples, Upham and Company, 1884); Stephen T. Robinson, *The Shadow of the War: A Story of the South in Reconstruction Times* (Chicago: Jansen, McClurg, & Company, 1884).

47. Peter Joseph Hamilton, *The Reconstruction Period* (Philadelphia: George Barrie & Sons, 1905), 9–11, 19, see also 22.

48. Schouler, *History of the Reconstruction Period*, iii, v.

49. Schouler, *History of the Reconstruction Period*, 32, 37, 114; on Schouler's service, see Edward Stanwood, "Memoir of James Schouler," *Proceedings of the Massachusetts Historical Society* 54 (April 1921): 283–88, 285; on his term as AHA president, see "Presidential Addresses by Year," American Historical Association, https://www.historians.org/about-aha-and-membership/aha-history-and-archives/presidential-addresses/by-year. On Dunning, see James S. Humphreys, "William Archibald Dunning: Flawed Colossus of American Letters," in Smith and Lowery, *The Dunning School*, 77–105, especially 78–81. For an instance in which Dunning briefly identifies himself and his audience as American, see the use of "our" on Dunning, *Reconstruction*, 237.

50. Hamilton, *The Reconstruction Period*, iii, vii, 22, 249, 504, 544, 550.

51. Schouler, *History of the Reconstruction Period*, 92–99, 134–38, 140–41, 155–56, 273–76, Chapter 2, section II, "Finance and Foreign Efforts"; Chapter 2, section V, "Treaty of Washington"; and Chapter 3, section IV, "Centennial Celebrations." Dunning, *Reconstruction*, Chapters 9, "Economic and Social State of the Nation"; 10, "A Critical Period in Foreign Relations"; 14, "Commercial and Industrial Demoralization in the North"; and 18, "The Nadir of National Disgrace."

52. For the influence of James Ford Rhodes, *History of the United States: From the Compromise of 1850 to the Final Restoration of Home Rule at the South in 1877*, volume 6 (Norwood, Mass.: Norwood Press, 1906) on Schouler, see Schouler, *History of the Reconstruction Period*, iii–iv. On the whole, Schouler agreed with Rhodes's interpretations, although he challenged Rhodes's negative view on Andrew Johnson; see Schouler, *History of the Reconstruction Period*, especially 2–3, 73; and Wharton, "Reconstruction," 307. For Schouler's personal experiences, see Schouler, *History of the Reconstruction Period*, 119–20, 144–45, 342–43n3.

53. Dunning's racism is well-known. On Schouler's view, see especially *History of the Reconstruction Period*, 33–34, 37, 42–43, 48–49, 96, 175–76, 178–79, 190, 245, 252, 253, 260–61, 355–56.

54. Peter Joseph Hamilton, *The Reconstruction Period*, 12–19, 221, Chapter 8, "A Study in Race Tendencies"; quotation from 3. Hamilton's editor held open the possibility that African Americans might yet prove themselves worthy of political equality and invoked the *Declaration of Independence*; see ix, x.

55. Dunning, *Reconstruction*, xv–xvi.

56. Dunning, *Reconstruction*, quotation from 16; see also 142–44, 220, 225.

57. On 1876, see Schouler, *History of the Reconstruction Period*, 283, 297–302; quotations from 356 and 302. On Schouler's patriotism, see "James Schouler," *Mississippi Valley Historical Review* 16, no. 2 (September 1929): 212–22; Novick, *That Noble Dream*, 83–84; Theodore Clarke Smith, "The Writing of American History in America, from 1884 to 1934," *American Historical Review* 40, no. 3 (April 1935): 439–49, especially 440, 443.

58. Hamilton, *The Reconstruction Period*, 3, 7, 11, 41, 503, 530, 537, 556–57.

59. Hamilton, *The Reconstruction Period*, 557.

60. See Henry Barrett Learned, Review of James Schouler, *History of the Reconstruction Period, 1865–1877*, vol. VII of his *History of the United States under the Constitution*, published in *American Historical Review* 19, no. 3 (April 1914): 665–67.

61. L. S. Rowe, Review of W. A. Dunning, *Reconstruction: Political and Economic, 1865–1877*, published in *Annals of the American Academy of Political and Social Science*, 32, (September 1908): 189–90; quotation from 190.

62. E. Benjamin Andrews, Review of W. A. Dunning, *Reconstruction: Political and Economic, 1865–1877*, published in *American Historical Review* 13, no. 2 (January 1908): 371–73; quotation from 373. See also Humphreys, "William Archibald Dunning," 87; Wharton, "Reconstruction," 299–300.

63. Walter Lynwood Fleming, *The Sequel to Appomattox: A Chronicle of the Reunion of the States* (New Haven: Yale University Press, 1919), 305.

64. William A. Dunning, Review of Peter Joseph Hamilton, *The Reconstruction Period: The History of North America*, and Philip Alexander Bruce, *The Rise of the New South*, published in *Political Science Quarterly* 23, no. 1 (March 1908): 129–32. Dunning neglected to mention that Hamilton's volume, like his own, had multiple chapters devoted to the making of federal policy toward the South.

65. David Y. Thomas, Review of Peter Joseph Hamilton, *The Reconstruction Period: The History of North America*, published in *The American Political Science Review* 2, no. 3 (May 1908): 490–92; quotations from 491–92.

66. Only two of Burgess's fourteen chapters focused on the South, while a final chapter on foreign affairs was tacked on by way of a critique of the Reconstruction-era Republican Party. Burgess, *Reconstruction and the Constitution*, Chapters 8, 12, and 14. On Burgess and Reconstruction historiography, see Shepherd W. McKinley, "John W. Burgess, Godfather of the Dunning School," in Smith and Lowery, ed., *The Dunning School*, 49–76, especially 53–54, 59–60, 61–64, 65, 67–68.

67. Hamilton, *The Reconstruction Period*, 3–4; see also 10.

68. See Hamilton, *The Reconstruction Period*, 67.

69. See Hamilton, *The Reconstruction Period*, 9, 12.

70. On this transition, see Smith, "The Writing of American History in America," 439–42; Hofstadter, *Progressive Historians*, 35–41.

71. On the differences between Dunning's national approach and his students' focus on southern states and localities, see Humphreys, "William Archibald Dunning," 91. For an overview of early monographic scholarship on Reconstruction, see Wharton, "Reconstruction," 300–4.

72. For a classic summation of the different perspectives fueling early revisionism, see Stampp, *The Era of Reconstruction*, 8–9. For an analysis of the subsequent decline of Beardian interpretations, see August Meier, "An Epitaph for the Writing of Reconstruction History?" *Reviews in American History* 9, no. 1 (March 1981): 82–87, especially 82–84. On the differences between Allen and Du Bois, see Eric Foner, "*Black Reconstruction*: An Introduction," *South Atlantic Quarterly* 112 (Summer 2013): 409–18, especially 415–16. On leftist interpretations of the Civil War and abolition during the 1930s, see Zimmerman, "From the Second American Revolution to the First International and Back Again," 323–29.

73. Humphreys, "William Archibald Dunning," 98; Wharton, "Reconstruction," especially 297–98, 308–10, 314; Novick, *That Noble Dream*, 225–34.

74. Thomas C. Holt, "'A Story of Ordinary Human Beings': The Sources of Du Bois's Historical Imagination in *Black Reconstruction*," *South Atlantic Quarterly* 112, no. 3 (Summer 2013): 419–35, especially 421–22, 428–33; and Thavolia Glymph in Foner, "Eric Foner's 'Reconstruction' at Twenty-Five," 20.

75. Thomas Fleming, "Robert Selph Henry," in Clyde N. Wilson, ed., *Dictionary of Literary Biography*, Volume 17: Twentieth-Century American Historians (Detroit: Gale Research Company, 1983), 207–8, 210.

76. See Henry, *The Story of Reconstruction*, 29, 30, 130, 181, 315, 363–65, 366, 435, 496–97; Fleming, "Robert Selph Henry," 210.

77. See Henry, *The Story of Reconstruction*, 61, 120, 386, 435, 597.

78. Fleming, "Robert Selph Henry," 209.

79. On white supremacists, see Henry, *The Story of Reconstruction*, 144–45, 149, 153–54, 204, 233–35, 335, 344, 356, 359, 433, 544; on the Republican Party, see 157–58, 237–38, 248, 315, 365, 421–22, 501, 560.

80. See Foner, "Black Reconstruction," 410–11.

81. See, for example, Henry, *The Story of Reconstruction*, 398; Foner, "Black Reconstruction," 412, 414, 416.

82. See especially Du Bois, *Black Reconstruction*, 187, 210–18, 580–86, 591–92, 595–97, 631–34.

83. Du Bois, *Black Reconstruction*, passim.; Henry, *The Story of Reconstruction*, 22, 28–31, 127–30, 143–49, 180–81, 233–37, 544–47.

84. Du Bois, *Black Reconstruction*, passim; Henry, *The Story of Reconstruction*, Chapters 3, "Home to Desolation"; 4, "Contrasts and Contradictions"; 15, "The Business of Living"; 20, "Memories and Hopes"; and 41, "Gains in Agriculture, Education and Transportation."

85. E. Merton Coulter, *The South After Reconstruction* (Baton Rouge: Louisiana State University Press, 1947).

86. On capitalism, see Du Bois, *Black Reconstruction in America*, passim, but especially 5, 17, 37–38, 634–35; Foner, "Black Reconstruction," 411, 414–15; on imperialism,

see Du Bois, *Black Reconstruction in America*, 9, 15–16, 30, 206, 632, 706; Foner, "Black Reconstruction," 411, 414–15, 416; Moon-Ho Jung, "*Black Reconstruction* and Empire," *South Atlantic Quarterly* 112, no. 3 (Summer 2013): 465–71, especially 467–68.

87. Quotation from Du Bois, *Black Reconstruction in America*, 708.

88. See Du Bois, *Black Reconstruction in America*, 3, 54, 126, 206, 698, 703.

89. See Du Bois, *Black Reconstruction in America*, 4, 12, 24–25, 41, 75, 694, 699.

90. For exceptions, see Du Bois, *Black Reconstruction in America*, 38, 47, 51, 87–91, 143, 148–49, 215, 386, 673. See also Smith, "The Past as a Foreign Country," 126.

91. See Foner, "Black Reconstruction," 417.

92. While Du Bois's work was widely reviewed, a preliminary examination of eight reviews indicates that none of them addressed Du Bois's balancing of the South and the nation, with reviewers of all backgrounds, perhaps unsurprisingly, more concerned with his defense of African Americans and his Marxian approach. These reviews are: R. J. Bunche, "Reconstruction Reinterpreted," *Journal of Negro Education* 4, no. 4 (October 1935): 568–70; Arthur C. Cole, in *The Mississippi Valley Historical Review* 23, no. 2 (September 1936): 327–28; Avery Craven, in *American Journal of Sociology* 41, no. 4 (January 1936): 535–36; Douglas Debevoise, in *North American Review* 240 (September 1935): 369–72; Rayford W. Logan, *Journal of Negro History* 21, no. 1 (January 1936): 61–63; Francis Butler Simkins, in *Journal of Southern History* 1, no. 4 (November 1935): 530–32; A. A. Taylor, in *New England Quarterly* 8, no. 4 (December 1935): 608–12; and R. H. Woody, in *North Carolina Historical Review* 13, no. 1 (January 1936): 91–95. The best discussion of the reception of Du Bois's *Black Reconstruction* is David Levering Lewis, "Introduction" in Du Bois, *Black Reconstruction in America*, xi–xvi.

93. Harry Williams, Review of Robert Selph Henry, *The Story of Reconstruction*, published in *The Journal of the American Military History Foundation* 2, no. 3 (Autumn 1938): 166–67; quotation from 167. Williams was among the scholars then interested in the influence of national economic developments on Reconstruction politics. Joseph G. Dawson III, "T. Harry Williams," in Clyde N. Wilson, ed., *Dictionary of Literary Biography*, Vol. 17: "Twentieth-Century American Historians," 435, 444.

94. R. H. Woody, Review of Robert Selph Henry, *The Story of Reconstruction*, published in *The American Historical Review* 44, no. 3 (April 1939): 659–61; quotation from 659–60.

95. W. G. Seabrook, Review of Robert Selph Henry, *The Story of Reconstruction*, published in *The Journal of Negro History* 23, no. 3 (July 1938): 386–88; quotation from 387.

96. Henry T. Shanks, Review of Robert Selph Henry, *The Story of Reconstruction*, published in *Social Forces* 17, no. 3 (March 1939): 450–51; quotation from 450–51.

97. W. B. Hesseltine, Review of Robert Selph Henry, *The Story of Reconstruction*, published in *The Mississippi Valley Historical Review* 25, no. 1 (June 1938): 119.

98. James Patton, Review of Robert Selph Henry, *The Story of Reconstruction*, published in *The North Carolina Historical Review* 16, no. 1 (January 1939): 83–85; quotation from 84.

99. Henry, *The Story of Reconstruction*, 398.

100. Henry, *The Story of Reconstruction*, 5, 8, 211, 219, 401, 592.

101. With narratives alone, a fuller account would need to address Fleming, *Sequel to Appomattox*, Claude Bowers, *The Tragic Era: The Revolution after Lincoln* (Cambridge,

Mass.: The Riverside Press, 1929); and Coulter, *The South During Reconstruction*, all of which shared a focus on the South.

102. See Novick, *That Noble Dream*, 348–54, 365–66; Franklin, "Mirror for Americans," 6–7.

103. Stampp, *The Era of Reconstruction, 1865–1877*, Chapter 6, "Radical Rule in the South." Portions of other chapters also addressed the South, see especially 195–205, but on the whole the federal policy remained at the fore.

104. David Donald, Review of Kenneth Stampp, *The Era of Reconstruction, 1865–1877*, published in *American Historical Review* 71, no. 2 (January 1966): 700–1.

105. Patrick, *The Reconstruction of the Nation*, vii–viii.

106. Patrick, *The Reconstruction of the Nation*, 210. I say mostly because Patrick occasionally made patronizing comments about former slaves; see 11, 12, 284, 286.

107. On Johnson and Congress, see Franklin, *Reconstruction*, Chapters 2, "Presidential Peacemaking"; 4, "Confederate Reconstruction Under Fire"; and 5, "Challenge by Congress." On Grant, 82–83, 147, 149, 150, 165–68, 172, 199, 202–3; on Liberal Republicans, 149.

108. On the South, see John Hope Franklin, *Reconstruction: After the Civil War* (Chicago: University of Chicago Press, 1961), Chapters 1, "The Aftermath of the War"; 3, "Reconstruction: Confederate Style"; 4, "Confederate Reconstruction Under Fire"; 6, "The South's New Leaders"; 7, "Constitution-making in the Radical South"; 8, "Reconstruction—Black and White"; 9, "Counter Reconstruction"; and 12, "The Aftermath of 'Redemption.'"

109. Franklin, *Reconstruction*, 146–51.

110. Franklin, *Reconstruction*, 14, 227.

111. See J. Ryan Beiser, Review of Rembert Patrick, *The Reconstruction of the Nation*, published in *American Quarterly* 20, no. 2, part 2 (Summer 1968): 374–75; quotations from 374.

112. See David Donald, Review of Rembert Patrick, *The Reconstruction of the Nation*, published in *Commentary*, September 1, 1967.

113. See Patrick W. Riddleberger, Review of Rembert Patrick, *The Reconstruction of the Nation*, published in *Journal of American History* 54, no. 3 (December 1967): 677–78; quotation from 677.

114. See W. R. Brock, Review of Rembert Patrick, *The Reconstruction of the Nation*, published in *American Historical Review* 73, no. 2 (December 1967): 610–11; quotation from 611.

115. See LaWanda Cox, Review of Rembert Patrick, *The Reconstruction of the Nation*, published in *Journal of Southern History* 33, no. 4 (November 1967): 577–79; quotation from 578.

116. As the first revisionist narrative of Reconstruction, and one written by an African American, Franklin's *Reconstruction* also prompted negative reactions from scholars committed to older racist interpretations. See John Hope Franklin, *Mirror to America: The Autobiography of John Hope Franklin* (New York: Farrar, Straus and Giroux, 2005), 195–96.

117. Benjamin Quarles, "Key to a Riddle," *Journal of Negro Education* 31, no. 1 (Winter 1962), 38–39; quotation from 39. Franklin's last sentence read: "In the postwar years the

Union had not made the achievements of the war a foundation for the healthy advancement of the political, social, and economic life of the United States"; Franklin, *Reconstruction*, 227.

118. Edgar Allan Toppin, Review of John Hope Franklin, *Reconstruction: After the Civil War*, published in *The Journal of Negro History* 47, no. 1 (January 1962), 57–59; quotation from 57. Hans Trefousse and Alan Conway heralded Franklin's book as the best synthesis of the period; see Hans Trefousse, Review of John Hope Franklin, *Reconstruction: After the Civil War*, published in *American Historical Review* 67, no. 3 (April 1962): 745–46; Alan Conway, Review of John Hope Franklin, *Reconstruction: After the Civil War*, published in *English Historical Review* 78, no. 309 (October 1963): 811–12.

119. Eric McKitrick, Review of John Hope Franklin, *Reconstruction: After the Civil War*, published in *The Mississippi Valley Historical Review* 49, no. 1 (June 1962): 153–54; quotation from 153.

120. Avery Craven, Review of John Hope Franklin, *Reconstruction: After the Civil War*, published in *The Journal of Southern History* 28, no. 2 (May 1962): 255–56.

121. On Franklin's earlier difficulties with southern archives, see Franklin, *Mirror to America*, 83–84, 119.

122. See Novick, *That Noble Dream*, 362–63, 377.

123. One strand of thinking within this debate became a part of the internationalizing trend, as evidenced above all else in Thomas Bender's scholarship.

124. Bernard Bailyn, "The Challenge of Modern Historiography," *American Historical Review* 87, no. 1 (February 1982): 1–24; Thomas Bender, "Whole and Parts: The Need for Synthesis in American History," *Journal of American History* 73, no. 1 (June 1986): 120–36; and Eric H. Monkkonen, "The Dangers of Synthesis," *American Historical Review* 91, no. 5 (December 1986): 1146–57.

125. Foner, "Reconstruction Revisited"; Foner, *Reconstruction*. Foner went so far as to claim that "historians have yet to produce a coherent account of Reconstruction to take its [the Dunning school's] place"; see Foner, *Reconstruction*, xxii. See also Eric Foner's comments in Foner, et al., "Eric Foner's 'Reconstruction' at Twenty-Five," 25.

126. Foner, *Reconstruction*, xxii–xxv.

127. On the relationship between these works, see Eric Foner's comments in Foner, et al., "'Reconstruction' at Twenty-Five," 24, 26.

128. Foner, *Reconstruction*, xxiv.

129. See especially, Foner, *Reconstruction*, xxiv, 110, 114–15, 117, 237, 539, 544–47, 598–600, 612.

130. Foner identified comprehensiveness as one of his own key criteria for the volume; see Foner, *Reconstruction*, xxii.

131. Michael Perman, "Eric Foner's *Reconstruction*: A Finished Revolution," *Reviews in American History* 17, no. 1 (March 1989): 73–78; quotation from 75.

132. C. Vann Woodward, "Unfinished Business," *New York Review of Books*, May 12, 1988, 22.

133. David Donald, "The Black Side of the Story," *The New Republic*, August 1, 1988, 41–44, quotations 43, 44.

134. David Herbert Donald, Jean Harvey Baker, and Michael F. Holt, *The Civil War and Reconstruction* (New York and London: Norton, 2001), 478, 479, 480–81. For a recent monograph that draws on this perspective, see Nicolas Barreyre, *Gold and Freedom: The Political Economy of Reconstruction* (Charlottesville: University of Virginia Press, 2015), 4–6, 235, 237.

135. Steven Hahn, *A Nation Under Our Feet: Black Political Struggles in the Rural South from Slavery to the Great Migration* (Cambridge: Harvard University Press, 2003), 6. Hahn's *A Nation* warrants further comment but is not a focus of analysis here because it is not a narrative of Reconstruction. Instead, it seeks to present rural southern African-Americans political action from slavery to the Great Migration as part of the history of black separatism. Like Foner, Hahn focused on southern African Americans, but differed from existing scholarship in refusing to locate the ultimate meaning of their struggles in their potential membership in the United States. Hahn sought to challenge what he took to be the "liberal integrationist framework" dominating the historiography on antebellum slavery, Reconstruction, and Jim Crow. This framework, he believed, misunderstood the nature of rural, southern African-American political struggle and, moreover, treated "Emigrationism, separatism, self-help, and racial solidarity" as the afterthought of African Americans frustrated in their search for equality, citizenship, and integration (6). As with Donald, Holt, and Baker's claim, Hahn suggests that a focus on integration limits attention to other topics that warrant attention.

136. The distinction here is slightly modified from the one used by Eric Foner in Eric Foner, et al., "Eric Foner's 'Reconstruction' at Twenty-Five," 25, and Downs and Masur, "Introduction," 3.

137. Heather Cox Richardson, *West from Appomattox: The Reconstruction of America After the Civil War* (New Haven: Yale University Press, 2007); Mark Walgren Summers, *The Ordeal of the Reunion: A New History of Reconstruction* (Chapel Hill: University of North Carolina Press, 2014).

138. Richardson, *The Death of Reconstruction*.

139. Richardson, *West from Appomattox*, 1–7. Richardson argues that the middle class also came to see Gilded Age robber barons as "special interests;" 232–37.

140. Richardson, *West from Appomattox*, 4; see also 349.

141. Richardson, *West from Appomattox*, 9–31, 39–63, 67–69, 82–92, 110, 149–50, 165, 168–70, 176–78; subsequent portions of *West from Appomattox* also address the South, but for years that fall after Reconstruction's conventional end date. We do not have to accept the conventional end date as the final word, but the point here is to compare her coverage of southern and federal developments central to earlier national narratives of Reconstruction.

142. James McPherson, Review of Heather Cox Richardson, *West from Appomattox: The Reconstruction of America After the Civil War*, published in *Western Historical Quarterly* 40, no. 2 (Summer 2009): 231–32; Andrew Slap, Review of Heather Cox Richardson, *West from Appomattox: The Reconstruction of America after the Civil War*, published in *Civil War History* 55, no. 3 (September 2009): 407–9; Michael W. Fitzgerald, "The Idealized West and Reconstruction," *Civil War Book Review* (Summer 2007). See also Brooks D. Simpson, Review of Heather Cox Richardson, *West from Appomattox:*

The Reconstruction of America After the Civil War, published in *Journal of American History* 96, no. 1 (June 2009) and Jane Turner Censer, Review of Heather Cox Richardson, *West from Appomattox: The Reconstruction of America After the Civil War*, published in *Journal of Interdisciplinary History* 39, no. 3 (Winter 2009): 455–56.

143. See Summers, *The Ordeal of the Reunion*, 5, and Chapters 8, "Conquered Provinces"; 9, "Passage to India"; 10, "On Every Putrid Spot"; 12, "Corruption Is the Fashion"; and 14, "Dead Sea Fruits, 1872–1874."

144. Summers, *The Ordeal of the Reunion*, 1–3, 5, 11, 13–14, 17.

145. Summers, *The Ordeal of the Reunion*, 4, 395–96.

146. See Michael W. Fitzgerald, *Splendid Failure: Postwar Reconstruction in the American South* (Chicago: Ivan R. Dee, 2007); and Douglas R. Egerton, *The Wars of Reconstruction: The Brief, Violent History of America's Most Progressive Era* (New York: Bloomsbury, 2013).

Afterword:
The Possibilities
of Reconstruction's
Global History

Frank Towers

This book showcases what a global history of Reconstruction looks like and points to what further study in this emerging field can offer. As Ian Tyrrell and David Prior explain, Reconstruction is a late bloomer in the global turn in U.S. historical studies. Prior's insightful history of the double meaning of the word "reconstruction" shows that whether considered as social transformation or national reunification, the focus has been on the internal dynamics of either the United States as a whole or more often the South as a region. Scholars who would make the case for the rest of the world's relevance to Reconstruction have to demonstrate their case against one impressive body of scholarship that has used Reconstruction to tell powerful stories about distinctly American narratives of race, violence, and region and another equally complex historiography on the state and Constitution.

If these obstacles created by these traditions weren't enough, more recently Reconstruction has become reconceptualized as a bridge in a uniquely American story rather than an era in its own right: a link between the antebellum antislavery struggle and the Civil War on one side and the "long" civil rights movement—a period that reaches back to the Jim Crow era—on the other. That story of continuity goes right up to the present as historians seeking to understand today's "American Dilemma" of the mass incarceration of African Americans punctuated by police executions of black civilians on little or no evidence look back to the origins of black prison labor in Reconstruction.[1] To paraphrase civil rights activist H. Rap Brown, (racial) violence is as American as cherry pie, and if you want to understand America, understand its violent resolution of the Civil War.

These factors help to explain why Reconstruction, the "dark and bloody ground" of the American past,[2] has had more staying power as an exceptionalist narrative—that is, a history of America that treats its history as unique—than more widely celebrated events such as the Revolution or the Second World War.

Surely there is something in the antiheroic story of promises broken, violence, and villainy that has fired imaginations from the Dunning school when the bad guys were Republicans, freedpeople, and industry, to the Foner school where the roles were reversed but the outcome no less disheartening.

As this volume demonstrates, the history of Reconstruction involved non-American actors, drew on international discourses, and was understood by its participants as part of a global historical moment. A global, comparative understanding of Reconstruction gives the period more relevance for American history because such a perspective makes a grounded claim for the place of America in the nineteenth-century world that does not rely on measures of political or cultural power.

This volume's three essays on European immigrants bring out the importance of German and Irish American transnational understandings of their own politics to figuring out their trajectory in Reconstruction America. Where immigrants lived (America's North, South, and West) profoundly shaped their politics, but where they came from (Ireland and Germany in these cases) did as well. As Caleb Richardson shows, being a Fenian in America had an entirely different connotation than it did within the settler colonies of the British Empire. With the movement akin to the myriad number of voluntary associations in the United States, an American Fenian could think of his or her attachment as a marker of both American civic pride and support for Irish independence. In Canada or Australia, openly supporting the Fenians risked prison, making the commitment to join more clearly an act of allegiance with revolution in Ireland. For this reason, Feniansim had a much larger base of support in the United States and a much shallower level of commitment, which helps to explain why despite dreams of a grand army of expatriates, those hoping to invade Canada in the name of Irish freedom found only a few hundred had turned out to take a stand, a number nonetheless larger than anything mustered on the British side of the border.

The authors in this volume showcase another development in recent scholarship that brings developments in the study of American politics to bear on global approaches to U.S. history. Several essays in this volume broaden the definition of politics to include the public sphere and civic culture as meaningful arenas for contesting questions of public policy and national identity. Even the Reform Act, a classic example of formal political legislative activity, mattered as much for what it said about the direction of democratic impulses as it did for the actual expansion of the franchise in England, which still failed to reach the levels set in the United States over the forty years previous. Fenian picnics, German casino clubs in Texas, Crummell's speeches and writing about Africa, among other examples drawn from this volume, show Americans using the broad politics of the public—manifested in voluntary associations, collective gatherings, and spoken and written debate—to shape political outcomes. As such, these essays join current trends in U.S. political history to the global turn in nineteenth-century studies.[3]

Global histories of Reconstruction might benefit from considering other recent developments in U.S. political historiography that have shared in the aim of getting beyond the narrow confines of electoral and legislative political history. The new institutionalism, or policy history as it also called, especially calls out for attention. Studies of seemingly mundane institutions such as the U.S. postal service have opened up new insights into the significance of the state as the promoter of civic culture in the first place. Similarly, histories of public works have shown how the public-private dynamic of governance helped to make the nineteenth century United States one of the strongest states in the world as opposed to its self presentation as a limited government committed to laissez faire.[4]

What would a transnational history of institutions in global reconstruction study? Certainly, transnational corporations come to mind as a source. Steamship lines, railroad companies, banks, and telegraphers all played crucial roles in the movement of people, goods, and ideas. In matters of war, arms dealers used new steamship and railway lines to increase access to weapons. Historians might also examine civil servants involved in the more mundane aspects of international relations: the state agents who managed customs, immigration, mails, telegraphs, and port clearings. Consular officers around the world often found themselves caught between competing sovereignties and local business interests that threatened to turn minor incidents into near casus belli, as occurred during the *Trent* Affair in the Civil War.

Another strand in this volume is transnational liberalism and its meanings in different global contexts. In hindsight and especially when viewed within the U.S. national framework as a vehicle for a true egalitarian, small "r," reconstruction of American society, liberalism was hardly revolutionary. In fact, the self-proclaimed Liberal Republicans who ran against Ulysses S. Grant in 1872 did so in part as a protest against federal support for African-American political and civil rights in the South.[5] Abroad, however, liberalism often looked more dangerous to the established order. Alexander Crummell, Domingo Sarmiento, and the supporters of the British Reform Act of 1867 drew on the American experience as inspiration for their efforts to reform Africa, Argentina, and Britain. Education for women in Argentina and Africans in Liberia and a broader franchise in England and Wales all challenged the established social order of their societies in ways similar to the aims of Republican policy in the South. Snay, Rothera, and Hetrick join Don Doyle, Patrick Kelly, Pablo Mijangos, and others who argue for the importance of the mid-nineteenth-century struggle against aristocracy in all its forms as a bond that united the ideals of the Union cause in the Civil War with related movements abroad and forged a dialog between liberal national heroes such as Benito Juárez, William Henry Seward, and Giuseppe Garibaldi.[6]

At the end of the nineteenth century, socialist revolutionaries sought to distinguish revolution from liberalism, which they viewed as a prop to capitalist exploitation. Yet in the 1860s, even Karl Marx could find in the Union a beacon of freedom against a slaveholding aristocracy.[7] Given the erosion of liberal gains in the late 1870s and 1880s, most clearly illustrated by the New Imperialism and the scramble for Africa, it is easy to dismiss the revolutionary potential of free labor, free soil, and free men during the generation that it held sway in the United States and around the world.

Why that revolution ended is one thread that future global histories of Reconstruction should consider. The defeat of Radical Reconstruction timed closely with Bismarck's union of blood and iron in Germany and the subjugation of the Taiping state in China, a movement that liberals in the United States and Britain saw as a kindred spirit and whose defeat destroyed a last viable effort to stop western exploitation of China in the nineteenth century. India's rebels of the 1850s could fit the same paradigm, as could Iranian nationalists.

In the aftermath of these defeats, systems of racial and ethnic hierarchy were recreated in the more "modern" extremes of legal segregation and varieties of unfree labor that stopped short of chattel slavery but relied on force and fraud to sustain global profits in commodities. And, far from disappearing, monarchy took on new, grander forms as Europe's kings and queens conquered new lands, acquired new sources of wealth, and promoted levels of global exploitation that matched or exceeded the brutality of earlier ages.

Viewed from the 1890s, the 1860s truly was a time of hope around the world for a more equitable global order. Imperialism's defeat of liberal nationalism closed a possible path toward preventing the era of world war between 1914 and 1945. To study Reconstruction as a piece of the global history of liberalism raises basic questions about how it emerged, why it fell, and whether the many permutations of these values had had enough coherence in terms of ideas and human networks to merit the label "global."

Patterns of settlement and conquest shed light on the Reconstruction era's complicated relationship between liberalism and imperialism. For the United States, historians would do well to consider its similarities to British imperialism. Historian James Belich's concept of a nineteenth-century "Angloworld" highlights the shared pattern of settler-colonial conquest in the United States and United Kingdom, which reached much higher levels than in other imperial systems. British and Americans used a unique governing system for conquest that emphasized local power over central planning and public-private partnerships as the spur to capitalist development. Railroads, steamships, mail services, and, as Alison Efford shows, even weapons distribution were run by private companies but relied on public monies and government policies to prosper. Furthermore, the "Anglo-world" followed a particular vision of land and its control as absolute that had dire consequences for original inhabitants on British and U.S. imperial frontiers. Finally, each of Britain's major settler colonies (Australia, Canada, New Zealand, and South Africa) went through a process of state-making and regional political adjustment not unlike Reconstruction, with the most proximate example, Canadian Confederation, occurring in a direct dialog with the U.S. experience.[8]

If the British Empire offers a familiar venue for transnational histories, China and East Asia present another rich but more unknown setting for tracing the ties between Reconstruction in the United States and the larger world. In response to the general global turn in U.S. history and Kenneth Pomeranz's sweeping reinterpretation of the rise of the West as a contingent outcome of what were parallel achievements in East Asia and Western Europe, China and East Asia have attracted the attention of historians seeking to put together the many competing themes of nineteenth-century history.[9]

The reach of nineteenth-century globalization meant that events in Asia had significant consequences for the United States, as did American Reconstruction for developments in Asia. China's Taiping civil war not only involved Southern filibusterers and Yankee missionaries, but also provided an opportunity for Britain to make up for profits lost from the cotton embargo and thus lessen the pressure for intervention in the U.S. Civil War. In the late 1860s and 1870s, merchants looking for cotton supplies branched out across the globe. They sometimes brought with them Southern experts in cotton cultivation and coercive labor. In fact, the Confederacy's defeat spurred a mini-diaspora of proslavery capitalists in search of plantation economies that paid better than their former homeland. Meanwhile the new, neither-slave-nor-free labor regime of the U.S. South fit into a global pattern of the New Imperialism's staple crop economies. A critical ideological prop to this system was the politics of settler-colonial white workingmen who put their producerist self-image up against a degraded "coolie" system from Asia.[10]

If historians can approach Reconstruction as a global phenomenon of the 1860s and 1870s, a period of renegotiating social and political relations in the wake of revolution, then perhaps that global era could be the subject of comparisons across time. Certainly, the interwar years of the twentieth century, 1920–39, lend themselves to comparison with the 1860s and 1870s. Similarly, the aftermath of the Napoleonic wars unsettled not only Europe but also the Americas, India, and ultimately East Asia. Going farther afield, one can ask whether there were comparable patterns in more distant historical epochs, such as the aftermath of the Thirty Years War in Europe that led to the Treaty of Westphalia, an important forerunner to the modern European order of states, or more recent ones, such as the collapse of the Soviet Bloc and its fallout in the 1990s. To take a very long view, did Reconstruction bear echoes of a more deeply imprinted pattern of human adjustment to crisis, such as the fallout from the Black Death in the fourteenth century? Very likely the answer to this last question is no, but with a clearer idea of what the larger picture of Reconstruction looked like in the mid–nineteenth century, historians will be better equipped to delineate its meaning for both the present and the more distant past. Surely there are broad comparisons to be made across moments where a political crisis raised possibilities for ground-level social transformations.

Notes

1. Douglas Blackmon, *Slavery by Another Name: The Re-Enslavement of Black Americans from the Civil War to World War II* (2008, rpr. New York: Anchor Books, 2009); Tomiko Brown-Nagin, *Courage to Dissent: Atlanta and the Long History of the Civil Rights Movement* (New York: Oxford University Press, 2011).

2. Bernard A. Weisberger, "The Dark and Bloody Ground of Reconstruction Historiography," *The Journal of Southern History* 25, no. 4 (1959): 427–47.

3. A prototype for a transnational history of civil society politics in Reconstruction is W. Caleb McDaniel, *The Problem of Democracy in the Age of Slavery: Garrisonian Abolitionists and Transatlantic Reform* (Baton Rouge: Louisiana State University Press, 2013). For other examples of historians who use civil society to study politics in the era of Reconstruction see Mary P. Ryan, *Civic Wars: Democracy and Public Life in the American City During the Nineteenth Century* (Berkeley: University of California Press, 1997); Susan Zaeske, *Signatures of Citizenship: Petitioning, Antislavery, and Women's Political Identity* (Chapel Hill: University of North Carolina Press, 2003); Stephen Kantrowitz, *More Than Freedom: Fighting for Black Citizenship in a White Republic, 1829–1889* (New York: Penguin, 2012); Kyle G. Volk, *Moral Minorities and the Making of American Democracy* (New York: Oxford University Press, 2014).

4. Influential examples of this scholarship include Richard R. John, *Spreading the News: The American Postal System from Franklin to Morse* (Cambridge: Harvard Univer-

sity Press, 1995); John Lauritz Larson, *Internal Improvement: National Public Works and the Promise of Popular Government in the Early United States* (Chapel Hill: University of North Carolina Press, 2001); William J. Novak, "The Myth of the Weak American State," *American Historical Review* 113, no. 3 (June 2008), 752–72; Brian Balogh, *A Government Out of Sight: The Mystery of National Authority in Nineteenth-Century America* (New York: Cambridge University Press, 2009). For a transnational case study, see Jay Sexton, "Steam Transport, Sovereignty, and Empire in North America, c. 1850–1885," forthcoming in *The Journal of the Civil War Era*.

5. Andrew L. Slap, *The Doom of Reconstruction: The Liberal Republicans in the Civil War Era* (New York: Fordham University Press, 2006).

6. Don H. Doyle, *The Cause of All Nations: An International History of the American Civil War* (New York: Basic Books, 2014); Patrick J. Kelly, "The North American Crisis of the 1850s," *The Journal of the Civil War Era* 2, no. 3 (2012): 337–68; Pablo Mijangos y González, "Guerra Civil y Esatado-nacion en Norteamérica (1848–1867)," in *El Poder y la Sangre: Guerra, Estado y Nación en la Década de 1860*, edited by Guillermo Palacios and Erika Pani (México, D.F.: El Colegio de México, 2014), 43–62. Also see Jay Sexton, "William Henry Seward and the World," *Journal of the Civil War Era* 3, no. 4 (2014): 398–430. For an early iteration of this thesis, see W. L. Morton, "British North America and a Continent in Dissolution, 1861–1871," *History* XLVII (1962), 139–56.

7. Karl Marx and Friedrich Engels, *The Civil War in the United States*, Richard Enmale, ed. (New York: International Press, 1937).

8. James Belich, *Replenishing the Earth: The Settler Revolution and the Rise of the Angloworld* (New York: Oxford University Press, 2009). For the importance of local sovereignty in the British Empire see John Darwin, *The Empire Project: The Rise and Fall of the British World-System, 1830–1970* (New York: Cambridge University Press, 2009).

9. Kenneth Pomeranz, *The Great Divergence: China, Europe, and the Making of the Modern World Economy* (Princeton, N.J.: Princeton University press, 2001); C. A. Bailey, *The Birth of the Modern World, 1780–1914* (Malden, Mass.: Blackwell, 2004); Jürgen Osterhammel, *The Transformation of the World: A Global History of the Nineteenth Century*. Trans. Patrick Camiller (Princeton, N.J.: Princeton University Press, 2014).

10. Stephen R. Platt, *Autumn in the Heavenly Kingdom: China, the West, and the Epic Story of the Taiping Civil War* (New York: Knopf, 2012); Sven Beckert, *Empire of Cotton: A Global History* (New York: Knopf, 2014); Andrew Zimmerman, "Cotton Booms, Cotton Busts, and the Civil War in West Africa," *Journal of the Gilded Age and Progressive Era* 10 (2011): 454–63; Gerald Horne, *The Deepest South: The United States, Brazil, and the African Slave Trade* (New York: New York University Press, 2007): Kornel Chang, "Circulating Race and Empire: Transnational Labor Activism and the Politics of Anti-Asian Agitation in the Anglo-American Pacific World, 1880–1910," *Journal of American History* 96, no. 3 (December 2009): 678–701. The far-sighted work of Alexander Saxton remains relevant to this debate. See *The Indispensable Enemy: Labor and the Anti-Chinese Movement in California* (Berkeley: University of California Press, 1971).

Contributors

Julia Brookins is Special Projects Coordinator at the American Historical Association.

Alison Clark Efford is an Assistant Professor of History at Marquette University.

Matthew J. Hetrick is currently a Visiting Affiliate Assistant Professor at Loyola University Maryland.

David Prior is an Assistant Professor of American History at the University of New Mexico.

Caleb Richardson is an Assistant Professor of History at the University of New Mexico.

Evan C. Rothera received his doctorate from the History Department at Pennsylvania State University.

Mitchell Snay is a Professor of History at Denison University.

Frank Towers is an Associate Professor of History at the University of Calgary.

Ian Tyrrell retired as Scientia Professor of History at the University of New South Wales, Sydney, Australia, in July 2012 and is now an Emeritus Professor of History.

Index

RECONSTRUCTING AMERICA
Andrew L. Slap, series editor

Hans L. Trefousse, *Impeachment of a President: Andrew Johnson, the Blacks, and Reconstruction.*

Richard Paul Fuke, *Imperfect Equality: African Americans and the Confines of White Ideology in Post-Emancipation Maryland.*

Ruth Currie-McDaniel, *Carpetbagger of Conscience: A Biography of John Emory Bryant.*

Paul A. Cimbala and Randall M. Miller, eds., *The Freedmen's Bureau and Reconstruction: Reconsiderations.*

Herman Belz, *A New Birth of Freedom: The Republican Party and Freedmen's Rights, 1861 to 1866.*

Robert Michael Goldman, *"A Free Ballot and a Fair Count": The Department of Justice and the Enforcement of Voting Rights in the South, 1877–1893.*

Ruth Douglas Currie, ed., *Emma Spaulding Bryant: Civil War Bride, Carpetbagger's Wife, Ardent Feminist—Letters, 1860–1900.*

Robert Francis Engs, *Freedom's First Generation: Black Hampton, Virginia, 1861–1890.*

Robert F. Kaczorowski, *The Politics of Judicial Interpretation: The Federal Courts, Department of Justice, and Civil Rights, 1866–1876.*

John Syrett, *The Civil War Confiscation Acts: Failing to Reconstruct the South.*

Michael Les Benedict, *Preserving the Constitution: Essays on Politics and the Constitution in the Reconstruction Era.*

Andrew L. Slap, *The Doom of Reconstruction: The Liberal Republicans in the Civil War Era.*

Edmund L. Drago, *Confederate Phoenix: Rebel Children and Their Families in South Carolina.*

Mary Farmer-Kaiser, *Freedwomen and the Freedmen's Bureau: Race, Gender, and Public Policy in the Age of Emancipation.*

Paul A. Cimbala and Randall Miller, eds., *The Great Task Remaining Before Us: Reconstruction as America's Continuing Civil War.*

John A. Casey Jr., *New Men: Reconstructing the Image of the Veteran in Late-Nineteenth-Century American Literature and Culture.*

Hilary Green, *Educational Reconstruction: African American Schools in the Urban South, 1865–1890.*

Christopher B. Bean, *Too Great a Burden to Bear: The Struggle and Failure of the Freedmen's Bureau in Texas.*

David E. Goldberg, *The Retreats of Reconstruction: Race, Leisure, and the Politics of Segregation at the New Jersey Shore, 1865–1920.*

David Prior, ed., *Reconstruction in a Globalizing World.*